Praise for *Dirty*

"Meredith Maran makes us fall in love with the teenagers she writes about."
—Anne Lamott, author of *Traveling Mercies*

"*Dirty* takes us on a level-headed, no-holds-barred tour of the netherworld of teenage life. Meredith Maran's heart-wrenching, eye-opening search yields sensible answers every parent should ponder."
—Daniel Goleman, author of *Emotional Intelligence*

"Today there are 900,000 African-American youth in jail, and only 600,000 in college. Disparate treatment by the criminal justice system and prosecution for drug offenses is a major way in which youth of color, especially, are funneled into the criminal justice system. *Dirty* provides policy makers, parents, and the community with critical firsthand information from inside this epidemic of injustice—and insightful ideas about what must be done to end it."
—Rev. Jesse L. Jackson, Sr. President and founder of Rainbow/PUSH Coalition

"Dirty is a useful, analytical, painful, and hopeful book about adolescent culture on drugs. Read wisely, this book has the potential to transform the cultural landscape of America."
—Dr. Mary Pipher, bestselling author of *Reviving Ophelia*

"*Dirty* is an accurate and realistic portrayal of teenage drug use. What kids do, how they do it, why they do it. Parents should read this book. Kids should read this book."
—James Frey, bestselling author of *A Million Little Pieces*

"Meredith Maran shares her hard-won knowledge as a journalist in the devastation of the drug war, and then goes further still to tell her story as a searching mom. Reading about these counselors and mothers and fathers and kids left me enraged and hopeful. *Dirty*'s news is as necessary as it is devastating, all the while staying close to the complicated heart."
—Adrian Nicole LeBlanc, bestselling author of *Rand Family*

"*Dirty* packs the dramatic punch of *Traffic* but tells the stories of real life teens and their families."

> —Lawrence H. Diller, M.D., author of *Running on Ritalin* and *Should I Medicate My Child?*

"*Dirty* is required reading for every parent of a teenager, and every teenager with a parent."

> —Lonny Shavelson, physician and author of *Hooked: Five Addicts Challenge Our Misguided Drug Rehab System*

"In *Dirty*, Meredith Maran writes with a journalist's instinct and a mother's heart. This meticulously researched, compulsively readable book takes us beyond the headlines and drug war rhetoric and into the minds of America's teenagers. Intimate, informative, and often heartbreaking, this book is a must-read for every parent, professional, or person who cares about the future of our children."

> —Debra Ginsberg, author of *Waiting* and *Raising Blaze*

"*Dirty* is a passionate, compelling cry for America to "get straight" about the real victims of the War on Drugs: our own kids. These real-life stories of teenagers in rehab tell a bigger story about America's priorities and how they need to change if we want our kids to have happy, healthy lives. A great read, too!"

> —Ben Cohen, founder, Ben & Jerry's; president, Business Leaders for Sensible Priorities; president, The True Majority

"An insightful, compassionate look at the mistakes we are making with our teenagers."

> —*Publishers Weekly*

HarperCollins books may be purchased for educational, business, or sales promotional use. For information please write: Special Markets Department, HarperCollins Publishers, Inc., 10 East 53rd Street, New York, NY 10022.

HarperCollins Web site: http://www.harpercollins.com

HarperCollins®, 📖 ®, and HarperSanFrancisco™ are trademarks of HarperCollins Publishers, Inc.

FIRST HARPERCOLLINS PAPERBACK EDITION PUBLISHED IN 2004

Designed by Kris Tobiassen

Library of Congress Cataloging-in-Publication Data is available upon request.

ISBN 0–06–073061–7

04   05   06   07   08   ❖/RRD   10   9   8   7   6   5   4   3   2   1

Dirty

A Search for Answers Inside
America's Teenage Drug Epidemi

Meredith Maran

HarperSanFrancisco
A Division of HarperCollins*Publishers*

FOR MARÍA DEL CARMEN ACOSTA RUÍZ

Gracias, comadre

Contents

PART 3: TESTING DIRTY
Does Any of It Work?

PART 4: GETTING OUT
How Can We Get Kids Off Drugs?

Prologue

Mike and his friend Jack are kicking it in Jack's room, drinking some beers, smoking some weed. It's the first night of Christmas break, freshman year of high school. Jack rummages through his sock drawer, pulls out a small white rock.

"What's that?" Mike asks.

"Crank," Jack answers.

"I heard that shit's tight," Mike says.

"Let's do it up." Jack shuts the door in case his mom comes home.

Mike hesitates. Smoking weed is one thing. Putting something up his nose—that's what junkies do.

"C'mon, dude," Jack urges him. He pulls out a mirror and a razor blade, chops the rock into powder. He snorts a few lines, chops up some more, passes the mirror to Mike. Mike closes his eyes and snorts his first line of crank.

Instantly he's filled with the feeling he's always wanted and never had: pure happiness. All his problems—in school, with his parents, even his zits—vanish as if they've been vaporized by the Star Trek laser gun he played with as a kid.

Mike snorts another line. He can't sit still. He jumps up.

"Got any more of that shit?" he asks, his heart pounding in his chest.

Sitting in the backseat of his mom's BMW, his mom chatting with his grandmother in the front, Tristan slips a double dose of Xanax to his stepbrother, Max, and the same to his stepsister, Caitlin. They pass a water bottle, gulping the pills down.

The Xanax kicks in just as they arrive at their cousin's birthday party. "Let's go smoke a bowl," Tristan whispers to his sibs. They sneak out, float to a park nearby, stuff a pipe with pot.

"This stuff is *hella* strong," Caitlin mumbles.

"We just got *dosed*, dude," Tristan giggles. "This shit is laced with something *serious*." Falling all over each other, laughing, they stagger back to the house.

Later that night while everyone's asleep, Tristan creeps into Caitlin's room. He takes her car keys and the two twenties he finds on her dresser. "She owes me that much for the pot and the pills," he tells himself.

Tristan drives Caitlin's VW to his friend Justin's house. He and Justin split a fifth of vodka. As Tristan's driving home—sideswiping a few fire hydrants and parked cars along the way—his cell phone starts ringing off the hook, his mom's number lighting up over and over on the screen. When he gets home she's in the kitchen, crying. Tristan promises her everything she wants to hear: he'll never smoke pot, drink, or drive without a license again.

"At least not till next weekend," he thinks, and falls into bed.

"We're the police. Don't make this any harder than it is."

Zalika freezes. Two cops are standing in front of her, one black, the other white, their faces lit by the liquor store's neon sign.

"It's over for me," Zalika thinks. All the time she's been selling rock on this corner, she never thought it would come to this. Marcus had told her what to do if the Five-O came up on her: swallow everything she had. But how can she do that now? She has sixty rocks of crack on her body—five in her mouth, twenty in her pockets, the rest in a baggie stuffed up inside her—and two cops in her face.

Zalika starts swallowing the rocks in her mouth, grabbing handfuls from her pockets. But there are too many to swallow. Too many to hold. The rocks spray from her mouth, her hands; they're bouncing off her Nikes. Going on pure instinct, she drops to the ground to pick them up.

The white cop pulls her to her feet. "We were just gonna send you home to your parents," he says, shaking his head sadly. "What are you, seventeen?"

"Almost fifteen," Zalika answers.

Two more cop cars arrive, lights flashing. Cops swarm all over, scooping up the rocks, the street junkies watching with their mouths hanging open as if the police are snatching their last meal. The black cop handcuffs Zalika. "You have the right to remain silent . . ."

Introduction

This is a book about why teenagers use drugs, what we're doing about it, why nothing seems to be working, and what we might do to solve—or at least look honestly at—the problem.

I've been writing books and articles about teenagers since I was one myself, driven then as now by the same Big Question—the question that drove me to smoke my first joint and write my first book in high school, the question that drives me still: How and why are things in America so different from the way they're supposed to be?

This question opens another one. What can the lives of teenagers—no longer cosseted as children, but not yet accountable as adults—teach us about the price of our broken promises?

I know the price. I've paid it, first as a raging teenager, then as the mother of one. I mean it when I say that this book started close to home: my home. It started with a mother's pain: mine. What drove me to write this book was not asking, first, where America had gone wrong, but where I'd gone wrong. What had I done or failed to do for my younger son, Jesse, that led him to spend his teenage years high on pot and alcohol, running the streets, in jail?

Jesse's first arrest was for shoplifting at age thirteen; his last was a DUI at age twenty. During the years in between, the only thing I could count on was the steady escalation of his arrests and school suspensions—from fighting on campus to joyriding; from stealing checkbooks and wallets to stealing bicycles; and finally, to breaking a bottle over a kid's head, sending him to the hospital. I lived through those years in a protracted state of shock: mid-traumatic stress I can still summon now just by writing about it. Sleepless nights blurred into bad-news days; brief interludes of "normal life" were shattered by phone calls summoning me and my ex-husband to principals' offices, police stations, emergency rooms, jails.

What, I asked myself and everyone else, did my suffering child need? Why couldn't I, or his devoted dad, or the many trained professionals we enlisted give it to him? Why was Jesse's one-year-older brother, Peter, gliding through adolescence—smoking plenty of pot, blowing off plenty of homework, but doing just fine in school, at home, in life—while Jesse rarely went a day without getting high, a week without a heart-stopping drama? From birth Jesse had been exceptional: brilliant, artistic, complex. Alternately horrifying and astounding his teachers with his precocious cartooning, satiric story writing, and razor-tongued wit, he was suspended from preschool for biting, from fourth grade for disrupting class, from junior high for threatening the dean. By the time Jesse got to high school, he didn't seem so exceptional anymore. He seemed like any other wanna-be thug.

At age twenty, after his final stint in jail, Jesse started going to church. He stopped drinking and smoking pot. He stopped committing crimes. Today, at twenty-three, Jesse lives a life of service to others. My son the teenage felon works, now, at a residential treatment program for drug-addicted teenagers. My son the (ethnic, if not religious) Jew is now the youngest and the only white minister at a predominantly African American Baptist church. He credits God with saving his soul, and his life.

I blamed myself for Jesse's problems, of course, just as I'd spent twenty years in therapy blaming my mother for mine. But as this admirable young man emerged from the tempest of his adolescence, I began to wonder where else the responsibility might lie. What did Jesse's struggle *mean* in the bigger picture of our nation's epidemic of teenagers in crisis?

The mistakes I'd made with Jesse were legion, but they couldn't explain why my home state of California, among others, was building more jails than schools; why business was booming nationwide for wilderness programs, therapeutic boarding schools, and adolescent rehab centers. Nor could my failings explain my friends' problems with *their* kids. My friends, I knew, were attentive, smart, loving parents—rich, middle-class, and poor; black, white, and brown; gay, straight, and other, raising their kids in all kinds of styles and cultures. Yet their teenagers were having trouble too, suffering in any of the myriad ways that teenagers in America suffer and manifest their suffering.

I'd talked my friend Stephen through hiring professional kidnappers to "escort" his heroin-addicted daughter to a therapeutic boarding school in the middle of the night. I'd told my friend Valerie to search her son's sock drawer, then comforted her when she found pot and bullets in an incense box there. I'd advised my friend Chris about what she could and could not bring inside when she went to visit her alcoholic daughter in Juvenile Hall. I'd mediated in the verging-on-violent screaming matches between my *comadre* María, the finest parent and the finest woman I knew, and her stoned and raging teenage son.

I knew that, like Jesse, my friends' kids had issues beyond drug abuse: psychological and social wounds deeper than the needle tracks on their arms. Where, I wondered, did those wounds come from? How can we—as families, communities, a nation—treat or, better yet, prevent them? And why are so many of our children in so much pain in the first place?

I've long believed that teenagers are the canary in America's mine: old enough to know what's wrong around them, young enough to name and condemn it unreservedly. Their alienation and their anger mirror and exacerbate our own. As William Finnegan says in the final words of his 1998 classic, *Cold New World*, "What young people show us is simply the world we have made for them."

What does our children's drug use show us—about them, about us, about the world we've made for them? By asking the Big Questions about teenage drug use, I went looking for Big Answers. I went looking for what I needed, a few short years ago, to help ease my son's anguish and my own.

This is what I found.

America's drug crisis is a runaway train. Keeping teenagers from jumping on board—or being flattened on the tracks—is the linchpin of the nation's efforts to stop it. Research shows that if you don't use drugs as a kid, you're less likely to use drugs as an adult. Keeping teens clean today, the logic goes, equals fewer adult addicts tomorrow. The strategy is a reasonable one. The problem is, it hasn't worked.

Despite countless attempts by governments, schools, churches, and families to contain the epidemic of teen drug use that exploded across the nation during the 1960s, the epidemic has been escalating (with an occasional downward blip) ever since. Thirty years into the government's multi-billion-dollar campaign to steer kids away from drugs and fifteen years since we were all mesmerized by that single egg frying in the pan—"This is your brain. This is your brain on drugs"—in turn-of-the-millennium America more teenagers are using drugs than ever in the history of this country, or any country in the world.

One-fourth of the high-school seniors in America today have problems with drugs and alcohol. Nearly two-thirds of the teenagers in America today do drugs before they finish high school—one-third of them by the time they're in eighth grade. (Do the math: we're talking twelve-year-olds.) Fifty-six percent of seventeen-year-olds know at least one drug dealer at school.

Nothing we're doing about it is working. Not the ads, not the DARE programs in the schools, not the after-school specials on TV. Not the glitzy rehab spas, the grimy public treatment centers, the fancy boarding schools. Not the Juvenile Halls, the youth detention camps, the jails.

By the time they're seniors in high school:

50 percent of teenagers have binged on alcohol (chugged five or
    more drinks in a row).
41 percent have smoked pot.
12.5 percent have taken tranquilizers or barbiturates.
12 percent have taken Ecstasy ("X" use was up 71 percent between
    1999 and 2001).
11 percent have used amphetamines ("speed" in its various forms).
10 percent have taken LSD.
9 percent have used cocaine, about half in the form of crack.
9 percent have sniffed inhalants.
4 percent have snorted or shot heroin.

Two hundred thousand American teenagers were arrested for drug violations in 1999, an increase of 291 percent over the past decade. Seven out of ten juveniles who get in trouble with the law test positive for drugs. Nine out of ten teenagers who need drug treatment aren't getting it.

These are your kids. These are your kids on drugs.

Welcome to America, where on any given day, one million people are in treatment for drug or alcohol abuse. The number one health problem in the nation, substance abuse causes more death and illness than any other preventable condition. Four times as many women die from addiction-related illness, for example, as die from breast cancer.

Nearly fifteen million Americans—6.3 percent of the population age twelve and over—are illicit-drug users. Half of them are under age twenty-six. All told, they spend $60 billion a year on the illegal stuff they smoke, snort, swallow, and shoot.

Whether you indulge or not, you're paying for the party. Drug abuse costs the U.S. economy $414 billion a year. Besides the health and productivity costs, President Bush's War on Drugs swallows $19.2 billion. Two-thirds of that is spent on law enforcement and interdiction (kicking in housing-project doors, making sure the people who get busted go to jail). With no apparent comprehension of cause and effect—only 3.6 percent of the War on Drugs budget is allotted for treatment, 2.4 percent for prevention—the Bush administration acknowledges that most people who need treatment aren't getting it.

More than one million people a year are arrested for drugs, contributing generously to one of our nation's most dubious achievements: the United States has the second-highest—and the fastest-growing—incarceration rate in the world. Sixty percent of the nearly two million people in our prisons today are drug offenders. If the prison population keeps increasing at its current rate (6.6 million Americans—one in every thirty-two adults—are currently incarcerated, on probation, or on parole), by 2053 there will be more Americans in jail than out.

This is your country. This is your country on drugs.

I began my research in the summer of 2001, talking with the teachers, therapists, coaches, and parents who'd helped me with Jesse and with *Class*

Dismissed, the book I published in 2000 about a year in the lives of three high-school seniors. These folks referred me to experts in adolescent drug treatment and to teen treatment centers. I explained that I was looking for a few different kinds of teenagers to follow through a few different kinds of drug rehab programs. By exploring a diverse array of "recovery" experiences, I hoped to understand how the most powerful social determinants—race, class, gender, geography, psychology—affect kids' proclivity to do drugs and what happens to them when they get caught. I wanted a representative mix of urban, rural, and suburban kids from different ethnic, economic, and family backgrounds who used a representative mix of drugs with a representative mix of results.

I told the program directors that I wanted to sit in on the kids' court appearances and therapy sessions and to follow them through their relapses and runaways. I promised to conceal the kids' identities, but warned I would conceal little else. Agreeing to participate meant that everyone involved—district attorneys, probation officers, public defenders, and judges as well as teachers, therapists, parents, and kids—would relinquish much: privacy, time, energy. For the next year or so I'd be everywhere, asking them about everything. Their only payoff? A chance to let the world in on the *real* war on drugs—the one they wage from the trenches every day. It speaks volumes about their dedication to this battle that all three of the programs and teenagers I selected agreed to expose themselves in this way.

To explore long-term residential treatment—the most intensive type, for the most seriously drug- and crime-involved kids—I chose Center Point Adolescent in downtown San Rafael. One of many "therapeutic communities" built around a rigorous routine of behavior modification ("Fake it till you make it," in addict parlance), Center Point is populated by fifteen to twenty mostly white, working-class boys from the northern reaches of small-town California, all of them placed in the one-year program as a condition of their probation.

I didn't have to look for a kid to follow at Center Point; my first day there, Mike chose me. A seventeen-year-old "tweaker" (methamphetamine user) from the blue-collar suburbs of Santa Rosa, Mike employed the resourcefulness that I would see so much of during the next year, systematically convincing the Center Point administrators, then his parents, then me that being in a book would be good for him, and vice-versa. Silly me. During my first weeks with Mike, sitting through his group and individual therapy sessions, hearing him saying all the right things at all the right times, I worried that he might be a little *too* clean and sober, a little *too* stable, to teach me what I wanted to learn about the rutted road to recovery. Little did I know how many miles and milestones Mike and I would end up covering together.

To learn more about the "recovery high school" treatment model—the only one designed specifically for teenagers—I chose Phoenix Academy, a public school in affluent Marin County. Well funded and professionally staffed, Phoenix serves up a blended curriculum of academics and therapy to suburban white kids and urban Latinos, rock stars' sons and immigrants' daughters. Some Phoenix Academy students are placed there as a condition of their probation; many are enrolled at their parents' request or their own.

At Phoenix I found Tristan sitting by himself at lunch, eating the curried lentils and raw spinach he'd brought from home, a cloud of orange curls framing his freckled, peach-fuzzy face. The grandson of a well-known artist, at sixteen Tristan had already been around the rehab block a few times, thanks to his taste for pot, mushrooms, vodka, and the pills he found in his friends' parents' medicine cabinets. When I met him, Tristan wasn't sure he wanted to get sober, but was sure that he never wanted to lie again—a remarkable commitment for a teenage kid to make; an even more remarkable one to keep.

Because Drug Courts are a growing and controversial national treatment trend ("Hug-a-Thug Courts," their critics call them), and because I was so moved by how much they do with the little they are given, I decided to explore the Juvenile Drug Court in the inner city of Richmond, California. All of this program's kids are on probation; most of them are African American, Latino, Asian, and poor; many are first-generation Americans from Contra Costa County's grittiest 'hoods. The Drug Court clients are lovingly monitored by the Drug Court Team: the judge, probation officer, prosecutor, and public defender who collaborate with the kids' counselors at the after-school drug-treatment center they're required to attend five afternoons a week.

By the time I met Zalika, I'd spent several months spinning in the Drug Court's revolving door, watching kids begging to be admitted, then disappearing, then showing up again. The director couldn't promise me that

Zalika would stick around (she didn't), but he accurately predicted that I would find her fascinating. Exceptionally bright and charming, the "bad seed" of her high-achieving, upper-middle-class African American family, sixteen-year-old Zalika had been turning tricks and selling crack since she was twelve years old. She was intrigued but ambivalent about my proposition, interviewed me for weeks before finally agreeing to let me into her life, and hasn't yet stopped testing me to decide if I deserve her trust. It's been a daily challenge to earn it.

And so we began. Mike, Tristan, Zalika, and their parents signed waivers relinquishing their confidentiality rights. I signed a form promising not to use the kids' real names or photographs. And then every day I went wherever they were: to school, to program, to court. To the mall, to Planned Parenthood, to the Zen center. To the police station, to two counties' Juvenile Halls, to the kids' parents' houses, and to the houses where they hid out from the law (but never, incredibly, from me).

I was with Mike when he swore he'd make it through rehab this time, and with him when he didn't. I was with Tristan at AA meetings, and when he had to tell his therapist that he'd relapsed—again. I was with Zalika when she ran from Drug Court, and when she walked back in to face the handcuffs.

Mike taught me how to blow a crank pipe, and how hard it is for a tweaker to go even one day without speed. Tristan taught me how to beat a drug test, and how to find the nugget of self within the lode of others' expectations. Zalika taught me the origami of cocaine packaging, and how to make just about anyone do what you want them to do, without even knowing they're doing it.

I grew to love them. They grew hella fond of me. I had a blast with them. And they, whether they wanted to or not, had me.

I was present for most of the events in this book. When I couldn't be, I verified, as thoroughly as possible, what I was told. Unless otherwise specified, the viewpoints expressed are those of the teenagers, although my opinions of their parents, counselors, friends, and situations were unavoidably affected by theirs. The names of all the teenagers mentioned, and of their families and the programs they attended before I met them, have been changed for two reasons: to protect the kids from negative repercussions, and because by promising to conceal some insignificant identifying facts I was able to gain access to deeper, more significant truths. The names of the three profiled programs and of most of the adults who work in them are real.

A caveat about the statistics you'll find throughout these pages: most of the agencies, organizations, and individuals that are funded to conduct studies of adolescent substance abuse do so, for better and for worse, to advance their own agendas. They want more money to be allocated for prevention, or treatment, or incarceration; they're looking to "prove" that stricter parenting, or legalization, or pharmaceuticals will solve the problem. Their numbers are based on only those teenagers who are arrested, sent to publicly funded treatment, and/or divulge to a stranger on the telephone that they use drugs, and which ones, and how often.

Not surprisingly, the research yields wildly disparate results. Two quick examples. One: different government agencies report variously that 7 percent, or 21 percent, or 41 percent of high-school seniors smoke pot; both the *San Francisco Chronicle* and Columbia University's Center on Addiction and Substance Abuse report that 47 percent do—and the teenagers I asked swear that just about all of their friends do. Example number two: the National Institute on Drug Abuse, the federal government's chief drug-research bureau, says that 9 percent of high-school seniors sniff inhalants. In a special segment on February 2, 2002, *Good Morning America* reported that 18 percent of teenagers are "huffers"—exactly double NIDA's finding.

Flawed as they are, the data help to paint the Big Picture, albeit in the broadest of strokes. Toward that end I've compiled the most current statistics available, drawing from a wide range of sources and cross-checking their accuracy wherever possible.

Finally, a few words about what this book is and isn't.

It's not an analysis of U.S. drug policy (although it seems pertinent that, as I write, those taxpayer-funded "Buy Drugs, Support Terrorism" ads saturate the media, while U.S. bombs fall on the Middle East, where a good deal of the heroin trade was launched and sponsored by the CIA. Which brand of terrorism, I wonder, are we supporting when we buy drugs?).

It's not an exposé of the possible ties between the pharmaceutical, alcohol, and tobacco multinationals, the drug cartels, organized crime, the multibillion-dollar rehab industry, and those politicians who continue to make obscene profits not only possible but inevitable for all of them.

It's not a scientific study of the physiology of addiction—nor of whether such a thing exists. In fact, this book isn't scientific at all. I wanted to know what causes teens to use drugs, what we offer them when they do, and what we can learn from our failure, thus far, to solve the problem. To find out, I reflected on my experiences as a teenager and as the mother of teenagers. I dug around to see what other researchers and experts in the field had to say. Most informatively of all, I accompanied three teenagers on a few miles of the journey that their drug use has compelled them to take.

Which brings us to what this book *is*: a shocking, revelatory, loud report issued directly from the mouths, hearts, minds, and central nervous systems of teenagers in (and out of) drug rehab. Mike, Tristan, and Zalika took a big chance and let me in. They showed me their secret stashes, their locked journals, their hidden wounds. They brought me with them to their hot boxes and house parties, their drug deals and shoplifting sprees, their therapy sessions and Juvenile Hall cells. And they talked to me about every bit of it, every step of the way. Thanks to the courage, openness, and irrepressible humanity of these three teenagers—and the willingness of their families, teachers, and counselors to allow me to go where no reporter has gone before—I can bring you there too.

As the mother of a kid in trouble, I spent many anguished hours eavesdropping on my son's conversations; searching his backpack, his pockets, his room; trying to trick his brother, his friends, his therapists into telling me something, anything, that might help me understand and help him. I didn't, as I was often reminded, have a clue. If this book accomplishes its purpose, it will offer you a few.

Remember, though, this book tells the unique stories of three unique teenagers. Their stories are representative, not comprehensive. There are as many reasons for, and treatments of, teenage drug abuse as there are teenagers. It's important—it would be world-changing—for us to recognize and act on that fact: to recognize that every teenager and every teenager's story is unique and deserving of our attention.

In our culture, teenage drug use is both misunderstood metaphor and telegraphed message. Whether kids are addicted to drugs, abusing drugs, or using drugs—crucial distinctions I explore throughout this book—and whether they do drugs to meet or to mute their emotional, spiritual, academic, or developmental needs, their drug use is a tool. Wielding it with varying degrees of self-awareness, they explore their pain, medicate their pain, reveal their pain, and get treatment for their pain.

When our kids get into trouble with drugs, that's one way—not the ideal way, but an effective way—for them to ask us for help. It is one way—neither the ideal way nor, for the most part, an effective way—for us to help them.

If there's one thing I learned from being a teenager, from mothering teenagers, and from writing books about teenagers, it's how necessary it is—and how far we have to go—to give every child not just what's easy for us to give, but what he or she truly and uniquely needs.

PART 1

GETTING HIGH
Why Do Kids Do Drugs?

MIKE

Running on Empty

"Butler to Release! Butler to Release!" Mike heard the guard's voice crackling through the two-way radio on his teacher's desk. "You're out of here, Mike," Ms. Johnson called to him across the Juvenile Hall classroom.

Mike high-fived the boys, hugged the girls, then positioned himself in front of the locked unit door. Shifting nervously from one foot to the other, his pulse racing, he jumped when Ms. Johnson buzzed the door open for a short, stocky man in a blue Nike turtleneck, black slacks, and black tassel loafers.

"How you doin'?" Danny Ramirez asked Mike.

"Aiight," Mike responded.

Last week Danny had spent a couple hours interviewing Mike for placement at Center Point, a rehab program an hour south of here in San Rafael. But now Danny was looking Mike up and down as if he'd never seen him before.

"Ka-ching, ka-ching," Mike thought, watching Danny watching him. "I know that's all you care about: that money you *think* you're gonna get paid for keeping me locked up."

"Ready to go?" Danny asked.

"Sure," Mike answered. He stifled a grin, thinking, "Dude—you're about to find out *how* ready."

Danny gestured for Mike to follow him down the walkway that led from the units to Release—as if Mike didn't know the drill, as if he hadn't been through this routine ten times before. As they passed it, neither of them glanced at the Juvenile Hall "Vision Statement" posted on the wall.

The care of children today determines the quality of life tomorrow.

Our vision is that every child experience positive and successful alternatives, safe surroundings, and caring support.

Since our actions and decisions affect children, our vision is to provide opportunities for change and the support necessary for change to occur.

A guard buzzed the two of them through the first set of locked double doors and into the Personals office. "You're leaving us, Mike. That's great," said Nancy, the nice woman who worked there. She handed Mike a bulky manila envelope and the plaid short-sleeved shirt, size 42 blue jeans, and black suede desert boots he'd been wearing when the Santa Rosa cops had handcuffed him and dragged him in here, zombied out and crashing off a three-day crank run. Mike changed in the bathroom, gave Nancy the dingy white T-shirt, navy blue nylon shorts, and beige Converse high-tops he'd been wearing ever since. "I don't want to see you back again, you hear?" she said.

"Don't worry. You won't," Mike replied distractedly, shaking the envelope's contents into his hand. He stuffed the ten-dollar bill into his pocket, peering eagerly at the scratched-up screen on his pager. Eleven new messages. Mike's pager had been his lifeline while he'd been on the run from the law—a long stretch that ended three weeks ago.

"You're gonna have to give me that pager and your money when we get to Center Point," Danny warned.

"I know," Mike said. "You wish," he thought. He turned back to Nancy. "Thanks for everything," he told her.

She nodded. "Just don't let me see you back here," she repeated. "That's all the thanks I want."

As Danny and Mike continued down the antiseptic-smelling hallway, they ran into Mary Graves, Mike's probation officer. "You're getting another chance, Mike," Mary said, waggling a finger in his face. "If you run this time, I swear I'll come and look for you myself."

"I won't," Mike waved her off. Of all the POs he'd ever had, Mary was the worst: old, mean, and—just like the others—full of empty threats. He followed Danny through the last set of locked doors and into the cramped room where parents were checked in, then searched, on visiting nights: first stop on the way in, last stop on the way out for every visitor and "resident" of the Sonoma County Juvenile Justice Center.

"Bye, Mike. Be good, okay?" said Alice, the woman who sat behind the glass partition there.

"I will," he said.

Alice pushed the buzzer and Mike burst into the hot, sunny June morning. Before Mike had even inhaled his first breath of fresh air, Danny grabbed him by the elbow and led him past the POs' cars in the parking lot—ten identical Ford Tauruses with state license plates—and unlocked his Ford Ranger.

"Your buddy ran on me yesterday," Danny said as they fastened their seat belts.

"I know," Mike replied. Within hours of his friend Garth's escape yesterday, word had traveled back to the Hall: Garth had taken off into the streets of downtown San Rafael as soon as he hit Center Point's front door.

"You're not gonna do that to me, are you, Mike?"

"Why would I run, man?" Mike answered. "I'm done running."

"You better be." Danny turned right out of the Juvenile Hall parking lot onto Pythian Road and cruised slowly past the sprawling Zen-landscaped grounds of the St. Francis Winery.

"If he turns left, I'll stay," Mike told himself as they approached the intersection of Pythian Road and Highway 12. A left would take them toward Sonoma, away from Santa Rosa and the safety of Mike's old stomping grounds. Experience had taught Mike not to try to outrun the law in unfamiliar territory.

"If he turns right, I'll bounce," Mike decided. A right would bring them straight into the Santa Rosa suburb of Rincon Valley, home of Mike's grandma and most of his doper friends. He wasn't sure how Grandma Myrtle would react if he showed up at her house on the run again, but he knew exactly what his friends would do: give him a place to crash, protect him from the cops, break him off a piece of whatever they were snorting, smoking, or shooting.

"So—what do you think will be your biggest challenge at Center Point?" Danny asked, slowing to a stop at the intersection.

"Umm . . ." Mike's eyes were riveted to Danny's left hand as he lifted it from the steering wheel to the turn signal.

"Down, I stay," he reminded himself. "Up, I go."

Except for his times in the Hall, it had been three years since Mike had gone more than a few days without crank. He had no reason to think he could stay clean for a year in residential treatment now. Running, on the other hand—that was something he knew how to do.

"Turn right," he willed Danny silently. And that's what Danny did.

"Yes!" Mike cheered silently as the truck turned west onto Highway 12. He started planning his escape as the truck sped beneath a lush canopy of mossy oaks, past wineries built like castles ringed by moats of pink petunias, past cattle grazing in sunburned fields. There were only two stoplights in Rincon Valley.

"Two lights, two chances to run," Mike calculated.

"You seem nervous or something," Danny commented. As the road widened to four lanes lined with convenience stores and auto-body shops, the acrid stink of diesel fuel replaced the grassy scent of fresh-cut hay and manure.

"I'm cool," Mike mumbled, his heart hammering in his chest.

"Turn red," he prayed when the first stoplight came into view. Sure enough, the light blinked yellow, then red.

Suddenly Mike's mom's face flashed before his eyes, crying over him the way she'd cried so many times before. For an instant, Mike considered staying in the truck, going to Center Point, doing his time, getting clean. And then the moment passed.

"I promised myself if he turned right I'd run," he thought. "I can't let myself down."

"I know you've been in treatment before, but . . ." Danny was still trying to engage Mike in conversation as he braked to a stop.

Mike grabbed the door handle and yanked it up, hard. "Later, dude. Thanks for the ride," he said.

He jumped out of the truck, slammed the door shut, and took off running as fast as he could.

———————

The last time Mike started running he didn't stop for seven months. It wasn't his fault, really, that he ran. He'd meant it when he told his parents, his PO, the judge, and anyone else who would listen that if they sent him to drug treatment instead of sticking him in the Hall, this time he'd make a real effort to get clean. "I'm ready to turn my life around," he'd told them, believing every word.

But of all the programs they could have sent him to, they made the stupidest possible choice: Vista Village in Rincon Valley. Mike's resolve started crumbling when the Vista Village van picked him up at the Hall, drove by the Seven-Eleven where Mike used to hang out drinking Slurpees, past the apartments on Rincon Road, where half of Mike's friends lived, and up to the front door of Vista Village. If they really wanted him to clean up his act, why had they brought him back to where he'd gotten into trouble in the first place?

The van driver left Mike alone in a room with a phone on the desk. He called his mom. "Are you by yourself?" she asked, sounding worried, as usual. "Shouldn't there be someone with you?" Hearing his mom's voice made Mike homesick. She'd sworn from the start that she'd never visit him in the Hall, so he hadn't seen her in weeks.

"I love you, Mom," Mike said, and hung up.

He was still telling himself that he could make it at Vista Village when the Intake woman came in and handed him a lame light blue T-shirt, even lamer light blue sweats, and a bottle of nasty-smelling lice shampoo. She sent him to take a shower. By himself.

"If they really expect me to stick around," Mike thought, "how come they're making it so easy for me to leave?" When he got dressed, he put the blue clothes on over his own shorts and T-shirt and stashed the Vista Village underwear in a pile of towels. Now he was prepared, whatever he decided to do.

Five minutes later Mike was sitting in his first group session, looking around at several tweakers he knew. He raised his hand and told the counselor he had to use the bathroom. "You'll need to take someone with you," the counselor said.

"Well, duh," Mike thought. This was only Mike's second residential treatment program, but everyone knew you couldn't do *anything* by yourself in these places.

"Hey, Jim," Mike asked a guy he used to get high with, "would you take me?"

As soon as they were out of earshot, Mike asked Jim, "What's the best way to bounce from here?"

"Just walk out the front door, dude," Jim whispered back. "It ain't locked."

"You think I'm dumb, man?" Mike hissed. "If they see me go, they'll follow me! What's the best way out so they won't chase me right away?"

Jim led Mike outside to a bathroom detached from the main house. "I'll wait for you right here," Jim announced loudly and turned his back. Mike took a quick look around. He saw that the fence was scaleable.

"Thanks, dude," Mike said. He sprinted across the lawn, scrambled over the fence, and landed hard on the other side. He ran down Middle Rincon Road past his grandmother's house, hoping she wouldn't happen to look out and see him, over the bridge where he used to play as a little kid, and into the Seven-Eleven parking lot. His chest heaving, he pulled off the blue sweats, used them to mop his face, tossed them into the Dumpster, and crossed the street to his friend Bobby's apartment.

"Hey, dude!" Bobby pulled Mike inside and handed him a cigarette.

Mike sucked hard on the Marlboro Red. He felt better already. You could snort crank or anything you wanted in the Hall, but smoking was just about impossible to sneak.

Bobby laughed, pointing to Mike's feet. "You still got your Chucks on, man." Sure enough, Mike still wore the telltale Chuck Taylors—the beige Converse high-tops issued to every Juvenile Hall inmate.

Bobby was tweaking, Mike could tell. "Got any shit, man?" he asked.

Bobby shook his head. "Did up all I had," he answered. "But I still got some bud. Let's smoke a bowl."

Weed alone never cut it for Mike, even after a couple of weeks without anything, when his tolerance was at its lowest. "Let's go get some beers," he said as soon as the pipe was empty.

"I ain't goin' out with you wearin' those Hall clothes," Bobby said. Quickly, Mike changed into the oversized jeans and Nike windbreaker Bobby gave him. They headed to the corner liquor store. The clerk there was a longtime customer of Mike's, a guy who used to talk recovery at the kids but now traded beer and cigarettes for crank. "I'll be by with something for you tomorrow," Mike promised, and the clerk handed over a six-pack of Schlitz Malt Liquor.

Three tall beers and another bowl of weed later, Mike had called most of his friends to tell them the good news. Only a couple of them gave him a hard time, telling him he was dumb to run. One offered him a place to stay.

Two hours after Mike ran from Vista Village he was at his new home getting high with Jeff, a twenty-five-year-old who had his own place, a girl-friend Mike really liked, and a cute two-year-old son, Gardner. Smelling the crank smoke as he walked into Jeff's made Mike's pulse race in anticipation.

As soon as he and Mike were settled on the couch, Jeff pulled a small rock of crank and a glass pipe out of the stash bag on the coffee table. He dropped the rock into the pipe, held a lighter beneath the bowl until the rock melted, then blew the "cut"—the stuff the dealers add to stretch the meth—off the surface of the melted liquid.

Mike was mesmerized, watching. He loved everything about getting high, the ritual almost as much as the rush. He waited hungrily as Jeff snapped the lighter shut, rolled the pipe between his hands to coat the bowl with the dope, then held a flame under it to melt the crank again. Finally it was time. Jeff offered him the pipe. Mike's hands shook with excitement. He inhaled deeply, then blew out a gray cloud of smoke.

Ahhh. The rush jolted through Mike's body. Yes! Even his fingertips felt good. His toes! His eyebrows! He and Jeff passed the pipe back and forth until the bowl was empty. Now Mike was ready for anything. "Got any beer?" he asked, jumping up off the couch and pulling open the fridge. Mike's favorite buzz was being drunk and sprung at the same time.

As Jeff and Mike sat drinking together, Jeff said Mike could stay with him and Connie for as long as he needed to. Mike wouldn't have to pay rent—just chip in for utilities, baby-sit Gardner once in a while, and con-tribute his share of the dope. Jeff said he'd hook Mike up with a job at Sky-Blue Detail, a car wash and detailing shop where Jeff got his Mustang cleaned. When Connie got home that night, the three of them sealed the deal with a pizza, another bowl of crank, and a few more six-packs of beer.

Mike started smoking weed and drinking when he was twelve, not long after he moved in with his dad. Being a good-for-his-age skateboarder, he'd always hung out with older kids, stealing his dad's beer out of the fridge, getting drunk, smoking blunts. His dad, Michael, warned him about the drinking—whenever Michael was fresh out of rehab, he admitted he was an alcoholic; when he was back to drinking, he said it ran in the family and nothing and no one could stop it.

Michael had done a lot of coke and speed back in the day. Mike suspected he still did. The excuse he gave Mike was, "We didn't know it was bad for us back then." But Michael didn't mind his son smoking weed. "I never heard of anyone smoking pot, then going out and beating someone up," he always said.

It took Mike hella long to convince his mom to let him move in with his dad. So when he saw her on weekends, Mike didn't tell her how cool his dad was about the pot. "You're just trying to get what you never had," she used to say before she finally let him move in with Michael. "And it's just not gonna happen, Mike."

Mike knew what his mom meant. After the divorce, Mike was supposed to spend every other weekend with his dad. But when Michael showed up he was usually drunk or high, or both. When he didn't, Mike would pace around his mom's house, hanging on to his suitcase as if that would make the weekend, his whole life, turn out the way it was supposed to. Mike grew up believing that if he just lived in the same house with his dad, his dream would come true.

His mom finally gave in when he was ten. By the time Mike was twelve, he and his dad were more like roommates than father and son. On Friday nights Michael would go out to play music with his band. "Stay out of trouble," he'd say on his way out. Or "If your room's clean when I get home, I'll give you some good bud." Mike would be smoking pot with his friends when his dad's friends would call, telling him to come pick Michael up. Mike learned to drive that way, maneuvering his dad's pickup truck through the Santa Rosa streets at two in the morning, his dad drunk and snoring in the passenger seat.

Pretty soon Mike gave up skateboarding, baseball, and everything else he'd been into; it all seemed boring and pointless. He started getting into fights, getting into trouble at school. He kept his dad off his back by threatening to tell his mom how Michael slapped him around when they got into one of their fights. He kept his mom off his back by promising to do better.

Then when he was thirteen, Mike snorted his first line of crank with his buddy Jack. And became a crank fiend, just like that.

Within a few days Mike had graduated from snorting crank to smoking it. He hadn't slept, except with his head on his desk at school, since that first night. "I'm turning into a fucking dope fiend," he told himself. "From now on I'll only get high once every two weeks." A week crawled by. All Mike could think about was tweaking. "Fuck it," he said finally, and snorted some more.

Mike stopped caring about everything except crank. He stopped going with his mom on weekends to see his grandma and his cousins. He stopped going to school—he'd always hated it anyway. He stopped going home most nights. After that Mike never went more than a few days without snorting, shooting, or smoking crank, unless he was locked up in the Hall.

Snorting got him the most wired in the shortest amount of time. Shooting was a smoother, shorter high. But smoking was Mike's method of choice. When he was still going to school, Mike made his pipes from test tubes he stole from the science lab. After he quit school, he started making them from the glass air fresheners they sell at every corner store. He'd peel off the paper label, then wash the cherry-, pine-, or strawberry-scented chemicals out of the tube. He'd hold the hissing torch—a Coleman gas canister fitted with a propane tip—to the glass till it glowed red in the heat of the flame. And then he'd do the trickiest part: blowing into the molten tube as hard as he could till the bottom expanded into a bowl with an air hole blown into it.

Mike was famous for his pipes. He could make one faster than anyone, and what tweaker wants to wait around to get high? Secretly, he considered himself an artist, like the glass blower he'd seen once on the Discovery Channel.

Why do teenagers do drugs?

Does Mike do drugs because his father does? Because he was wounded by his parents' divorce? Because he struggled in school? Because he dropped out? Because he stopped playing sports and started hanging with stoners?

Maybe Mike does drugs because his parents are too lenient, or too strict; or because they make too many demands on him, or too few.

Maybe it's because addiction runs in Mike's family, or because enough people have told him it does that he's resigned himself to that fate.

Maybe Mike's drinking and cigarette smoking led him to try pot, and his pot smoking led him to try crank.

Maybe, living as he does in the methamphetamine capital of the world, smoking crank for Mike is like a kid in a brewery town drinking beer: doing too much of what the locals do, teenage thrill seeking he'll soon grow out of.

Or maybe speed will kill Mike. And maybe—having nothing to look forward to beyond his next high, seeing little in his future that's worth growing up for—he doesn't care if it does.

We'll never know—how could we?—what Rubik's Cube of causes turned crank into Mike's best friend. But that doesn't keep us from trying to figure it out. As well we should. Without understanding the causes of teenage drug use, how can we hope to treat or prevent it?

Many government agencies are dedicated to researching this question. Their studies yield lists of contributing factors—some commonsensical, some seemingly contradictory, many condemnatory—that shape the strategy of the prevention programs our tax dollars fund so generously.

The National Institute on Drug Abuse (NIDA) attributes youth drug use to "chaotic home environments; ineffective parenting; lack of mutual attachments and nurturing; shy and aggressive behavior in the classroom; failure in school performance; poor social coping skills; affiliations with deviant peers; and perception of approval of drug-using behaviors in the school, peer, and community environments."

Children most often begin to use drugs at age twelve or thirteen, NIDA says, beginning with illicit use of legal substances (tobacco, alcohol, inhalants), then progressing to illegal drugs, most commonly marijuana. According to NIDA, kids who smoke cigarettes or drink are sixty-five times more likely to smoke pot.

The Substance Abuse and Mental Health Services Administration (SAMHSA) finds increased risk among "adolescents who dropped out of school or who reside in households with fewer than two biological parents." The Parents' Resource Institute for Drug Education reports that teens who live in single-father homes are almost twice as likely to use drugs as are kids who live with both parents. Teens who live with father and stepmother are at second-greatest risk, followed by those who live with mother and stepfather, and mother only.

The Office of National Drug Control Policy (ONDCP) tells us that the estimated eleven million children whose parents abuse alcohol or illicit drugs face heightened risks of drug abuse themselves.

A government-funded Harvard University study reports "far higher" rates of drug use among gay and bisexual teens (understandable, considering the study's other finding: more than 30 percent of gay and bi teens said they'd been threatened with a weapon during the past thirty days; about one-third had attempted suicide during the previous year).

The Center on Addiction and Substance Abuse at Columbia University (CASA), while acknowledging that its research, "like any telephone survey, most likely underreports the extent of use of illegal drugs," found that only one-quarter of American teens—30 percent of white kids, 18 percent of African Americans, 23 percent of Hispanics—live with "hands-on parents" who "establish rules and expectations of behavior." Those teens, CASA says, are at one-fourth the risk of teens living with "hands-off parents" who "fail to consistently set down rules and expectations." CASA also reports that two of the most important factors leading to youth substance abuse are the availability of drugs and perception of risk in using them. According to SAMHSA, race has an impact on that critical availability factor (and on virtually every other aspect of teenage drug use and treatment, as we'll see).

What does the research say about what keeps kids from turning to drugs?

"Since 1991, drug use has been increasing among America's youth," a NIDA drug-prevention brochure acknowledges, adding optimistically, "Now it is possible to describe the basic principles derived from drug abuse prevention research . . . so that they can be applied to successfully prevent drug use among young people."

What are these prevention principles? According to the ONDCP, the "resiliency factors" believed to help kids resist drugs are "stable temperament, high degree of motivation, strong parent-child bond, consistent parental supervision and discipline, bonding to pro-social institutions, associations with peers who hold conventional attitudes, and consistent, community-wide anti-drug-use messages and norms."

"When youth are strongly connected to school and successful in school," NIDA's Household Drug Survey found, "they tend to associate with peers who do not use substances and tend not to use them themselves." The

ONDCP says that a young person involved in sports is 49 percent less likely to get involved with drugs.

Although only one-third of American families regularly share meals together (half of them with the TV on), CASA says that teens of "hands-on parents" who eat dinner with their teens six or seven nights a week aren't nearly as likely to smoke pot. "It is time for every parent to look in the mirror rather than look outside to what everyone else can do," CASA asserts. "Parents need to ask themselves every day: 'What am I doing today to keep my kids drug-free?'"

To the worried or guilt-prone parent, this list of "prevention principles" is a to-do list marked "Urgent." Studying it, any good mother, father, or guardian will yearn to raise only heterosexual, athletic children of stable temperament, parenting them soberly and effectively in a nonchaotic home headed by their two biological parents and located in an antidrug community, ensuring that they are neither shy nor aggressive and always academically successful in the classroom, surrounded by peers who do not use substances and who hold conventional attitudes.

Let's see: How many items on that checklist have I myself accomplished?

I was bonded to my sons and they to me—and more than one trained professional suggested that our "enmeshment" was part of Jesse's problem. I was short on discipline, but no teenager was more supervised than Jesse: unlike most parents, both of his were self-employed, so we could and did stay on him, as his friends said, like white on rice. I put a home-cooked dinner on the table every night at six, but it often grew cold while I drove around the Oakland streets looking for my missing son. As for sports—don't talk to me about sports. Despite his gift for basketball (as a high-school junior he was the only white player in the renowned Oakland Athletic League), Jesse was kicked off more teams than most kids ever join.

Much of what the studies advise parents to strive for makes perfect sense. But given the real-life realities of parenting adolescents in these United States, the guidelines seem cruelly idealistic at worst, easier said than done at best. For starters, the lists don't address the fundamental mystery and miracle of parenting, of human nature itself.

Why does one child turn toward self-destruction while his brother turns the other way? Why is Jesse, unlike anyone else in our family, a brilliant artist? A former menace to society? A devout Christian? Would living with both of his biological parents, or being Hispanic or gay, or having different friends have made him more or less so?

By framing the causes and deterrents of teenage drug abuse strictly within the realm of the personal, the prevalent research directs our attention away from the equally relevant impact of the political. Yes, families in America today are falling apart, with disastrous effects for our children. Yes, quaint as it sounds, we *do* need to eat dinner with our teenagers—maybe not every night, but often, and always with the TV off. We *do* need to know what's going on in our kids' classrooms, their lives, their hearts. We *do* need to reweave the web of community that once held children and families firmly in place.

But as parents we cannot accomplish these things alone. Sweeping societal as well as personal changes are in order. What decent parent (and yes, there are many who, in many ways and for many reasons, do not fit that definition) wants any less than the ideal childhood for her child? And how many parents can achieve that dream within the bounds of our profit-driven, family-unfriendly, child-neglecting society, in which the number of children living in poverty—and in Juvenile Halls—rises steadily, while the money spent on children's health, education, and welfare steadily falls? How can we blame parents for their kids' drug use when the number of hours worked by middle-class parents rose, between 1989 and 1998, by six full-time workweeks a year; and having a baby or even leaving work early enough to cook dinner can threaten a parent's job?

Without venturing a remedy, former Secretary of Health, Education and Welfare Joseph Califano acknowledged in 2001 that "national efforts to keep schools drug-free have failed, primarily because drug-prevention lessons don't address the factors that lead students to experiment with drugs."

What are those factors, really? Until we begin to understand the root causes of our own failings—as parents, yes, but also as a society—we won't understand our teenagers'. And until we—government and employers as well as parents and voters—show our children that there is simply nothing more important to us than they are, we won't give them what the smoke signal of their drug abuse tells us that they need: parents with time and energy to know and nurture them; schools equipped to engage and educate them; a world and a family that welcomes and makes a place for them.

————————

On the run, Mike lived the life he'd dreamed of all those long nights in the Hall, in rehab, in his own bed under house arrest, the monitoring bracelet on his ankle keeping tabs on him like a PO who never slept. Detailing cars was fun—especially with the free-flowing crank that kept Mike and his fellow workers *seriously* attentive to detail—and his nine-dollar-an-hour paychecks more than covered his expenses. He loved taking Gardner to the park, teaching him new words, tossing him a ball. On weekends Jeff and Connie took Mike to Reno or Tahoe, where he got to go jet skiing and partying with older girls—strippers, sometimes.

Soon after he moved into Jeff's, Mike called his mom, then his dad, to tell them where he was. He didn't want them to turn him in, but he didn't want them to worry either. At first his mom threatened to call the cops, but Mike knew she wouldn't go through with it. "We're gonna see if you can handle your business, stay out of trouble for once," his dad told him. "Maybe being on your own will teach you some responsibility."

A few weeks later, Mike showed up for Christmas at his uncle Jerry's, where his mom's family always gathered for holidays. They all knew he'd run away, that there were warrants out for his arrest. His cousins were cool with that, but some of his aunts and uncles gave him dirty looks. So Mike didn't stay long. When he hugged his mom good-bye, she had tears in her eyes.

Over the next seven months Mike had a few scares. He'd be driving a friend's car and run into a friend of his mom's who knew he didn't have a license, that he was wanted by the police. Or a cop car would pull up to the Seven-Eleven when Mike was inside, and he'd have to run out the back. One day his boss at Sky-Blue Detail told Mike the cops had been in looking for him. Being a tweaker too, Tony was cool: he just gave Mike his last paycheck and told him to come back when the heat was off. A few weeks later when Mike ran out of money, Tony took him back, no questions asked. The cops never showed up there again.

Mike had a superstition that worrying about getting caught would make it happen. So he kept himself from worrying most of the time—including the day he was coming off a three-day crank run, crashing and broke, when

Heather, a friend of Jeff's, offered him a stolen checkbook that hadn't been reported stolen yet.

Mike didn't hesitate. He called Ken—one of his younger, dumber friends, a kid with a real ID and no warrants—and told him they could make some money, fast. "All I need is a ride," Mike said. When they got to the check-cashing place, Mike had Ken write out the check for three hundred dollars and sign it. Mike promised Ken ten bucks for his trouble and sent him inside. "I'd cash it myself," Mike explained, "but you know I got warrants."

Feeling twitchy and depressed, the way he always did when the crank started wearing off, Mike sat in Ken's car waiting. And waiting. Five minutes took an hour to go by. "What's taking so long?" Mike started getting mad. "Can't that punk do *anything* right?"

He drummed his fingers on the dashboard, turned on the car radio, turned it off. All Mike could think about was getting the money, getting some crank, getting back to Jeff's and his pipe. Finally he jumped out of the car, slammed the door behind him, took one step toward the check-cashing store—and stopped dead in his tracks.

Cop cars were coming from everywhere. "I'm fucked," Mike thought. Struggling to stay calm, he started walking away as slowly as he could.

"Get your hands up!" a cop yelled. He dragged Mike into the store, yanked his hands behind his back, and cuffed him. Ken was cuffed too, and he wouldn't meet Mike's eyes. Mike realized Ken had ratted him out. Looking at Ken, in his baggy pants and shaved head, Mike could see his own mistake. The kid looks like a skinhead gangster, he thought. No wonder the store had called the cops.

"I didn't do anything!" Mike told the cop who was guarding him.

"That's not what your little friend says," the cop snapped back. "We've got you on at least two felonies: passing fraudulent checks and commercial burglary." He took out his notepad. "What's your name?"

Mike's mind spun like a CD off its track. "David Warren," he answered. Dave was a good friend. Mike figured he knew enough about him to answer any questions they came up with.

"Your friend here says you got the checks from some girl named Heather," the cop said, shoving him into his car. "Let's see what she has to say."

The cops sped over to Jeff's house, dragged Mike out of the car, and pounded on the door, yelling "Police! Open up!" When no one answered, they pushed the door open. They grabbed Heather as she was running out the back, searched her pockets and purse, found a pipe and some crystal meth.

"You motherfucker!" Heather screamed at Mike as the cops cuffed her and led her outside. "I did you a favor! And you ratted me out!"

"It was Ken," Mike mumbled. Heather had never been in trouble before. And now she was in *big* trouble. Just like Mike was.

One of the cops took Mike back outside and patted him down. He found four Vicodins and one Vitamin E horse capsule that Mike used for cutting crank. "I can get rid of these for you," the cop murmured, slipping the pills into his pocket. "So you don't get charged for them too." Then he put Mike back into his car and drove him down Highway 12 and up Pythian Road to Juvenile Hall.

"You need to take this kid to the hospital," the admitting supervisor told the cops. "He's having a drug reaction." Mike made his teeth chatter and his hands shake even harder than they already were. The cops drove him to a hospital in Santa Rosa, where he sat on a gurney for two hours, handcuffed, still tweaking, and thirstier than he'd ever been in his life. No one would bring him any water.

"Fuck, man, I made it seven months," he thought. "I knew it was gonna end sometime." He told himself that he'd use the time in the Hall to catch up on his sleep.

Finally a nurse checked Mike's pulse and blood pressure and told the cops they could take him away. "Just another speed freak coming down," she said.

Back at the Hall, they ran Mike's prints through a new electronic fingerprinting machine, then booked him under his real name for two felonies and a misdemeanor: conspiracy to commit commercial burglary, conspiracy to pass stolen checks, and offering false ID. "That'll get you three years minimum," warned the cop who'd taken Mike's pills. Aside from the new machine, it was strictly same old, same old at the Hall: two days in the holding cell, then a court date and the offer of a deal.

Mike's mom was in the back row of the courtroom, as always; his dad wasn't there, as always. Mike's "public pretender," as Mike called the lawyers they gave him, told the judge that Mike had agreed to plead to one felony in exchange for the other charges being dropped. The judge scheduled Mike's sentencing for a date in two weeks, warned Mike that he might be headed for some serious time, pounded his gavel, and sent Mike back to his cell.

At the sentencing hearing, Mike's lawyer asked the judge to give him ninety days in Probation Camp, a county-run jail way out in the boonies that was one step worse than the Hall, but not as bad as CYA—the California Youth Authority, where the kids who are murderers and rapists go. When Mike heard that, he saw what would happen next as if he were watching a movie. They'd send him to Camp, which was minimum security. He'd run away. He'd get caught. They'd bring him back to the Hall, where he'd be on Intake status for forty-five days, which wouldn't even count against his sentence.

"I don't need Camp," Mike told the judge. "I need drug treatment."

The judge looked at Mike's mom. "Mrs. Butler. Are you in favor of sending Mike to treatment? I see here that he's already been through a twenty-eight-day program as well as Drug Court, and nothing seems to have done the job."

Mike looked at his mom, begging her with his eyes. "I think Mike might finally be serious about getting off drugs," she said. "Maybe treatment could help him do that."

"Thank you," Mike mouthed to his mom. He turned back to the judge, trying to make eye contact. The judge ignored him.

"What do you think, Ms. Graves?" the judge asked Mike's PO.

"He definitely needs drug treatment," she said. "We don't stand a chance of rehabilitating this young man until he's free of his addiction to methamphetamines."

The judge sighed. "All right, Mike," he said. "I guess you're going to treatment. I can only hope that this time you'll take advantage of it."

"I will, Your Honor," Mike said. "I promise."

The next day, Danny Ramirez showed up to interview him for placement at Center Point. A week later, Mike was on his way there in the truck with Danny. And then Danny made that fatal mistake, turning right instead of left. So Mike just had to get out and run.

TRISTAN

Why Are We Here?

Sitting on a plane for Bend, Oregon, a Kid Rock CD blasting into his head-phones, Tristan was trying hard not to cry. He knew where he was going—to Journeys, the same hard-core wilderness program that his older brother got sent to a few years ago. And he knew why: because he'd just gotten kicked out of boarding school. Still, he felt confused, as he often did, as if his life was a train whizzing by him, not stopping to let him on.

The past few days were a blur. The dean at Cragmont Academy saying, "You can come back after you get some help with your addiction." ("Addic-tion?" Tristan stammered. "What does that mean?") The Cragmont chaplain driving him to the airport. His mom, Marian, meeting him in San Francisco with that totally freaked-out look on her face, telling him he was going to Journeys the next day. Begging his parents to let him stay home, promising to do better. His older brother, Luc, telling him that Journeys wasn't all that bad. His stepfather, Rob, telling him he'd come back a better person. Then his mom driving him back to the airport this morning, crying as she put him on the plane, saying, "It's only three weeks. It'll go by fast, I promise."

Kid Rock was just making Tristan's confusion worse, all that "pimpin' girls" noise in his ears. He switched to a Jimi Hendrix CD, hoping to find some wisdom in Jimi's lyrics. Everyone said Jimi was "hella deep," but Tristan couldn't even make out the words of his songs. How lame was *that*? "Lame-ass punk," he heard the boys at Cragmont taunting him. "Fat-ass pussy."

The pilot announced that they were landing. Tristan looked out the window. He couldn't believe his eyes. There was snow *everywhere*. "It's gonna be fucking *freezing* at this place," Tristan realized. In his fourteen years, Tristan had only seen snow at the Sierra ski resorts where he and his friends went snowboarding on winter weekends. When they got cold, they could sit in the lodge and drink lattés. Tristan was pretty sure they weren't going to be serving lattés where he was going.

"Fuck!" Tristan cursed as he ran across the icy tarmac in the shorts, T-shirt, and beach sandals he'd put on at home in Marin County this morning. By the time he got inside the airport he couldn't feel his toes. He was digging through his backpack, hoping his mom had packed him a jacket, when a huge, scary-looking guy came up to him and said, "I'm Rodrigo. Follow me."

Rodrigo didn't even offer to help Tristan with his bag. "You got any cigarettes, lighters, weed, grenades, dynamite?" Rodrigo asked as they climbed into the Suburban.

"No!" Tristan shouted. Was this guy kidding? He felt like he was in a bad movie.

"You better not be lying," Rodrigo warned him. "They'll strip-search you when we get to the ranch house." Rodrigo handed Tristan a bunch of forms on a clipboard. "Fill these out," he said, and started driving.

Tristan tried to focus, but the words were flopping around like fish on the page. "Um . . . what month is this?" he asked.

Rodrigo shot him a dirty look. "The one between Halloween and Christmas," he snapped sarcastically. "Can you figure the rest out all by yourself?"

As soon as Tristan walked into the Journeys office, another buff guy came up to him. "I'm Sancho," he said. "Take your clothes off." Tristan looked around. A couple of kids were mugging him already. "Pull down your boxers and bend over," Sancho barked.

Tristan had been teased about his chubbiness at Cragmont so much, he'd stayed in his room for the first week he was there. He hadn't even eaten until a nice teacher started bringing him his meals. Now they expected him to start his time here *naked?*

"Can we do this in the bathroom, please?" he asked Sancho politely. The kids snickered. "Drop 'em. Now," Sancho snapped.

"I'm in the wrong place," Tristan thought. "When my parents find out how bad this is they'll take me out of here."

Tristan had been suspended from school plenty of times, in trouble with his parents for years. Ever since he started drinking and flunking classes in sixth grade, then smoking pot and flunking classes in eighth, he'd been dragged to therapists and educational consultants and psychiatrists and doctors who'd tested him for learning disabilities and dyslexia, diagnosed him with ADD, and put him on Ritalin. He'd even been driven home in a police car once, when he and some friends got caught stealing cigarettes from a Seven-Eleven. But Tristan had never been arrested, let alone strip-searched, before. He couldn't believe his mom had done this to him.

"I'll run away," Tristan decided. Then he looked at Sancho's bulging, tattooed arms. "This dude's gonna kick my ass," he thought. He closed his eyes, as if that would keep the people in the room from seeing him, pulled his clothes off, and bent over.

The next night Tristan and nine other boys—all of them dressed in the Journeys uniform: glow-in-the-dark orange pants and jackets and camouflage underwear—were driven to the Journeys base camp 160 miles away. The "barracks," where meals were cooked and served, was one room in the middle of nowhere, with a pump for water, a generator for electricity, a woodstove for heat, and an outhouse in the snow. The counselors slept in the barracks. The boys slept in a tent outside.

"My mom's paying eight thousand dollars a month for me to be here. I'm not eating that gross-ass food," Tristan said, scowling at the plate of macaroni and cheese that the kid on dinner duty put in front of him.

"You're gonna want that shit so bad in a week . . ." the kid said. "Anyway, you have to clean your plate." After cleanup the kids sat around on their cots in the big tent and told Tristan, the only new kid, how the program worked.

"Forget running away," advised one boy, who'd been sent to Journeys for counterfeiting ten thousand dollars on his mom's laser printer. "We've all tried it. No one's ever made it farther than Bend. Sancho calls the cops, says we got another one on the run, and they come looking for you."

"Why would I run away?" Tristan said. "I'm getting out in three weeks."

The other kids laughed. "Dude, your parents lied to you," said an eighteen-year-old who was there for forging checks. "Everybody who comes here says that shit."

"Trust me. I'm leaving in three weeks," Tristan insisted.

"My parents told me I was going on a canoe adventure for a week," a skinny boy said. "I've been here four months."

Before lights-out the counselors gave out journals and pencils with blunt tips and told the kids they had to write in them each night.

DAY 1

Very worried that my parents will change their mind and have me stay here longer than planned. the toilet is gross, disgusting and smelly I'm kinda scared to use it! This place is way worse then I thought. Just setting down on my small bed with no mattress a million miles away from everything I miss and crave!

During his first week at Journeys, Tristan kept thinking he was as miserable as he could possibly be. Then he got more miserable. First it was "Work Ethic": chopping and carrying wood, building rock paths in the frozen dirt, digging holes with shovels that snapped in the cold. Then the twenty-five-mile, five-day camping trip called "The Trek": teams of four kids carrying not only their own heavy backpacks, but a stretcher filled with a hundred pounds of supplies. At night the counselors broke out the rations: powdered milk, tuna fish, peanut butter. Every morning Tristan woke up with his arms aching, swearing, "No way I'm gonna do this again today." Every day he walked farther, carried more than he had the day before.

DAY 3

I'm very clueless of the reason why mom and Rob sent me here, compared to everyone else here I feel like a goodie-goodie who never does nothing wrong. I could have went to intencive therapy and easily passed it and went back to Cragmont without problem. Now I have risked every chance of me succeeding and being happy. I'm trying to think of Journeys as something to look back on and say, "oh man that was a great experience," but all I see is hard work, bad food, no relaxing so basically nothing like home. Hopefully things will get better but if they don't do I keep working my hardest or just say fuck it?

The counselors checked the kids' journal entries each morning. Once Tristan realized that what he wrote in his journal, like the things he said in group sessions, would affect how soon he got to go home, he started using the same formula for his entries that he used when he spoke in group: mixing bits and pieces of what he actually felt (mad and betrayed) into big batches of what the counselors wanted him to feel.

DAY 7

Dear Me,

I am looking forward to my solo, it sounds really hard but I think I'll have a feeling of freedom. If you make a mistake out there then it is your own fault, not the way your parents brought you up or because you got fucking ADD or anything. No rules, no laws, I am in control.

On the eighth day, the boys were loaded into the Suburban and driven to their "solo sites": a barren patch of snow-covered sagebrush where each of them would spend five days alone, five miles from each other. Rodrigo gave Tristan a tarp and a rope to make his tent, a shovel to dig his shit hole, a sleeping bag, a list of journal assignments, and five days' worth of Ritz crackers, peanut butter, granola, powdered milk, and water. Rodrigo told Tristan to ration his food carefully and not to go more than fifty feet from his tent. Then he took Tristan's boots just to make sure he couldn't go.

DAY 9

I lay here in my tarp all day long with my eyes wied open, thinking about some weird ass shit that I never thought I would ever think about. Thinking about how much more I need to be talking and spending time with everyone in my family and all this other crazy ass shit.

By the third day of his solo Tristan had eaten everything but the crappy granola, and he'd lost track of time. He only ventured out of his "tent" to hobble to his shit hole. When he peed, crouched on his knees with the sleeping bag wrapped around him, the pee froze as soon as it left his body. At night Tristan was terrified, listening to the coyotes barking in the darkness. The last few nights he thought he heard people talking and laughing. But there was no one anywhere near him, except once a day when Rodrigo or Sancho drove past Tristan's site, waving at him from fifty feet away to make sure he was still alive.

Tristan tried to distract himself by working on his journal assignments. The first was called, "Why Am I Here?"

"Because my fucking parents kicked me out of the house—that's why!" Tristan yelled, his voice bouncing off the canyon walls. And then he rubbed his fingers together to warm them and settled down to write.

WHY AM I HEAR?

Growing up in a family of 4 children, there was a lot of competition going on. Thru my whole life I was always the one that was the slowest or that got the bad grades or that got in trouble the most. The one that always needed the special help and all that crap. So I always got all the attention and never had to do to much for myself. When I was about 11 years old, my mom realized what she had been doing my whole life. She stopped feeling sorry for me when I screwed up. That was all I knew was to be cared for by my mom.

Doing his assignments made Tristan think back on his life. He'd been in special ed from kindergarten on—extra embarrassing because his step-brother, Max, was the same age and in the normal classes. Tristan had always been chubby, and he'd always been teased about it. Most of all, Tristan had always been mad.

Mad because his childhood sucked, starting when he was four years old. His parents split up, and Bruce, his dad, moved two hours away and came out as gay. Then his mom got together with Rob, and Rob and his two kids moved in with them, and they moved from Berkeley to Marin.

Tristan got along fine with Max and Caitlin—Caitlin was older than Tristan and Max and younger than Tristan's real brother, Luc—but Tristan and Luc both wished that their stepfather would just disappear. Whenever Tristan didn't get his way, he'd threaten to go live with his dad. Whenever Tristan's mom got mad at him, she'd threaten to send him there. After a while Tristan barely knew his dad; he only saw him once every few months, when he and

Luc took the train to see him for the weekend. Sometimes they had such a bad time at their dad's, listening to him trashing their mom, they'd come home a day early. After the divorce, they weren't a family—they were teams in a war. It was Rob and Mom versus Dad, with both sides saying nothing but evil things about the other.

As Tristan got older, everything just got worse. In sixth grade he got expelled for bringing his stepfather's sword to school and flashing it at some kids who'd been calling him names. He didn't fit in with all the snobby people at his middle school in Ross, one of the richest towns in rich-as-hell Marin. The only thing that made the other kids like him was when he started acting crazy, talking back to the teachers, saying "Fuck you" to them when he really felt like saying that to Rob.

When Tristan was in eighth grade, Marian brought him to a therapist to see if he had Attention Deficit Disorder. The therapist asked him whether he ever forgot where he put his backpack ("Yes"), whether he smoked pot (he did, but he said he didn't) or used drugs (ditto). She asked if he wanted to go on Ritalin (he said he did) and why. Tristan told her he wanted to be able to study better, so he could be in the "smart room" at school with Max. The truth was, he thought it might get him high. Tristan stayed on Ritalin for two years. It made him feel a little more cloudy than usual, but it didn't help him study, and it didn't get him high.

Then Tristan found a way to feel less like a loser. Along with the beer and vodka he'd been drinking on weekends, he started smoking pot every day. Getting high mellowed him out, but it didn't mellow out his teachers or his parents. He kept getting suspended for disrupting class, cutting class, smoking pot. His mom took him to an "educational analyst" in San Francisco—the same one she'd brought Luc to when he started screwing up. The woman showed Tristan a bunch of flash cards and asked him what they meant, which made Tristan suspect that it wasn't just his academic level she was analyzing. The analyst told his mom to send him to Cragmont, a fancy boarding school in Utah.

Tristan begged his mom not to send him away, but she wouldn't change her mind. She told him that being at Cragmont would help him deal with his anger and his smoking and drinking. She told him she'd already made a fool of herself, begging her father for the thirty thousand dollars that a year at Cragmont cost. She put him on a plane with two duffel bags and a house-plant for his dorm room. When he got to the Salt Lake City airport, no one was there to pick him up. He sat on his duffel bags at the baggage carousel, holding his potted plant and crying.

At Cragmont the other boys kept teasing him, so Tristan went to his room and stayed there for a week. Then he got assigned a roommate who was even fatter and dorkier than he was. Tory was Tristan's ticket to popularity. He started making fun of Tory to the other kids, pushing him down the stairs and laughing when he fell, putting shit on his toothbrush and entertaining his classmates with imitations of the look on Tory's face when he saw it. Now Tristan was invited to walk to town with the cool kids, to smoke pot, and pay the townies to buy them booze and beer.

Two months later, Tristan and his friend Alex had just come back from sharing an eighteen-pack in town when the dorm parent confronted them. "Confess," he said, "or I'll Breathalyze every kid in the dorm."

Tristan knew he'd get kicked out of school if he admitted he'd been drinking, that his grandfather's thirty thousand dollars would be wasted, that his mom might make him go live with his dad, or worse. He also knew that other kids had been drinking that day and that his hard-earned popularity would be down the tubes if he got his dorm mates in trouble.

So Tristan confessed. And that's when everything started moving really fast. He went before the Discipline Committee, he begged for a second chance, the chaplain drove him to the airport, and his mom put him on a plane for Journeys. And now here he was: alone in the snow.

DAY 11

When I go back I'm gonna be totally honest with Mom and Rob and I'm gonna spend time with Max actually doing stuff with him. They really will be amazed at this, I can't wait to see the look in there eyes when I actually do these things! Mom said the only expectation she had was no more control battles but I'm gonna show her more than that.

On the sixth morning of his solo Tristan heard the Suburban roaring through the frozen desert. "Time to go," Rodrigo told him. "Pack your stuff out. Don't forget your water." Then he drove off.

"Fuck that," Tristan said. He poured out the water he had left so he wouldn't have to carry it and set off on the three-hour hike to base camp.

DAY 12

I think I've improved a lot with the physical work here. Its kinda funny because no one expected anything from me but I have a lot of suggestions to tell everyone that I think will really make a difference. Thinking about presents to get everyone for Christmas. I hope that I'll have enough time when I get home to buy all the presents.

Sitting around the campfire in group that night, Tristan talked about how much he'd learned from his solo, how glad he was to have been sent to Journeys, and how ready he was to go home. "Bull-*shit!*" Sancho spat his favorite word across the circle. Then he handed Tristan a letter.

DAY 13

Just read letter from mom telling me that I have to stay here over Christmas and then do another 21 days. I already knew Sancho was gonna tell them that I was doing shitty, and like always Rob would take complete control and fuck me over sideways. They don't know what there doing. I don't know what I'm doing wrong out here so how do I change that. how do I let people know I'm trying if they don't give me a chance to? No way out of confusion, no way in to realization.

Two months later and thirty pounds lighter, Tristan left Journeys, went back to Cragmont, and finished out the semester. In September 2000, the start of his tenth-grade year, he got what he'd wanted all along. Marian enrolled him at Marin Pacific High, the "normal" high school a few miles from his house. That's when the real party started.

Pot, Ecstasy, mushrooms, alcohol. Vicodin, Xanax, Valium, codeine. At age fifteen Tristan's life was all about what he could find, beg, or steal to drink, swallow, or smoke. He woke up high, spent the day getting higher, and went to sleep high. When he showed up at his classes his teachers hassled him, asking why his eyes were so red, why he couldn't stay awake. So he dropped his first class of the day—who wanted to get up at eight in the morning anyway?—and then his second—who wanted to get up at nine-thirty?

Soon Tristan was visiting Marin Pacific High only to conduct his drug transactions: buying an ounce of pot and selling half of it at enough profit to buy another ounce; trading the pills he stole from his friends' parents' medicine cabinets for fake IDs to use at the liquor store and fake ATM cards to use at the cash machine.

When his parents asked why he was staying out so late, he told them he'd signed up for night classes with a friend. When he ran out of pot, he told them he needed money for books. Everything Tristan could get his hands on turned into drugs: the foreign money his grandparents brought home from their travels, the cash stupid kids left in their unlocked lockers, the change his friends' parents left lying around their houses. Once, he snatched fifteen dollars out of his mom's purse, then stood there remembering that same purse lying on the car seat between them when he was a little kid. He put the money back, horrified that he'd almost stolen from his own mother. Later that night, broke and crashing, he wished he'd taken it.

In need of two hundred dollars to buy an ounce, Tristan and his friend Corbin—who'd been at a rehab in Idaho while Tristan was at Journeys—decided to do what several kids they'd met in rehab had done: print their own money. Corbin had a brand-new computer, scanner, and printer in his room, so they went to his house and printed up some twenties. Then they rode their skateboards down the hill to Long's Drugs, bought one Snickers bar apiece at separate registers, and tried to keep from howling out loud when the clerks handed them change for their twenties. Tristan and Corbin worked their way through the shopping center, using their twenties to buy pizza at Papa Murphy's, lattés at Starbucks, and a second round of Snickers at Safeway.

Then they took some twenties to Charley's Mini-Mart. Tristan got in line behind Corbin. Corbin handed Charley a Snickers bar and a twenty. Charley took the money and held it up to the light.

"Don't run," Tristan told himself, his heart hammering in his chest.

"Come with me." Charley took Corbin to the store's back room. Tristan ran to the safest place he could think of, falling into the flow of the two thousand students in the halls of Marin Pacific High.

Tristan couldn't sleep that night, imagining Corbin in Juvenile Hall, wondering if Corbin would rat him out. But the next day at school Corbin handed Tristan the rest of the twenties and said his parents—both of them lawyers—had gotten him a sweet deal: probation and therapy, no Juvenile Hall time at all.

The next week, in the middle of a school day, Tristan and a few friends were smoking in his hotbox—the closet in his room that he'd tricked out with a red lightbulb, some beanbag chairs, and Bob Marley posters—when suddenly his mom yanked the closet door open. Pot smoke billowed into her face. His friends scattered.

"You told me you wouldn't smoke anymore!" his mom yelled, tears running down her face. "You're a cheat and liar!"

When Rob got home from work that night, he and Tristan's mom went into their bedroom and locked the door. A few minutes later his mom came downstairs and told Tristan to pack his things. "You have two choices," she told him, her eyes swollen into slits. "Either you go to your dad's for two months, or you go back to Journeys for a month."

"Fuck Journeys," Tristan said.

"Fuck Journeys," he said again the next morning, when his mom drove him to the Amtrak station, turned to him, and begged, "Please go to Journeys. *Please*. It'll be so much better for you." Tristan snatched the wad of money from her hand, grabbed his bags from the backseat, slammed the door in her face, and stomped away.

When he got to the ticket window, Tristan glanced back at his mom. She looked so pitiful, sitting there crying. He felt like he was slipping down a mountain, grabbing at branches that kept breaking off in his hand.

Tristan walked back to the car. He opened the door. He hugged his mom and told her he'd go to Journeys. The next morning, one year after Tristan had arrived at Journeys for the first time, his mom took him to the airport and put him on a plane for Bend again.

FROM: Journeys Ranch [mailto:ranch@Journeys-bend.com]
SENT: October 26, 2000
TO: Marian
SUBJECT: Letter from Tristan

Peeps,
    Hey whatsup peoples, how's life? I hope everything is alright.
Not to much excitement here, days seems like months and an

hour is like a week but I'm doing good. I walked a Lama yesterday which was much fun and relaxing.

I miss all of you much and I apologize for ignoring you all as much as I did, I'm sorry for lying and for all the distrust and frustrations that I have caused in the past, believe me that it will never happen again. I'm glad that you all care for me as much as you do otherwise I wouldn't have come here.

Love,

Tristan

FROM: Marian Winthrop
SENT: October 31, 2000
TO: ranch@Journeys-bend.com
SUBJECT: Letter for Tristan

10 Reasons to try Phoenix Academy

1. Phoenix Academy has only 6–8 students per class, gentle teachers, and is similar to Team
2. The Team Program at Marin Pacific High is being expanded to 2 years (so you can go there after you finish at Phoenix)
3. Rob's early-morning coffee
4. Running in the rain to Corte Madera creek
5. Sturgeon at Lark Creek Restaurant
6. Fresh crab
7. Thanksgiving at home
8. A puppy
9. Drums
10. For Tristan

FROM: Bruce Mercer
SENT: November 04, 2000
TO: Journeys Ranch [ranch@Journeys-bend.com]
SUBJECT: Letter for Tristan

Tristan,

It would appear that, if things aren't going well at your mother's place, then the next logical step is to try living at your dad's. I feel that this would generally be the normal next step in such situations, but it seems you consider this the worst thing that can happen to you.

You tell me I have no say in the matter as the money is coming from your mother's family, but this is not true as your mother is trying to bill me for half of all costs.

I remember last summer you told me how all your friends have been through Journeys or a similar program and these programs are a joke. You have told me a couple of times that you know what parents and family want to hear and you know to say these things even though Journeys has had no effect on you. You say that you are still you and you will do what you want.

So, you can see why I am a little dismayed at the idea of your just all of a sudden heading to Journeys for a second time.

As you know, you come from an impossible situation. Your mother and I do not speak, and the last thing she would want is to admit that she is having a problem as a mother. Then there is the odd dynamic between her and Rob and their competing visions of what the house rules should be. This situation with the two adults in your house in disagreement about many matters lets you manipulate the situation and affords you an unusual degree of independence at 15 years old.

So where do we go from here? That is for you to decide. You told me last summer that you wanted to attend a top-rated college like Harvard but then your subsequent actions at the beginning of this school year would appear to have led you in an opposite direction.

I am here for you, but my solutions are not to ship you away out-of-state for other people to solve my/our problems. I am here for you if you will let me be, but not in an off/on context. Are you ready for a program or goals, and if so what are they?

Love,

Dad

JOURNEYS
PO BOX 7849
BEND, OREGON 97708
TEL: (541) 385–7538
E-MAIL: OFFICE@JOURNEYS-BEND.COM

January 3, 2001

Mrs. Marian Winthrop

62 Madrone Way

San Anselmo, California 94905

Dear Marian,

Your son, Tristan Winthrop-Mercer, participated in the Journeys Wilderness Program in the winter of 1999. After the Wilderness Program, Tristan participated in the Journeys Residential Program for two months. Unfortunately, Tristan did not complete the Journeys Residential Program and returned home (the typical stay is 4–6 months). After almost exactly one year, Tristan returned to Journeys as a consequence for disrespecting his parents and continued marijuana use. He remained in the Journeys Residential Program for one month. Tristan needs at least six consecutive months to address his emotional and drug issues. Until Tristan makes the commitment to change, the same issues will keep coming up for him as summarized in the following paragraph.

Tristan's ability to rationalize and manipulate to get what he wants protects him from being confronted about responsibility. Tristan presents as indifferent when frustrated and uses this to keep others from seeing his real fearful feelings of inadequacy. Tristan avoids his true feelings with self-destructive behaviors such as excessive drug use and splitting techniques between his parents. Tristan's emotional needs equal his need for some sort of drug and alcohol treatment.

Journeys recommends Tristan participate in a structured, emotional-growth program that can address his feelings of inadequacy and drug use. Tristan also needs a small-school environment that can address his academic needs. In order for any program to be effective, Tristan will need to buy in and make the commitment. It is unknown at this time where Tristan stands for his future. If you have any further questions, please feel free to call me. Thank you.

Respectfully submitted,

Grace Wilbur

Journeys Residential Program Manager

Why are we here?

How has it come to this: children of affluence, banished by their distraught parents to patches of barren land where they're stripped of everything their parents so badly wanted them to have?

Thirty years ago when Tristan's parents were his age, they (and millions of other teenagers, including me) were doing what he's doing now, exploring their passions, altering their consciousness, and individuating from their parents. In other words, sex, drugs, and rock 'n' roll.

Unlike our kids—forced to tread in their parents' footsteps even when they do drugs to rebel against their parents—we believed that we were inventing it all. Surely before we came along, no generation had crossed so many frontiers, challenged so many institutions, done so many drugs (at least not until our kids came along and did even more of them).

But hundreds of years before we mediagenic 1960s kids had secured our place in history, drugs stirred consciousness and controversy in America. Marijuana played a starring role from the start. Grown here since before the states were united, in the 1600s it was sold as a medicinal herb in pharmacies and general stores. After the Mexican Revolution of 1910, Mexican immigrants taught gringos to light up and turn on for more entertaining purposes.

In the 1850s opium arrived with Chinese railroad workers and quickly became the rage of the upper class. Most who used it began in their teens, horrifying the upstanding populace and triggering the nation's first antidrug campaign. When increased importation tariffs on opium failed to stem the flow, the 1914 Harrison Act—aimed at saving young women from "being ruined morally and otherwise"—made opium illegal except by prescription. As is true to this day, when drugs are outlawed, only outlaws have drugs: a prescient 1918 study of opium-addicted inmates at San Quentin prison found that 48 percent of them had first used the drug between the ages of fifteen and twenty-one.

Eager to profit from the American appetite for opiates—especially the new German import, a "safe and nonaddictive" formulation called heroin—

in the early 1900s the drug companies of the day stepped into the void. Before there was Bayer Aspirin there was Bayer Heroin, sold over the counter in drug kits complete with hypodermic needles. Ad campaigns promoted heroin as the cure-all for everything from alcohol withdrawal and cancer to depression, tuberculosis, and old age. By 1925, five years after the Dangerous Drug Act made nonprescription sales of heroin and morphine illegal, there were two hundred thousand heroin addicts in the United States.

Marijuana returned to center stage when the Volstead Act of 1920 dramatically hiked the price of liquor. Overnight, pot was transformed from the favored high of the marginalized—Mexican immigrants and Negro jazz musicians, mostly—to white America's drug of choice. By 1930, "tea pads," where potheads could get high legally for twenty-five cents, had sprung up across the country; more than five hundred flourished in New York City alone. Then the Great Depression hit, and with it a surge of the anti-immigrant jingoism that so often accompanies economic downturns. Mexicans were blamed for joblessness; pot use was blamed on Mexicans. And so the Marijuana Tax Act of 1937 became the first in a series of antimarijuana laws that account for just under half of all drug arrests today.

Morphine and heroin use rose again after World War II, carried home in the duffel bags and veins of the GIs who got hooked in the killing fields. Triggered by GI addiction and by the beatniks' reintroduction of pot to the white middle class, in the 1950s new laws were passed imposing stiffer penalties for drug offenses. Once again youth became the target of a government antidrug campaign. Evoking images of beret-wearing, Marxism-spouting, heroin-injecting beatniks, government propaganda portrayed heroin and marijuana as equal and inseparable twin menaces. The campaign's credibility-crushing scare tactics were later blamed for helping to inspire the all-out drug rebellion of the 1960s.

If you remember the 1960s, they say, you weren't there. But I remember them well, and so will we all, as the most paradigm-shifting few years in modern history. Between 1965 and 1970 arrests for marijuana possession leapt 1,000 percent; a 1970 poll revealed that twenty-four million Americans had smoked pot. But while we hippies at home skipped through the aisles of the 1960s drug supermarket, taste-testing LSD and peyote, hashish and mescaline, our brothers and boyfriends in Vietnam were taking a far harsher trip. Estimates of "in-country" heroin addiction among GIs were as high as 25 percent, or more than sixty thousand young men—many of whom came home strung out as well as traumatized.

By the late 1960s, "Speed Kills" flyers flapped on telephone poles in youth culture enclaves like the Haight in San Francisco and New York's Lower East Side. Former psychedelic voyagers were losing their minds and their teeth, now, to methamphetamines and junk. Flower power continued to shrivel throughout the 1970s, when suburban kids took to inhalants and psychosis-inducing PCP ("angel dust") ravaged the poor.

In the 1980s, methamphetamine labs started springing up in the white working-class hamlets of the West, and middle-class kids in cities raved their nights away on "designer drugs" like Special K, GHB, and Ecstasy. Throughout the next decade the "classics"—pot, speed, LSD, inhalants, pills, coke, and heroin—remained on the adolescent menu, and Ecstasy became what it is today: the fastest-growing drug among teenagers in America.

But no drug has ever hit America with the deadly precision of crack's attack on the urban ghettos in the 1980s—a genocidal carpet-bombing orchestrated by none other than the CIA. A 1996 *San Jose Mercury News* story—widely challenged but ultimately substantiated—reported that the CIA-backed Contras funded their overthrow of Nicaragua's socialist government with blood money sucked from crack addicts at home.

"Nicaraguan Contras, run by the CIA, delivered tons of cut-rate cocaine to a young Los Angeles drug dealer," the *Mercury News* reported, ". . . who turned the cocaine into crack and supplied the Crips and Bloods street gangs, which saturated the market with crack and used the profits to arm themselves with automatic weapons." The story called the deal "one of the most bizarre alliances in modern history: the union of a U.S.-backed army attempting to overthrow a revolutionary socialist government and Uzi-toting 'gangstas' of Compton and South Central Los Angeles."

As marijuana use has climbed among adolescents of all races—between 1992 and 1998, it increased by more than 50 percent; twice as many teenagers now use pot than all other drugs combined—the rate of new victims claimed by crack each year has slowed slightly since its apex in the 1980s. Still, crack continues to wreak devastation, particularly in African American ghettos.

Slinging Rock, Turning Tricks

Zalika felt like she was on some crazy-ass TV show. But, no, this was real. One minute she was out there selling crack, same as always. The next minute she had two cops surrounding her and sixty rocks flying out of her hands, her mouth, her pockets. And then the cold, hard slap of the handcuffs on her wrists.

The two cops led her around the corner of 16th and Mission, past all the other people selling crack and heroin, speed and weed, past all the dope fiends waiting to buy it. When the black cop put his hand on her head to bend her into the backseat of their squad car, his touch felt gentle, as if he cared.

Zalika could read people like a book. That's how she'd made it pretty much on her own since age twelve. And she could tell that for some reason the cop felt bad about arresting her. Maybe she had a chance after all.

"It's my fifteenth birthday tomorrow," she told the black cop, realizing as she said it that it was true. "Please, would you let me go?"

"Can't do that, young lady," he said. "We already called it in."

"I swear I'll never do it again," she begged. "I don't like being out there no way."

The cop turned around and looked at her. "Why you doin' it in the first place?" he asked in a kind voice.

"Where are your parents? Where do you live?" the white cop asked.

Zalika was good at having conversations with older people, especially when they could do something for her. So she told the cops everything that might help them decide to let her go. She explained that she'd run away from her parents' house across the bay in El Sobrante (so they'd know she came from a good middle-class suburban family, not some ghetto housing project). She told them she lived with a friend in the Fillmore (but not who that friend was: C-Note, a twenty-seven-year-old drug dealer). She told them she was on that corner just trying to get by. She told them this was her first time in the back of a police car.

"Who put you out on that corner?" the black cop asked.

"Some dude I just met," she lied. "I just got started before you came."

The cop must have believed her; he started talking to her like she didn't know what was going on. He told her how the big dealers sell to the little dealers, how the little dealers get kids like her to take all the chances, how girls like her get killed out there all the time.

"Tell me something I don't know," Zalika thought as the cop went on and on. In her three months on 16th and Mission, she'd seen fourteen people get shot and too many people OD'd to even count. She'd seen people stabbed with broken bottles and beaten with baseball bats, drunks and dope fiends fighting each other till they dropped.

She herself had been robbed at gunpoint five times—the last time a week ago, when she was pulling an all-nighter. At three in the morning, just six rocks left, she was sitting at the bus stop, pretending to be waiting for the bus. A guy sat down next to her, poked something sharp into her side.

"Hand over the shit or you're dead," he said. Zalika gave him the hundred dollars from her bra.

"Quit fucking playing," he said, so she handed him the three hundred from her left shoe. The guy stood up in front of her then, pointed the gun at her head. He's gonna blow me away, Zalika thought. So she gave him the six rocks too, even though she knew it would make C-Note hella mad that some fool got his crack for free. It worked: the guy took the rocks and ran.

C-Note *was* mad—all Zalika had for him was the two hundred she still had in her right shoe. But he didn't hit her, just told her to make up the four hundred the next night. C-Note only had her out there for his little petty money anyway. His fat cash came from those briefcase-sized bags of crack he cooked up and left the house with every night.

Zalika asked the cops questions, responded politely to theirs, showing them that she wasn't some 'hood rat, that her background put her on their level, or higher. She thought it was working. Then they pulled up to San Francisco Juvenile Hall.

Zalika was terrified. She'd heard so much about that place: girls getting jumped and stabbed, getting torn up in gang fights, committing suicide. Zalika was so freaked out, she didn't even trip when the guard pulled the bobby pins and extensions out of her eighty-dollar hairdo, took her hundred-dollar jeans, her fifty-dollar Guess top, and her brand-new Nike Air Maxes, strip-searched her, and made her cough until the sack of rocks fell out of where she'd hidden them inside her.

After a few days Zalika realized that the Hall was just a big day care full of girls like her, out there selling dope for their men. Still, she cried every night, worrying that they'd take her away from her parents for good—even though she'd run away three months ago and had no intention of going back, even though she didn't know if her parents would even take her back.

When the guard made Zalika call her parents, her mom said they'd been waiting for a phone call to hear if she was dead or alive. Her dad told her there was nothing they could do for her now. "You're safer in there," he said. "If you come home you'll just run away again." Zalika wanted to ask them to come visit her, but she couldn't get the words out of her mouth. The whole two months she was in there, waiting for San Francisco County and her home county, Contra Costa, to decide what to do with her, her parents never did show up.

So Zalika had nothing to do but lie on the thin, hard mattress in her ten-by-ten cell and think about how stupid she'd been. She couldn't forgive herself for not just leaving those damn rocks in her pockets. The cops couldn't have searched her without a warrant. And they never would have picked her up as a runaway—there were too many kids on the streets for that. You could sell drugs all day in San Francisco; the cops didn't even care. If she hadn't choked, she could still be out there making that good money.

After a few days her probation officer, a nice black lady named Laverne, came to talk to her. Laverne asked the same questions Zalika had been asked a million times before by the therapists her parents had been sending her to since she started getting in trouble. Zalika told Laverne the same story she'd told the others.

When she was little, Zalika was "Baby ZaZa," the first child her parents had together, the favorite of her grandmothers, aunties, and uncles. Her family was happy then, living near her dad's people in San Francisco, her dad's two older daughters staying with them off and on. Zalika and her dad had a special bond; everyone knew she was Daddy's girl.

Then a month after Zalika's little sister was born, a woman came to their door with a month-old baby in her arms, saying that Zalika's dad was the father of her child. After that it was nonstop drama at home: her mom crying, her dad yelling, the move from their apartment in San Francisco to a totally different world, a house in the upper-middle-class, racially mixed East Bay suburb of El Sobrante.

From then on, except when her little brother was born, both of her parents were working all the time—her dad running an engineering company; her mom commuting an hour and a half each way to her job as a city planner in San Francisco. Even with her dad gone so much, he and Zalika stayed tight. When she was eleven he told her a secret—that she was his favorite of all his six kids. Zalika knew another secret she didn't tell anyone, even him. She'd overheard her dad on the phone, and she knew there was at least one other woman in his life.

When she was still eleven Zalika started having some drama of her own. Bored by kids her own age and bored at school, where she stayed on the honor roll without even trying, she started hanging out with her twenty-year-old neighbor Katrina and Katrina's twenty-three-year-old boyfriend, Tyrone.

One day Tyrone slipped Zalika his phone number. Zalika called him that night. He told her he wanted her "tight little body." Zalika liked the way his words made her feel—like she was special and beautiful and grown. They went on like that for a few weeks, whispering sweet nothings over the phone. Then Tyrone asked Zalika to meet him after school. They went to his place, and, just before her twelfth birthday, Zalika lost her virginity in his bed.

"Where the hell have you been all night?" her dad screamed when Zalika got home the next morning.

"None of your fucking business," she yelled back. When her daddy started beating her, Zalika felt like her heart was cracking open. She was his favorite; he'd never done anything like that to her before. Then she went numb.

That night when her parents fell asleep, Zalika jumped out her second-story bedroom window and ran to the corner to meet Tyrone. "I don't care if I ever go home again," Zalika told him, climbing into his car.

Tyrone said he was taking her someplace special. As they crossed the Bay Bridge, the lights of San Francisco glittering before them, he handed Zalika a purple lipstick. "Put this on," he said. "Where we're going, you need to look grown." They parked in front of a copy store on Mission Street. Some Mexican men standing in the doorway asked Zalika if she wanted a fake ID. Zalika nodded, and the men told her to go inside and get her picture taken. She came out with a California State ID that said she was twenty-two.

The special place Tyrone took her to was a club called The Theater. Zalika used her new ID to get in. On the club's tiny stage, topless women danced around a pole while men drank and stuffed twenty-dollar bills into their G-strings. "You see all that money?" Tyrone asked Zalika. "You could be doing that."

"Sounds good to me," Zalika said. Tyrone asked to see the manager, who asked to see her ID.

"You're hired," the manager said, and told her to start tomorrow.

To celebrate, Tyrone took Zalika to Foxy Lady, a store that sold strippers' outfits. He bought her three bra-and-miniskirt sets—classy black and red silky ones, none of that tacky shiny stuff. Then they went to a hotel and made love over and over. Tyrone told Zalika he'd never felt like this about any woman. She told him she'd never felt like this about any man. He took her back to The Theater.

Zalika watched a few of the dancers, then got the signal from the emcee and strutted onto the stage. She closed her eyes, started moving her body to Mary J. Blige, running her hands over her face, her hips, her breasts, the way Tyrone did when they made love. "*Heck* yeah!" Zalika thought, as the men started cheering and throwing money at her. "This is *hella* fun!"

That week Zalika danced every night. She slept on a cot in the Theater locker room during the day, went out to dinner with Tyrone when he came around at night. After five nights she'd made seven hundred dollars. She gave the money to Tyrone. He gave her back a hundred and told her it was time for her to "put in an appearance" at home.

Zalika crept up to her house at ten the next morning, hoping her parents would be at work. But her dad threw the door open, his eyes wild with rage. "We thought you were dead," her mom sobbed behind him. Her dad had called the police and the local newspapers, the TV and radio stations. He'd printed up stacks of missing-child flyers with Zalika's picture on them. "Dang—you were that worried about me?" Zalika thought. Even with her parents screaming at her, that felt kind of good. Especially coming from her dad.

"Where were you?" her dad shouted over and over. Zalika was sure her dad would kill Tyrone if he found out, so she kept quiet. Her dad smacked her around. She still wouldn't tell. He hit her harder. Finally she spit out Tyrone's name.

Her dad called the police. When they got there, he told them to charge Tyrone with statutory rape. The officer sat down next to Zalika. "It wasn't your fault," he told her. "You're just a little girl."

"I really like that guy. I wanted him," Zalika said angrily. "He didn't make me do *anything*."

"You're saying you *wanted* to have sex with that man?" the officer asked Zalika. Looking right at her dad, Zalika said, "Yes. And I still do."

Tyrone went on trial. Zalika told the DA she couldn't stand to watch, and he arranged it so Zalika didn't have to testify. Tyrone went to prison for two years. Katrina stopped speaking to Zalika. Her parents stopped speaking to each other. Her dad moved out of the house. And the special bond between Zalika and her dad was broken.

After that Zalika didn't feel like a little girl anymore. There was nothing she was afraid of, nothing to keep her at home. She started taking the bus to San Francisco, kicking it with the people who hung out near her dad's family in the Fillmore. She smoked her first weed. She sold her first ten-sack. To the people around her, ghetto life was normal; it was all they'd ever known. But to Zalika, coming from boring-ass El Sobrante, it was different, exciting. She loved boosting bottles of Smirnoff Ice and packs of Black-and-Milds from the corner store, rolling blunts, getting drunk and high. She loved knowing that anything could happen anytime. The wild feeling of the streets matched the wild feeling inside her.

Zalika started cutting classes, then whole weeks of school. She was spending nights at different boys' houses, days at home in between. One morning just after her thirteenth birthday, she dropped by her house. Her parents told her they were driving to San Diego to visit her stepsister in college. "If you want to come," her dad said, acting like he didn't care whether she did or not, "you better pack your stuff and come on."

Ten hours later they arrived at the campus. They went into the office to get directions to her sister's dorm. As soon as they were all inside, Zalika's parents slipped out. A white lady locked the door behind them. "This isn't your sister's college," she told Zalika. "It's a Christian home for girls in trouble with drugs and alcohol. You'll be here nine months. We hope you'll make the most of it." Zalika screamed and cried, banged on the door, threw chairs across the room. But she was stuck there.

For three months Zalika seethed at her parents on the inside and played by the rules on the outside. She did schoolwork every morning, sat through group therapy every afternoon, went to church on Sundays. She felt like she was walking in her sleep—not a good feeling, but not a totally bad one either. Then one day as group was ending, a girl named Cindy whispered to Zalika, "Me, Rachel, and Jamie are running away. Wanna come?"

Suddenly Zalika felt like herself again. "*Hell* yeah," she whispered back. The four of them ran across the campus, out the unlocked gate, and all the way to town. Zalika called her mom collect from a pay phone. She told her mom that if she didn't send her a plane ticket, she would hitchhike home by herself. Her mom said she'd send a ticket the next day.

As Zalika stepped out of the phone booth, a police car pulled up. The cops said the school had reported the girls as runaways. Zalika told the police she was waiting for a ticket home, but they took her to a center for abandoned children. Finally the ticket came, and the police drove her to the airport.

When she first saw her mom, Zalika felt so much bitterness she almost threw up. "You don't trick a person like that," Zalika told her. "You don't take your child way the hell down to the Mexican border and leave her there alone." Then she changed her clothes and took off for San Francisco.

The next day Zalika met C-Note. He offered her a place to stay—no sex; she'd just be his dope girl—and a lot more money than she'd ever made selling weed. Zalika was good at what she did, and C-Note was good to her in return. He took her to Mary J. Blige and Mariah Carey concerts. He bought her outfits, meals in nice restaurants, a lavender Camaro with eighteen-inch rims. Her life was just fine—until the night the cops rolled up on her and ruined everything.

Two months after her fifteenth birthday, handcuffed and shackled, Zalika appeared in San Francisco juvenile court. The judge told her they were transferring her case to Contra Costa County and sent her to Juvenile Hall in Martinez, ten miles up the freeway from El Sobrante.

Three weeks after that the Contra Costa judge found her guilty of "accessory to sale of crack cocaine" and sentenced her to a hundred hours of community service, a hundred dollars in restitutions, mandatory drug testing, a curfew of six o'clock on weeknights and ten on weekends, and individual and family counseling. Zalika was ordered to go to a special school, a day-treatment drug program called the Sun and Moon Center. Worst of all, Zalika was put on JEM, Juvenile Electronic Monitoring. She had to wear an ankle bracelet that kept track of her twenty-four seven—which meant that except when she was at school, in counseling, or doing her community service, she had to be at her parents' house.

Mad as she was, Zalika tried. Not because any of it was fair, not because any of it would do her any good, but because she knew that if she violated her probation she'd end up in CYA, California Youth Authority, where she did not want to be. So she went to school most days. She pissed the teachers off—they accused her of bragging to the other kids about her life in the streets—but she got good grades anyway. She went to the counselor the county sent her to, even though it took her two seconds to realize the woman was about half as smart as she was.

She even tried to get her community service hours in. But they put her by the side of the road, way out in the cuts, pulling weeds—not a job for a person who takes pride in her appearance. The dirt ruined Zalika's new jeans and white tennis shoes. Dust got all up in her just-braided hair. She stopped coming. Then she missed a few appointments with her new PO.

The judge issued a warrant for her arrest. If she went home now, the cops would come and get her.

The old feelings had come over her anyway. Zalika was bored. She'd never forgotten the way being with Tyrone had made her feel. To get that feeling again, she had to run away again. So she went to San Francisco, asked some people she knew to help her get out of town. They drove her across the Golden Gate Bridge to San Rafael. The town was mostly rich white people—Zalika would have stood out like a sore thumb—but they dropped her in the one poor, mostly Mexican neighborhood called the Canal.

Zalika had known since age eleven that she could use what she had between her legs to get what she needed. And that's what she did to get by in San Rafael. She met men. They took her home with them, bought her dinners, gave her a place to sleep. When she felt they were getting tired of her, she moved on to the next one.

After a while, all that moving around got old. Zalika thought about going home, but she had that warrant hanging over her. The longer she stayed away, the less it seemed that she could ever go back.

Three months after Zalika arrived in San Rafael, she was buying a box of condoms in the Circle K when a dark-skinned, handsome man started talking to her. He said his name was Marcus, but she could call him MC.

Zalika went home with Marcus that night, and they were never apart—not by choice, anyway—again. Marcus was selling dope the smart way: a few nights in San Rafael, a few in Novato, then a run in San Francisco. When things got hot in those places, he'd go chill somewhere dead like Santa Rosa till the heat died down. He stayed in hotels, kept himself mobile.

Zalika felt like they were married. They slept together every night, made love two, three, sometimes four times a day. Marcus cared about her so much that he made Zalika call home at least once a week, so her parents wouldn't worry. He took her with him to see his mama in Pittsburg, even to see his baby's mama in Vacaville. Finally, Zalika thought, she'd found the right person.

So when Marcus started saying that selling dope wasn't getting it, that they needed more money to live the way he wanted them to, naturally Zalika started thinking about what she could do to help. "I met this girl at the gas station," she told Marcus one night in San Francisco. "She said she was ho'ing around the corner, that she makes hella money every night."

"You ready to do that, baby?" Marcus asked her, looking at her so sweetly Zalika thought she'd melt. "I'm out here anyway," she told herself. "I might as well do something. What could it hurt?"

Zalika said yes, she was ready. So Marcus sat her down and taught her the ropes. He told her how to talk to johns, to find out what they wanted—a trashy-acting ho' or a lady, a little girl or a grown-up woman. He showed her how to put the condom on, how to use her body language to get the most money out of a guy. He told her to remember that she was running the show, that for anything to go down it had to happen her way. Then he took her to Macy's and bought her two thousand dollars' worth of pantsuits and dresses. He took her to the wig shop and bought her ten wigs to go with them. He said she needed classy outfits to work where she was going to get her start: the best-paying stroll in the Bay, the Mission district of San Francisco.

"It's a business," Marcus told her, turning Zalika around in the Macy's mirror. "You need to dress like a businesswoman."

At first ho'ing was exciting, like something you'd see on TV. Doctors, lawyers, big-time businessmen pulling up to her in their cars, wanting her enough to pay for it. Getting them to agree to her price, the thrill of the cash, always up front, in her hand. The sex itself was the smallest part—whether they did it in the guy's car or went to a hotel, it never took more than an hour. The biggest part, the part Zalika liked best, was having the confidence to know a man five minutes and take off her clothes—to run the show, as Marcus had taught her.

And sure enough, she was making mad money: two hundred dollars a trick, five, six, seven tricks a night. Marcus would drop her on the corner of 20th and Shotwell at eleven or twelve, then wait for her at the donut shop on Mission and 20th, where all the pimps hung out, till she got done at seven the next morning As long as she broke a thousand, Marcus didn't push her; she could quit whenever she got tired.

Their real life together started when Zalika came in for the day. She'd hand over the cash. Marcus would check them into a hotel on Nob Hill or Union Square. Then he'd rent a Cadillac Escalade or a Mustang convertible, buy a few bottles of Courvoisier, and make up a pack of blunts. They'd go cruising, smoking four blunts by noon every day, drinking till Zalika was falling-down drunk. They drove to Reno and Vegas, Oakland and LA, doing donuts in the street, buying matching outfits, showing off what they had. Marcus's dope and Zalika's body were like their own mobile ATM, spitting out cash everywhere they went.

Even so, after a month, ho'ing started getting old. A couple of times the cops stopped her, asked her how old she was, threatened to call her parents. And then there was the night her dad went looking for her and found her— on the stroll.

"Zalika!" She couldn't believe it, but there he was, sitting in his car watching her in her miniskirt, spiked-heel boots, and wig, tears running down his face. "Get in," he said, throwing the passenger door open.

"No," Zalika said, and turned her head.

"Zalika," her dad sobbed like a crazy person. Then he slammed the car door shut and drove away.

"I'm hurting the people I love most," Zalika thought, watching him go. "I'm hurting myself, wearing down my body, closing down my mind so small." Her dad had been in the Black Panthers when he was young. He'd taught her about Malcolm X and Miles Davis, hung Afrocentric art all over their house. He'd raised her to do good things for the world. "This is ruining me as a person," she thought.

"Are we in the grip of a teen crisis? Not exactly," Salon.com reported in an August 2000 story, "Whose Crisis Is This, Anyway?" "Statistics show that teenagers aren't really acting up or out more than they have in the past. Instead, we are more likely in a crisis of parenthood." In previous eras, the Salon story explained, parents were guided by "dominant directives about raising children," from "habit training" in the 1930s to the 1950s "permissiveness" of Dr. Spock.

A brief history of those directives:

Spare the rod, spoil the child.

—Age-old adage

Never hug or kiss your children, never let them sit in your lap. Shake hands with them in the morning.

—John B. Watson, *Psychological Care of Infant and Child,* 1928

Children who get into trouble are suffering from lack of affection rather than lack of punishment.

—Dr. Benjamin Spock, *Baby and Child Care,* 1968 edition of the 1946 original (America's second-best-selling book ever, after the Bible)

Beating children teaches short-term obedience, but in the long term, only violence and anxiety.

—Alice Miller, author of *The Drama of the Gifted Child,* 1979

Your children are either the center of your life or they're not, and the rest is commentary.

—Calvin Trillin, *Family Man,* 1999

Adderall (mixed salts of a single-entity amphetamine product) typically improves attention span, increases the ability to follow directions, and decreases distractibility among children ages three and older. Adderall may also decrease impulsivity, stubbornness and aggression.

—Ad for attention deficit/hyperactivity disorder (ADHD) medication, 2002

What's a parent to do?

"No clear directives exist today," the Salon story acknowledged. "Limited time for parenting, overburdened two-income parents with fragile emotional ties, fear for our children's future and a generation of 'Peter Pan' parents are some of the factors that contribute to today's 'crisis in parenthood.'"

Child psychiatrist Dr. Lawrence Diller, among many others, blames that crisis on the anti-authoritarian parenting style that Americans hungered for in the post-Nazi aftermath of World War II. "The child's immediate need for gratification took precedence over instilling the discipline required for adult life," Diller writes in *Running on Ritalin: A Physician Reflects on Children, Society, and Performance in a Pill*. "Parents were supposed to talk to their children and listen to them, before taking action or making decisions about them."

Diller asks, "Does this 'politically correct parenting' lead to ADD-type behavior in a child?" He cites research showing that Americans' antipathy about our children's behavior is rising, along with ADD diagnoses and Ritalin prescriptions. "Politically correct parenting for ADD-type children only adds to the challenge of raising them," Diller concludes.

No group has taken to anti-authoritarian parenting with such fervor as the parents Salon calls "flower children parents, boomer parents . . . [who] don't set limits [and] want to be friends with their children."

It's true: the sixties legacy lives in our teenagers—but they live it in a changed world. Marijuana was much weaker when we were their age, the context in which we smoked it much stronger. Zalika's dad, Mike and Tristan's moms, and I weren't just getting high, as our kids seem to be doing now. We were fighting for racial and gender equality, ending a war, changing the world. We weren't just mouthing off to our parents; we were building a new society from the ashes of the old. Whatever the particularities of our paths, we children of the sixties grew up questioning authority, fighting for democracy, opposing hierarchy.

So how can we tell our kids not to smoke pot? Apparently we can't.

According to a July 2002 story in the *New York Times*, one in five teenagers say they've used drugs with a parent—not entirely shocking, considering that up to 10 percent of parents with kids eighteen or younger smoke pot themselves. In the same story, CASA president Joseph Califano advises parents to be honest about their past use, while blaming the boomer generation for "inflicting its habits on its children."

"We're torn, ambivalent, hypocritical, self-flagellating," *Newsweek* writer Jonathan Alter says in an AlterNet story on what boomer parents tell their kids about drugs. "Sometimes we lie, sometimes we tell a little bit of the truth. We're a big soppy mess when it comes to dealing with drugs."

What our children have inherited from their messy parents is the rage, the unsettledness, the hedonism of the sixties: the mocking disdain for the teacher, the parent, the law; the joint (or blunt, bong, or pipe) in the mouth. What they're missing is the sense of purpose that steered us and the authoritarian parents who contained us. But when they get into trouble, all parenting paradigms fade away, and we bleed for them, just as our parents bled for us.

Whichever child-rearing fad is currently in vogue, when your kid's in trouble, the "parenting crisis" is felt as the chronic clutch of fear in the chest, the unrelenting ache of sorrow in the bones. Flower power notwithstanding, there is no mother who has sat in a courtroom facing a judge over her son's jump-suited back, no father who has found a baggie of cocaine in his daughter's backpack and not asked, "How could I love this kid so much and screw up as a parent so badly?"

To parents of kids like Zalika, Tristan, Mike, and Jesse, the "experts" offer a crippling one-two punch: an abundance of trendy advice and parent-blaming and an utter dearth of family-supportive policies and compassion. In the face of all this, self-examination is fraught with peril. But if we are to do the best we can for our children—even if all we've got to work with is love, determination, and some frayed-around-the-edges ideals, even when the very world that makes our job so tough is telling us that we're failing at it miserably—examine ourselves we must.

We must know for ourselves what we need in order to do the best job possible with our children: more time with them; fewer hours of away-from-home labor required to provide for them; schools and services that better serve them. And then—defying this parenting fad and that, using everything the sixties taught us about changing ourselves and changing the world—we've got to mobilize ourselves to get it.

Ho'ing became nothing more than a job Zalika hated. If she broke the rules—looked another pimp in his face, looked at another black man, gave Marcus reason to think she was holding out on the money—he would bust her upside her head. Zalika didn't like Marcus hitting her, but she didn't take it personally. She needed Marcus just like every ho' needs her pimp: to keep other pimps and the police away from her, to hold the money when she had too much on her, to buy the drink and rent the cars and drive her around. Besides, it could have been a whole lot worse. One night she watched a pimp kick his ho' in the head till she was damn near unconscious. Zalika wanted to yell at him to stop, but she couldn't take the chance. If the girl got up, Zalika knew, she'd just go back to him anyway.

Bad as the pimps were, it was the johns you really had to worry about. Sometimes when Zalika tried to get out of the car, the guy would try to grab her. Once a john kidnapped her halfway to San Jose before she tricked him into stopping the car. That cost her a whole night's work and a $150 cab ride back to San Francisco.

Then one night a Latino man approached her at her usual spot. He said he wanted her to strip in front of him, then jack him off. He handed Zalika three hundred dollars, drove into the cuts, and parked the car. Zalika had just gotten the condom on him when he jumped on top of her. He ripped her clothes off, choked her, and forced himself inside her.

It felt like the man weighed two hundred pounds. "I'm gonna die in this car if I don't do something," Zalika thought. So she acted like she was loving the sex, sat laughing with the guy in the backseat when he was through. Then she told him she'd lost an earring and bent down to look for it on the floor. Praying to a God she wasn't sure she believed in, she grabbed the car door, pulled up the lock, and threw herself out of the car.

The john ran after her, grabbing at her from behind. Luckily Zalika had run track in school, so she could outdistance him. She hid behind a bush, panting. His footsteps slowed, stopped. He walked back to his car. It seemed like he circled the block fifty times before he finally drove off.

Scratched and bleeding between her legs, her clothes in tatters, Zalika walked the streets till she found a parked cab. "I'm through for the night," the driver said when he saw how she looked.

Zalika yanked the door open. "The hell you are," she said. "My pimp's on Mission and 20th. Take me to him *now*."

Crying with relief, Zalika ran into the donut shop. Marcus jumped to his feet, grabbed her arm, dragged her out past all the other pimps, and tossed her into their car.

"How dare you let all those niggaz in my business," he shouted, the veins standing out on his neck, "goin' in there looking like that!"

Zalika was crying, begging Marcus to listen. "You can't do *shit* right," he fumed. "Get the fuck away from me."

"The dude raped me," Zalika sobbed. She showed him the blood running down her legs. Finally Marcus believed her. He drove to San Francisco General Hospital, parked in front of the ER, then shook his head. "I can't bring you in there," he said. "They're gonna ask too many questions."

Instead, Marcus drove north to his mother's house in Pittsburg. "Take a bath, clean yourself up," he told Zalika. She told him she needed a rest, so the next night he drove her to San Rafael instead of putting her out on Shotwell. The money wasn't as good in the Canal, but the work was less stressful. The johns were mostly Mexicans, construction workers who worked hard for their money, so Zalika didn't mind letting them get some for eighty or a hundred bucks.

One night Marcus dropped Zalika off at eight o'clock a few blocks from the Circle K where they'd first met. He told her he'd wait in the parking lot as usual. She set off in her Canal outfit: a cute little T-shirt, jeans, tennis shoes, and a puff jacket—no need for the professional wardrobe she wore on the San Francisco stroll.

Zalika was heading back to the car around eleven when sirens exploded all around her. Cop cars were everywhere. Two cops jumped out. One grabbed her. The other one cuffed her.

"What are you doing out here?" they shouted. She knew that if they patted her down they'd find what they were looking for: some cocaine one of her clients had given her, which she'd been planning to share later with Marcus, a roll of condoms, and nine hundred and forty dollars.

"I'm out here visiting my friend," Zalika told them.

"Sure, sure. And what's this?" one cop asked, pulling the coke out of her jacket pocket.

"And these?" asked the other cop, pulling a long strip of condoms from the back pocket of her jeans. "Looks like cocaine possession and soliciting for the purpose of prostitution to me," he smirked.

The cops put the condoms and the coke into a plastic bag, threw her in their car, and took her to the Marin County jail.

Report and Recommendation to the
Juvenile Court of Contra Costa County

COURT DATE: 10/24/01

MINOR'S NAME: Bey, Zalika

AGE: 15

WHEREABOUTS OF MINOR: Juvenile Hall

SOCIAL STUDY AND CASE ASSESSMENT

When this deputy visited the minor in Juvenile Hall, she refused to discuss any details of her activities while away from home. She asked for another chance to return home, and said she was doing well in school, but once she tasted freedom she did not want to follow her parents' strict rules or conform to their high expectations for her.

She said she didn't understand why she behaved as she did, but that she did not want to be with the type of people who go to group homes, and if she did she would have to give up her hopes for college and a normal life. When this deputy suggested that her best chance for a normal life and college was to find out what was motivating her behavior, she said she had gone to counseling and it did not work.

It was suggested that some of the problem might not be her fault, and might be related to things that happened to her before she became a teenager. She wept copiously and said she didn't want to remember those things. She said she had gotten tired of being "out there" and wanted to come home, but hadn't been able to figure out how to do that.

DRUG AND ALCOHOL ISSUES

She has previously admitted to some use of both marijuana and alcohol but claimed she hadn't used either in excess. Neither parent sees drug usage as the first issue to be addressed. They feel sure that she has a "pimp" to whose company she would return if able.

CASE NEEDS

Despite maximum effort on the part of her parents to control her, this 16-year-old [*sic*] remains defiant. She has neither responded to therapy nor corporal punishment, nor extensive opportunities for enrichment. She is exceptionally bright, poised and charismatic. She is currently using these positive attributes to deceive and manipulate others. Zalika is behaving in a manner that puts her life at risk. She does not have the judgment to survive even in an illegal lifestyle. It is not felt that she will be able to address the underlying reasons for her runaways and sexual acting out without being in a controlled setting. It is felt that she is capable of engaging in a therapeutic relationship and that she will not access her excellent potential if she does not do so.

SERVICE PLANS

Probation's attempts to rehabilitate the minor while she remained in the community have been unsuccessful. A review of family dynamics indicates that placement is appropriate at this time. The family is not willing to have the minor return home until successful completion of an out-of-home program.

PRIOR RECORD

Please see attached.

Respectfully submitted,

Robert P. Vendana, County Probation Officer

PART 2

GETTING CLEAN

What Do We Do for Kids Who Do Drugs?

MIKE

Good Morning, Family

No one knows, really, why kids do drugs—or why some kids do worse drugs than others, or use them more destructively, or have a harder time giving them up. Not knowing doesn't keep parents, counselors, or government agencies from speculating, but it *has* kept us, for the most part, from coming up with solutions that work.

The adolescent drug-treatment industry is adolescent itself. Twenty years ago there were few rehab programs for teenagers; now there are thousands. Correction: now there are thousands of programs with teenagers in them, but all too few that are *for* teenagers, that is, tailored to their particular issues, styles, and proclivities. All too many adolescent rehab programs are "adult lite" adaptations that make about as much sense to kids as high-school sex ed would if it focused on, say, maintaining postmenopausal passion.

One such program is the "therapeutic community" known as Center Point Adolescent. I find myself at this eight-year-old offshoot of its thirty-year-old adult counterpart, Center Point, Inc., one 90-degree August morning.

"Focus up, gentlemen!" Tom, the Center Point Adolescent group therapist, calls to order the first session of the day. "This is Relapse Prevention," he reminds the teenage boys—one of them African American, three of them Latino, twelve of them white—sitting in a circle of metal folding chairs.

Although they've been awake and busy since six-thirty this morning, most of the fifteen- to eighteen-year-olds seem half asleep, still, at nine: bodies slumped, legs outstretched, their faces pimple-blotched masks of resignation. In contrast, the two new boys—one from the Oakland ghetto, one from the mountain town of Ukiah, both delivered by their respective county sheriffs to Center Point this morning—are erect in their seats. Hyperalert, eyes wide, feet twitching, they're taking it all in. Or maybe just coming down off whatever got them sent here.

"Hey, Tom. Can we open a window, man?" asks Rafael, a handsome Latino boy with a shaved head. "It's hecka hot in here." Like most of the other Center Point clients, Rafael swaggers when he walks, wears a logo-splashed sweatshirt over gargantuan blue jeans, and speaks in the wanna-be–rapper drawl of the street. Unlike most of the others, though, he's lean and muscular, his complexion clear. A former small-town heroin addict and gang member specializing in armed robbery, Rafael is in the final, "Reunification," phase of the Center Point program. So he gets forty-eight-hour weekend passes that allow him to eat noninstitutional food, breathe noninstitutional air, pump iron at the gym. After twelve months here, Rafael is scheduled to graduate in three weeks, a triumphant reversal of his several previous failed rehab attempts and return engagements at Juvenile Hall.

"Sure," says Tom, a fifty-year-old white man with a shock of snowy hair, a silver stud in his left ear, and an air of sardonic detachment that mirrors—or perhaps models—the mood of the boys. As Rafael cranks the casement window open he gazes down longingly at the San Rafael streets two stories below: bathed in morning sunlight, bustling with commuters in gleaming BMWs and Lexus SUVs scurrying to the concrete canyons of San Francisco, fifteen miles and a galaxy away.

One of the new boys raises his hand. "I gotta go to the bathroom," he mumbles.

"Get some support," Tom replies.

Sitting in the corner, typing furiously into my laptop, I take this down. Get some support? To go to the *bathroom*? It's one of many "Huh?" moments I've had since I first came to Center Point a few days ago.

"I'll support you," volunteers Henry, a longtime client. He leads the new boy, who looks as confused as I remain, down the hall of the second-story apartment that doubles as Center Point's school and therapy offices and into the bathroom.

"Who wants to start?" Tom asks. Immediately Mike raises his hand. Mike told me this morning that if he's going to get out of here faster than anyone ever has—which has been his plan since he arrived here in escape-proof shackles five weeks ago—he'll need nothing but good reports from Tom. Especially since he got into trouble yesterday for using his roommate's hair gel without permission.

The consequence of Mike's transgression was what's known at Center Point as a "Learning Experience." Receiving an "LE" required Mike to take the following steps: choose one from Center Point's list of Key Concepts (Effort, Initiative, Completion, Integrity, Open Channel, Pride, Support, Empathy, Responsibility, and Trusting). Memorize its definition. Write a five-hundred-word essay on his interpretation of the concept. Read the essay to the Center Point "community" and appreciatively receive feedback (which Mike did at this morning's eight o'clock Good Morning Group). Recite the concept at the start of each of the five group-therapy sessions that all Center Point clients attend every day (except Saturdays and Sundays, when they attend only two).

"When-I-behave-in-an-honest-responsible-and-accountable-manner-I-am-choosing-to-live-my-life-with-integrity," Mike's words run together as he rushes through them for the second time this morning. "In-order-to-live-my-life-with-integrity-I-must-develop-a-keen-sense-of-right-and-wrong."

His LE obligation thus fulfilled, Mike begins to share, tailoring his presentation to fit the topic of the group. "Yesterday me and Stanley were out on food pickup," he says, running a hand through his now ungelled, but still erect, dirty blonde buzz cut. "This drunk dude started talking to me about a movie or some shit . . ."

"Language, Mike," Tom interjects dully. Like all Center Point policies, road-tested hourly by the out-of-control adolescents they are meant to contain (and eventually, it is hoped, to change), the no-cursing rule must straddle the gap between regimentation and what might reasonably be expected to work.

"Sorry." Mike continues. "The drunk dude has a Heineken in his hand. One of those little sixteen-ounce kegs. And it looks hella good . . ." Mike's crystalline blue eyes glaze over; he slips into a reverie.

Ever alert for "triggers"—drug memories that can set off a chain reaction of cravings in a group of dopers like this one—Tom urges Mike along. "And?"

"And . . . I kinda wanted that Heineken. At the same time I saw how stupid the dude looked, spilling his beer, drooling all over himself and shit."

Several boys snap their fingers in the air, the Center Point–approved expression of agreement while someone else has the floor. "I'm gonna have people like that around me when I get out," Mike continues. "My dad and his friends get hella drunk whenever we go out in his boat. One of them fell on me one time, pushed me into the fuck—the damn lake. The issue is, I don't know how to deal with people like that. And pretty soon I'm gonna have to."

"Did you get some support for that?" Tom asks.

"I talked to Stanley," Mike answers. "That beer looked hella good," he repeats.

Hands are waving around the circle. "My feedback for you is, just keep your head high, make the right choices," advises Stanley, a one-time speed freak like Mike, now one of Center Point's star clients. "You'll see how happy your parents are, how happy you are when you keep on that track. You'll be all right."

Mike snaps his fingers, signifying that yes, he'll keep on that track and yes, he'll be all right.

"Feedback, George?" Tom calls on a sixteen-year-old white boy. "When you see somebody using like you did, it's easy to remember the good times," George tells Mike. "But you gotta remember the bad times too."

"I've had people smoking weed around me when I was on pass, know what I'm sayin'?" Rafael offers. "My next-door neighbor tryin' to offer me coke . . . As the years go by you'll develop tools to handle all that. Yes, your feelings come up, know what I'm sayin', but you settin' yourself up for relapse if you start thinkin' 'bout those behaviors."

"I've seen sh—stuff like that before and not tripped off of it," Mike responds. "I don't know why it got to me this time." He looks around the circle, his gaze landing on Tom. "I just wanted to bring it out, look at what happened, identify my negative thoughts."

Typing and listening, I feel I've landed in a parallel universe. Where on earth do teenage boys with peach-fuzzy faces, gel-sculpted crew cuts, and late-model Nikes sit in a circle sharing their childhood experiences, examining their negative thoughts, offering each other support in flawless, if Ebonics-accented, psycho-speak?

At Center Point they do. Because whichever corner of California these boys came from—its rural hamlets or hardscrabble city streets, its hardworking families or heartless foster homes—whatever definitions of success have shaped and scarred them, for these boys, now, there is only one measure of success, only one way out. And "out" is what they want, even more than they want their pipes and their needles, their fast cars and their willing girlfriends, their Cap'n Crunch in the morning and their moms' home-cooked dinners at night.

So this, then, is what they do. Learn the lingo and speak it. Learn the rules and obey them. Swab the toilets, divulge on demand, line their sneakers up at right angles in their closets. In rehab parlance, they "work a good program" in hopes of becoming one of the chosen few, the Center Point clients who graduate, get off probation, and go home free to make a whole new set of good choices, or bad ones.

I find myself on a wild roller-coaster ride, sitting in on these groups. I'm amazed, watching these incarcerated adolescents plumbing each other's pasts, wielding a battery of psychological tools so sure-handedly in service of their own healing, and each other's. I'm impressed by the persistence of the staff, many of them former addicts, all of them working for poverty wages, swallowing down daily doses of disappointment, the AWOLs and relapses reminding them regularly of the odds against the boys' success, and their own.

And I'm gripped, unexpectedly, by grief, as witnessing other mothers' sons stumbling down the road to recovery tosses me back into turmoil about my own. Why didn't I find Jesse a program like this? What might have happened—and not happened—if Jesse had had a chance like this?

Then I catch a sour note of insincerity in one boy's soul-baring confession, a whiff of blatant brown-nosing in another's, and I'm stung by skepticism. I remind myself that every kid in this room was given the same no-brainer choice, one that Jesse was never offered: months or years locked in a cell at Juvenile Hall, or twelve months sharing in group-therapy sessions here.

Are these boys becoming better human beings, I wonder, or just better hustlers? After all, what brought them to Center Point was lying, stealing, manipulating, using, whatever it took to get their fix. This program, these confessions, now, are what stand between them and the next one. Do any of these boys mean a word they say?

"Over the months you stay here you'll find out what kind of relapse triggers you have," Rafael is telling Mike. "For me it's gang-banging and everything that came with it: the females, the money, the drugs, the violence. You need to find out what it is for you, know what I'm sayin'? When it happens, you want to talk to someone, reach your hand out for some support."

Snap, snap around the circle. Beside me, a boy is jerked awake by the sound.

"You already went AWOL, man. You got a second chance." Rafael's eyes are locked on Mike's, his voice low, reassuring. "Now you got an LE. Happens to everyone. But don't trip, know what I'm sayin'? You be aiight."

"There might be times you have to take yourself out of a situation, like with your dad and his friends," Tom adds. "Maybe hang out with someone who's clean instead."

Tom checks his watch. The rigidity of the Center Point schedule, I've learned, makes the operation of Swiss trains look erratic by comparison. Relapse Prevention ends at ten-fifteen, followed by Snack (Sun Chips and juice on Mondays, apples and Doritos on Tuesdays . . .). Boys' Group begins promptly at ten twenty-five.

"Anything else for Mike?"

"I'm aiight," Mike says quickly. Dominating a session, taking more support than you give, is one of the many no-no's in a therapeutic community like Center Point. Every member of a TC is supposed to care just as much about every other member's recovery as he does about his own. And just to make sure everyone acts as if they feel that way, in a TC *everyone* gets in trouble when *anyone* screws up. After Mike ran away from Vista Village, he heard later from a kid in the Hall, the staff called a meeting, told the kids that if they'd given Mike more support while he was there he might not have gone AWOL, and put the whole place on lock-down. That kind of thing happens in TCs all the time.

"I'm cool," Mike repeats now.

"Good," Tom says. "Next?"

Serving a one-year, court-ordered sentence at a residential therapeutic community is one way in which teenagers recover (or don't) from drug abuse. As Mike himself has experienced, there are many other ways to do it (or not do it).

Like Mike, most kids who have serious problems with drugs (and therefore, often, with school, their parents, the law) cycle through myriad treatment scenarios on their twisted switchback paths to "recovery"—the elusive pot of gold that is rehab's rainbow's end. Some teenagers miss it by "aging out" of juvenile treatment options, graduating at eighteen to the meaner world of adult addiction. Some fail one too many court-ordered placements, sitting out what's left of their childhoods in cinder-block Juvenile Hall cells. Some extricate themselves from whatever rehab process they've been forced into, reducing or concealing their drug use enough to placate, bamboozle, or wear out their parents, counselors, and/or probation officers. And then there are the tiny number of teenagers in drug treatment who actually stop doing drugs.

Did I mention that, mostly, that's not what happens?

When a teenager is identified as having a drug problem (almost always by an adult), a progression of interventions unfolds. Various people get in the kid's face waving various threats and consequences. The particulars depend largely on factors outside the teen's control: the income and race of his parents, where he lives, how "hands-on" a family he has. (I say "he" for a reason: around 80 percent of kids busted for drugs and sent to drug treatment are boys.) Also relevant are the types of drugs he uses, how often he uses them, what happens when he does, and how he got caught.

Whatever gets him there, when a teenager is sent into treatment he joins the hundred and fifty thousand American kids admitted each year to publicly funded rehab programs—85 percent of them in outpatient day treatment like Phoenix Academy and the Richmond Drug Court; 12 percent in a short- or long-term residential like Center Point; 3 percent as hospital inpatients.

Three-quarters of these kids, as well as the untallied others in private programs, are being treated for abuse of marijuana and/or alcohol.

For poor and working-class kids like Mike and kids of color like Zalika, the incident that puts them on the road to recovery (or at least to enforced treatment) is more likely to originate with the police than with their parents. When kids like Mike and Zalika get sent away it's usually a judge, not their parents, who sends them. (Sometimes it's both, as when Mike was court-ordered into rehab, and his parents sent him to the only one their insurance would cover, the twenty-eight-day "ReTreat" program in Santa Cruz. There, Mike told me, he smoked smuggled-in pot and snorted Ritalin with the ADHD [attention deficit / hyperactivity disorder] kids, who stashed the pills the nurse gave them to swallow, then chopped them into lines for a post–group therapy amphetamine buzz.) .

For kids like Mike and Zalika, "rehab" usually begins in the back of a cop car; "counseling" is first administered by a probation officer. On inner-city street corners and suburban high-school campuses, in gang-infested projects and low-budget malls, for dealing and for stealing, they get arrested. They get booked. They get locked up. From that moment forward they are, as is always said with a rueful shake of the head, "in the system."

Unlike Jesse and all too many teenagers, Mike and Zalika were lucky. They were arrested in counties with diversion programs for juvenile offenders whose criminal behavior is related (or is said to be related) to substance abuse. Whether they wanted it or not, whether they needed it or not, they were offered drug treatment as an alternative to detention.

Affluent white kids like Tristan in affluent white communities like Marin County don't, for the most part, need that kind of luck. The way the scenario tends to play out for them is pretty much the way Tristan's has played out for him. After endless denying of the now undeniable, the parents realize that their son's drug use is out of control. They send him to therapy. The therapist recommends psychological testing and Ritalin for the kid and, true to the therapeutic imperative (one good session deserves another), family therapy in various configurations for everyone else.

The kid keeps drinking and drugging. His grades tumble. He has new clothes his parents didn't buy him, new friends whose eyes are always red. Terrified and exhausted, the parents decide to send him away. Maybe there's a relative who lives in a "safer" place, or maybe the therapist recommends a $200-an-hour educational consultant, who recommends an $80,000-a-year boarding school. The kid goes to the school. He gets kicked out. The parents send him to an $8,000-a-month wilderness program in Utah or Oregon. The kid comes home changed, or unchanged. His troubles are over, or he slides even deeper into self-destruction. A psychiatrist prescribes antidepressants.

If things don't get too much worse, the kid's parents live on the prayer that someday he'll get better. It's a reasonable hope. For middle-class kids like Tristan—especially those who make it through adolescence unscarred by the indelible mark of the juvenile justice system—things often do. At the kid's college graduation, his grateful parents will realize that, much to their surprise, growing up turned out to be the most powerful treatment program of all. Was all that money, all that worry wasted? They'll never know. They hardly care. Their child is saved.

The problem for parents like Mike's, Tristan's, and Zalika's is, they don't know if they'll get that happy ending or they won't—until they do, or don't.

I met Mike Butler five weeks after he ran from Danny's truck, four weeks after he turned himself in to the Sonoma County sheriffs, who shackled and delivered him—successfully this time—to Center Point. As Mike was settling into his new placement, I was talking to Center Point administrators about which of their clients might make a good subject for my book.

One day in August Danny called to say he'd identified three candidates, all of whom met our agreed-upon criteria. The boys were new to the program but had made it past the first, volatile weeks, when most kids who are going to run away do. All three were talkative and articulate in groups. And all three were willing to participate in the book—nice, Danny explained, but unnecessary. Since the Center Point clients are incarcerated wards of the court, the staff—not the boys' parents—are their legal guardians, authorized to sign away their confidentiality rights, among others. "The parents had their chance with these kids. They blew it," Danny told me. "Now it's our turn."

Hearing Danny's flat indictment roused a choir of ghostly voices in my head. The junior-high dean, calling to inform me of Jesse's third suspension that month: "Did you raise your son in a barn, Mrs. Maran?" ("Obviously not," I kept myself from saying. "A cow with a firm hoof would have done a better job.")

The doctors: "Why haven't you had him tested for epilepsy?" ("I have.") "For ADD?" ("He forgot to take his Ritalin.") "For Tourette's?" ("Oh, please.")

The high-school counselors: "Have you ever considered therapy for Jesse?" ("If there's a child psychologist in northern California he *hasn't* seen, please hand over the referral.") "For yourself?" ("Oh *that* must be his problem. A session a week for ten years hasn't been quite enough.") "For the family?" ("My kids' father and I have spent a not-so-small fortune rehashing our ancient marital miseries in the presence of their innocent victims, our joint-custodial children.")

The therapists: "Jesse needs limits, and you won't set them." ("He's an artist! Won't limits squash his creativity?")

The juvenile-court judges: "Who's running your family, Mrs. Maran— you or your son?" ("Must be him. We have ample evidence that it isn't me.")

And finally, the probation officers: "I'm pulling the plug on your son," the last one told me when he pounded on our door at seven-thirty on a school morning and found Jesse still in bed. "If you won't give him consequences," he sneered, "the system will."

"Why don't you come to the house tomorrow, meet the kids, see if you find a match," Danny suggested. So I hushed the clanging voices, pulled myself back to the present, and arranged to spend the next day at Center Point.

"The house," I'm surprised to discover as I pull up in front of it, is a two-story, stucco and brown shingle, archetypal American family home, complete with arched picture window, white picket fence, and tidy squares of green lawn. I'd expected something institutional, dilapidated; after all, Center Point isn't one of those $33,000-a-month Hollywood treatment spas where movie stars are Rolfed into recovery. Ninety-five percent of Center Point's clients—most of them imports from less affluent counties than Marin—are placed here by the juvenile justice system. Kids whose parents can afford good lawyers, prestigious therapists, or high-end rehabs don't, as a rule, end up here.

Sandwiched between a French patisserie and a discount gas station, the Center Point Adolescent house is indistinguishable from others in its neighborhood, a relatively low-rent district of mostly high-end San Rafael, the seat of Marin County, the wealthiest county in California. Center Point is a private nonprofit with headquarters in San Rafael and treatment centers in several California counties—including five in state prisons. Established as a twelve-bed, coed facility in 1993, Center Point Adolescent went boys-only in 1995 and expanded to twenty-two beds in 1997. The facility occupies two neighboring sites. The "house" is where the kids eat, sleep, shower, do chores, and watch TV. "School" is the apartment above a mattress store across the street where they attend therapy groups each weekday from nine to noon and classes from one to five.

Danny greets me at the front door of the house, leads me down the driveway to the back. I take in the basketball hoop bolted to the cement patio, the clothesline festooned with several pairs of Shaq-sized jeans, the scraggly tomato plants struggling to survive in a patch of cracked dirt—and the wide-open back door. "I thought these boys were incarcerated," I say as I follow Danny up the back steps and into his tiny, airless office.

"They are," he says. "But we don't lock them in. For the program to work, they have to want it. Whether they stay or go is up to them."

"And if they go?" I ask.

Just that morning, Danny tells me, one of my candidates did just that. Danny outlines the protocol that's triggered by an "AWOL." He calls the police, the parents, the PO, then calls a special meeting so the "house" can process the event. "Sometimes kids run before they even get here," Danny says. He pulls out Mike's file, tells me Mike's story. "Let's go meet him and the other boy. We told the kids about your project. They're expecting you."

We pass through an immaculate kitchen, a gleaming dining room, a freshly vacuumed living room. Everything that can be painted white has been; there isn't a speck of dust on the mantel, a scuff on a floor, or a smudge on a wall. Glancing into a bedroom, I see two oak twin beds flanking a matching nightstand. I'm sure I could bounce a quarter (or, more fittingly, an eighth) off the hospital-cornered bedspreads.

"How do you keep this place so clean?" I ask.

"We don't," Danny answers. "The clients do. This is a therapeutic community. We're a family here. The clients learn to take care of the family and the house while they're learning to take care of themselves."

Danny and I cross the street to the school. "The boys are in art therapy," he says, ushering me through the unlocked apartment door. This place too is spotless, if sterile. The fireplace is Sheetrocked over; the crown moldings, banisters, and built-ins all painted that ubiquitous white, as if the spirit of the house too is incarcerated.

The thirteen Center Point clients are assembled in one of the apartment's two classrooms. The art therapist, a thin woman with a lined face and a warm smile, tells Danny and me that the theme of this morning's session is "Saying Good-bye."

"Why'd you draw this, Shane?" asks Brian, the boy who's leading the group. Danny whispers to me that Brian is one of my two remaining candidates.

Then Danny ducks his chin at a baby-faced, stocky white boy in a plaid button-down shirt sitting alone in the back. "That's the other one," he says quietly. "That's Mike."

As I glance at Mike, he meets my eyes, smiles, holds my gaze with his. Who's choosing whom here? I wonder. I see the eagerness on his face, the intelligence in his eyes. I see that he's charming and determined. And just like that, I'm hooked.

Brian points at one of the pictures Scotch-taped to the wall: the word "LATER" written across the page in vivid colors. "Shane—what's up with that?" he asks.

"Right before I got locked up, I was talking to my best friend on the phone," Shane answers tonelessly. "We said 'Later' and hung up. He OD'd and died that day. I never saw him again."

"I'm curious about the bright colors," the teacher comments. "Can you tell us why you chose them?"

Shane shrugs. "Black woulda been hella boring," he mutters.

"What's yours about, George?" Brian goes on to the next drawing: a bottle of beer being poured over a crudely drawn house.

"My whole family being messed over by my dad's drinking," George says.

Brian squints at an unsigned picture of a frowning stick figure behind the bars of a jail cell, syringes and pipes floating in a cloud above his head. "That's mine," Mike calls out. "'Cause practically everyone I used to use with is either dead or in jail now."

When the session ends the boys tumble out of the room, headed for the snack that awaits them in the small kitchen down the hall. Some of them greet me on their way out; some look me over curiously or challengingly. Only Mike stays behind. "When are you gonna decide?" he asks me without preamble.

"I take it you want to be in the book?"

"*Hell*, yeah," he answers. "My story's hella good. And I already talked to my mom. She's cool with it. So—when you gonna pick someone?"

When I come back to Center Point the next day, Danny tells me that Brian went AWOL before breakfast. Then he hands me a Confidentiality Release form with Mike's signature on it, right above Danny's. The decision has been made. I've been chosen.

Mike and I settle into a routine, getting to know each other in a strange, yet oddly intimate way. I leave my house in Oakland several days a week, driving across the Richmond–San Rafael Bridge—worrying, now, as I pass the menacing turrets of San Quentin, about another boy's future, just as passing any prison used to make me worry about Jesse's. I sit through Morning Group first, then the others: Anger Management, Grief and Loss, Conflict Resolution, Cultural Sharing, Problem-Solving Skills—all except Boys' Group, from which I am politely excluded.

I engage in the mealtime ritual that unfolds in silence each day at seven-thirty, noon, and six-thirty. The Table Setting Crew unfolds the tables and chairs in the dining room. The clients file into the kitchen. The Cooking Crew portions out cold cereal and milk for breakfast; cold cuts, sliced bread, and salad for lunch; beef stew and white rice for dinner. Then the silent meal: the passing of the pitchers of bright red juice, the boys lining up at the sink to rinse their plates and stack them in the dishwasher.

After lunchtime chores each weekday the boys' teacher, a sweet, burly, bear of a man they call Stevo, arrives at the house, greets them affectionately, and herds them across the street to school. As if they were a class on a field trip or upright citizens out for an afternoon stroll, Stevo walks them to the corner to wait for the green light (jaywalking is forbidden; even staff, dashing between school and the house, don't do it). They march past the liquor store (What must that be like for them, I wonder), through the blue door beside the mattress store and upstairs to the white apartment. Each boy picks his textbook from the shelf. Some of them are working on fifth-grade math, some on eleventh-grade history. A few, it appears, can barely read at all.

"What kind of math can you do?" Stevo asks Miles, who arrived earlier today. Miles looks at Stevo blankly. "What's the last math you were doing?" Stevo persists. Again, Miles says nothing. "When was the last time you were in school?" Stevo asks.

"Eighth grade," Miles mumbles.

"How old are you? Seventeen?" Miles nods sheepishly. "Not to worry. We got a bunch of eighth-graders your age here," Stevo reassures him, plucking a textbook from the pile. "You know algebra?" he asks. Miles nods. "That's great!" Stevo says. Miles's face brightens a bit.

Stevo goes on to Hakim, the other client who's new today and the only African American boy in the house. "You're from Alameda County, right? Cool!" Stevo says. "What math were you doing?"

"Pre-algebra," Hakim answers. He recoils as Stevo tries to hand him a textbook. "I got straight F's," Hakim protests.

"Just take it from the top," Stevo tells him. "We'll get you into it. Don't worry." Looking only slightly mollified, Hakim takes the book and saunters off to a corner table.

Stevo explains to me that Center Point is classified as an "alternative school," one of many euphemisms, like "continuation school," "community school," etc., for the school that every school district has, where kids are sent after they've bombed out of the mainstream high school but before the district has given up on them entirely. Such schools have special provisions for getting kids through. As does Stevo, who awards his students credits based not on grades, but on the hours they spend doing the work, with twelve to sixteen hours required for each unit instead of the eighteen hours required by mainstream high schools.

"I give them two credit hours for art therapy, double credit for school-work they do over the weekend, extra credit if they work for it," he tells me. "I'd never have a graduate if we went by normal standards. A lot of my kids haven't completed a single year of high school. The average guy comes in here with a hundred credits, tops. The school district requires two hundred twenty for graduation."

A caring, motivated teacher, a student-teacher ratio of sixteen to one, an educational plan and pace tailored to each student: the Center Point school offers much to its students, and they respond in kind. As soon as they arrive, the boys divide themselves into the two classrooms, take seats at the folding tables, and get quietly and seriously to work. Stevo moves among them answering their questions, praising their progress, granting bathroom breaks (with support, of course). Each boy holds in his head the number of credits he needs to earn his diploma; each hour spent under Stevo's tutelage brings him one step closer to that goal.

"Can I work in a room by myself?" Henry asks. "I gotta get six credits today if I'm gonna stay on track." Permission is enthusiastically granted.

Kids who fail in school are more likely to do drugs. Kids who do drugs are more likely to fail in school. Researchers study the connection.

One conclusion: kids need more of the drugs we give them—Ritalin and other amphetamine derivatives—so they won't flunk school and turn for solace to the drugs they get on their own.

"Substance abuse overlaps significantly with learning disabilities and behavioral disorders," announced a White Paper issued by the Center on Addiction and Substance Abuse (CASA) in September 2000. According to CASA, no less than 20 percent—that's 10.8 million—of the 54 million school-age children in the United States suffer from learning and/or behavioral disorders: mostly dyslexia and attention deficit / hyperactivity disorder (ADHD). Millions of kids are diagnosed with both. Up to half of the 5 million or so kids diagnosed with ADHD, CASA says, "self-medicate" with illegal drugs and alcohol.

Ah, ADHD. Known in the 1960s as "hyperactivity," called "ADD" from 1980 until recently, the disease and its diagnosis remain as ambiguous as ever. There is no test for ADD, no gene, no defining characteristics, leading many to believe that there is in fact no such disease. As pediatric behaviorist William Carey acknowledged to a 1996 conference of his peers, "The current status of the ADD diagnosis is an embarrassment."

Nonetheless, CASA calls on parents, teachers, and pediatricians to "identify learning disabilities in children as early as possible [and] deal with them promptly" in order to reduce kids' odds of abusing illegal drugs. Nothing wrong with that, you might say, and you would be right—except when a learning disorder is confused with a behavioral disorder, which it often is, and a behavioral-disorder diagnosis leads to a prescription, which it often does. And so today we have 4 million children—90 percent of those diagnosed with ADHD—taking Ritalin or other pharmaceutical amphetamines.

Since 1990 there has been a 700 percent increase in the amount of Ritalin produced in the United States (which produces and ingests 90 percent of the world's stimulants), yielding profits that have increased 500 percent in that period of time. Novartis, Ritalin's manufacturer and the world's third-largest pharmaceutical corporation, makes about $450 million a year from Ritalin alone.

In the past forty years, the "syndrome" now known as ADHD has been the nation's most studied pediatric psychiatric condition; Ritalin the most studied pediatric psychotropic drug. Given the results of all that research, we must wonder why—besides the profits involved—more and more schoolchildren are lining up for their Ritalin in principals' offices across the country each day.

"Children who took stimulants for hyperactivity over several years did just as poorly in later life as a group of hyperactive children who took no medication," Dr. Lawrence Diller reports in his 1998 book, *Running on Ritalin*. "Both groups were less likely [than nonhyperactive kids] to have finished high school or to be employed, and more likely to have had trouble with the law or to have drug or alcohol problems."

There is no doubt that the effects of learning disabilities and the amorphously labeled "behavioral disorders" bear greatly on the risk factors for adolescent drug abuse: "reduced self-esteem, academic difficulty, loneliness, depression and the desire for social acceptance," in CASA's words. But in the current frenzy to slap medical diagnoses onto schoolchildren's antipathy, other diagnoses—social as well as a biological—are being wrongly disregarded.

"Something is awry, all right. But something not entirely medical in nature," writes esteemed child psychiatrist and author Dr. Robert Coles in *The Mind's Fate*, as quoted by Dr. Diller. Indeed: our children are not as compliant as we want them to be, not as compliant as we think they need to be to survive in the world we have made for them. But is medicating them into compliance the answer?

Many symptoms attributed to ADHD—kids' restlessness, twitchiness, short attention spans—are symptomatic not of chemical imbalance alone, but of the poor match between what kids *want* to do with their minds and energies versus what's offered to them in the place where they spend most of their waking hours: today's overcrowded, underendowed classrooms. In *Running on Ritalin*, Dr. Diller tells of teachers encouraging parents to get their kids diagnosed and medicated in hopes of making classrooms more manageable; of parents whose overscheduled lives, worries about their kids' futures, and relief at being taken off the hook for their kids' now neurologically diagnosed problems send them begging for that prescription.

"What does the greatly expanded use of such a drug say," Diller asks, "about the institutions traditionally charged with the 'nurture' of children: our homes and families, our schools, our health-care systems?"

Diller's question is apt. After all, it's not just kids with learning disabilities, ADHD, or drug habits who can't or won't sit still in a classroom, who are bored by, flunk, quit, or just plain hate school. And even those kids who are well suited to classroom learning, even those kids who love school are painfully aware of the minimal investment society makes in their success. It's not just kids who are failing school—it's schools that are failing kids.

"Kids know that their schools very often, as they would put it, suck, that a high-school diploma is increasingly worthless, that their prospects when they leave school . . . are darker, on the whole than their parents' were," William Finnegan writes in *Cold New World*.

"The official and political neglect of children," Finnegan continues, "particularly poor children, includes a brutal squeeze on public school funding in much of the country (most spectacular in California), as taxpayers increasingly shirk their traditional obligations to the young." Indeed. While we've been wringing our hands and funding studies about kids flunking school and doing illegal drugs, between 1980 and 2000 the share of all state and local funds devoted to prisons nationwide grew by 104 percent, while the share allocated to higher education shrank by 21 percent. In constant dollars, the increase in state spending on jails was nearly double the increase in spending on higher education: $20 billion for "corrections," $10.7 billion on higher education.

"Over the past generation, government has withdrawn support for education, poor children, public works," Finnegan writes. And what has the government done with the money it's been withholding from our communities, our schools, our kids, thereby contributing to adolescent and adult drug abuse? Built jails to hold drug users, that's what.

"[America's] grotesque orgy of imprisonment," Finnegan says, "is driven primarily by the politically irresistible, utterly ineffective 'war on drugs.'"

Mid-afternoons when his day's schoolwork is done, Mike and I sequester ourselves in one of the therapy offices down the hall and sit facing each other in orange plastic chairs, my tape recorder whirring on the Formica table between us. Over and over, Mike reaffirms his determination to stay clean. "I know I've got a long road ahead of me," he says. "I miss my mom—I've never gone this long without seeing her. But my mind's made up. I'm staying here. I thank my grandma for talking me into turning myself in."

After running from Danny's truck, Mike tells me, he spent three days and nights smoking crank with his friends. Then he went to his Grandma Myrtle's house. "She was hella happy to see me." He smiles tenderly, remembering. "We ate some peaches and vanilla ice cream together. We sat on her porch and watched the sunset. She told me, 'Mike, you're hurting yourself. Go back to Center Point. You won't be in there that long.'"

It wasn't the first time Mike had been given that advice, but that night, eating peaches and vanilla ice cream with his grandma, "Something clicked," he says. The next morning, July 4, his dad drove him out Pythian Road to the Hall. A week later he was granted a second chance at Center Point.

"I'm ready to take responsibility. To deal with my shit I got to deal with," Mike tells me. He runs his hand through his buzz cut, a now familiar habit. "I still go through struggles in here. I still think about using." The hand through his hair again. "I know I'll be thinking about using for a long, long time."

Sometimes Mike brings a binder with him to our sessions and shows me the checklists he's been filling out, the essays he's been writing.

Recovery Exercise #1

STABILIZATION CHECKLIST

Do you believe you are addicted to alcohol or drugs? (Please explain your answer.)

Yes, because I can't go without thinking about them and using them without being in an unstable mood. And it runs strongly in my family.

Do you want to totally abstain from alcohol and drug use?

Yes, because I have tried to use them casually but it doesn't work. Besides my last 5 years of my life have been out of control. Another example would be that I wanted to get off probation and I had three opportunities to and I couldn't quit using so I ended up in a instatution called Center Point.

Do you experience "Magical Thinking About Use" ("When I think about what would happen if I use alcohol and drugs in the future, I create very positive fantasies in which alcohol and drug use instantly solve many of my problems.")

YES.

Please check any Post Acute Withdrawal symptoms that apply to you

- ☑ Difficulty in Thinking Clearly
- ☑ Difficulty in Managing Feelings or Emotions
- ☑ Difficulty in Remembering Things
- ☑ Physical Craving for Alcohol and Drugs

Each time we meet, Mike counts down the number of assignments he still has to finish before he starts earning privileges: visits from his parents, passes to go home on weekends. He tells me with great pride about the fights he walks away from now, petty arguments he would have gotten caught up in before. "They gave me this idiot for a Little Brother. This is a therapeutic community, so when he gets in trouble, it's on me. I told the kid his rug wasn't vacuumed good enough, and he started talking hella shit to me, trying to start a fight. I was like, 'You're willing to go that far to get your life thrown away?'"

And Mike the escape artist predicts which kids will go AWOL. "You can tell who's gonna run. They keep to themselves. They don't say shit in group." He names the boys he assures me won't be here next week. "You got to open yourself up to be here. Some people here don't get it. They don't want it. That's why I'm not running. I get it. And I want it."

To an outsider like me, the daily rituals of Center Point's therapeutic community seem strange, nearly cultlike—starting at eight o'clock with Good Morning Group, in which each boy robotically chants "Good Morning, Family" until everyone in the circle has had his turn.

But the therapeutic community is no fringy California fad. In fact, it's the most common method of residential drug treatment in the United States today. According to Dr. Lonny Shavelson's 2001 book *Hooked*, a hundred thousand men, women, and adolescents are living in TCs, starting and ending their days reciting "Good Morning, Family" and "Good Night, Family" to their "brothers" and "sisters."

The National Institutes of Health sanctions the TC, defining it as "differing from other treatment approaches principally in its use of the community as the key agent of change. . . . Strict and explicit behavioral norms are emphasized and reinforced with specific contingencies (rewards and punishments) directed toward developing self-control and responsibility." Federal agencies—the Department of Health and Human Services, the Department of Labor, the Justice Department, among others—fund therapeutic communities like Center Point, which also receives state money to run its five programs inside California prisons.

Now a mainstream treatment paradigm, the TC is the direct descendant of Synanon, a defunct institution that was anything but. Synanon was founded in southern California in 1958 by Chuck Dederich, the former Alcoholics Anonymous member who coined the phrase "Today is the first day of the rest of your life." First an innovative drug rehab center, then a commune, finally a religion of sorts, according to *The Rise and Fall of*

Synanon, by Rod Janzen, Synanon attracted twenty-five thousand members and spawned five hundred spin-off communities before its collapse in 1991. In all-night encounter groups and daily interactions, Synanon "communities" used "attack therapy"—described by one former devotee in *Hooked* as "emotional surgery without anesthetic"—to "break" addicts' denial. Despite its ultimate reputation as a paranoid sect—in its most infamous act, the group planted a rattlesnake in the mailbox of an antagonistic attorney—thousands of former addicts credit Synanon's confrontational techniques with saving their lives.

Today's TCs are works in progress, struggling to replicate Synanon's successes while leaving its more outlandish practices behind. Maybe the TC is still the dominant mode of residential treatment simply because no one's come up with anything better. Which isn't saying much: although Center Point claims that two-thirds of its adult clients complete their program, according to Shavelson, only 10 percent of adult addicts who enter therapeutic communities make it through the year it takes to finish. More than half, he says, leave within thirty days.

Center Point Adolescent claims a higher rate of success. The program's director told me that 75 percent of clients who make it past the thirty-day mark go on to finish out the year. (I was unable to verify this claim, since their records are confidential.) But Center Point won't say how many kids are kicked out before they get that first month in—or how many kids avail themselves of the ultimate diversion program: the life on the run that beckons so seductively beyond that unlocked door.

Early in September, for his Fifty-Day Project, Mike writes letters of apology to his parents.

> Dear Dad,
>
> I am writing this letter to apologize for all the times that I've let you down and make you worry. . . . I would also like to apologize for all the times you would stay up and be waiting for me all night. . . . I'm telling you now that I look back and feel bad for everything I've done. I feel apart of my apology is by completing this program and continuing to do good when I leave.
>
> Love, Mike

Dear Mom,

You mean more to me than anything in the world. I would like to apologize to you for when I would make you break down and cry because it makes me feel horrible now when I think about it. The worst of all things I think you went through was having to come out to court and then visit me in a little room that stinks. I will follow through with my apology by changing my ways at Center Point and by staying that way when I get out and continue to treat you with the respect that you deserve.

Love, Mike

Soon after Mike and I start working together I have my first conversation with his mom. Ten minutes into the conversation, Barbara and I are old friends. After all, we have the most important thing in each of our lives in common: a son we love to pieces, who's broken us into pieces.

"It feels good to me that you're gonna be spending time with Mike," Barbara says right away. "Every kid needs at least three moms. Especially a kid like Mike."

Barbara, forty-seven, is an attendant who works with special-needs children. She and Dave, the man she's been living with for three years, recently moved from Santa Rosa to the small Lake County burg of Pleasantville. "I'm making a new start," she says. "My new neighbors have never heard my son screaming obscenities at the top of his lungs. They've never seen the sheriffs in front of my house. They've never seen my son dragged out of my house in handcuffs. And I plan to keep it that way. I told Mike he can come live with me when he completes the program and he has no legal charges on him."

Barbara says she's "cautiously optimistic" about Mike's stay at Center Point. "This is the first time we feel like he's ready to do the work, to make changes." She pauses, laughs, and adds, "Knock on wood."

"Mike's an only child. His dad and I divorced when he was two years old. He was the easiest, most precious little baby, with these curly blonde locks—almost like a spirit from another place. A good-natured, independent, hilariously funny little boy. So much personality, and he got tons of love from everywhere . . ."

When Barbara speaks again her voice is thick with pain. "Since age twelve Mike's been pretty much out of control. Cutting school, flunking school, kicked out of school for fighting, for disrupting class, for just not giving a damn. Then the drugs. Pot and booze. Rave drugs. Crank.

"There's addiction on both sides of our family," Barbara says. "And Michael's pretty heavy into his booze thing. There is that genetic factor. But in my belief, it all boils down to this. Every soul who comes into the world has certain things to work with. Some people have charmed lives. Some people don't."

I ask Barbara about her relationship, and Mike's, with Mike's dad. "Michael and I have definitely not seen eye-to-eye on how to handle things. Michael has always treated Mike as a peer, not a son. I kept telling myself their relationship is their thing, and I gotta let go of it. But when your little boy is sitting on the curb with his suitcase waiting for his dad, and his dad doesn't show . . .

"Sometimes I'd think about taking Mike and leaving, going to hide in the Midwest or something. But I thought Mike needed a male role model in his life. That's why I finally caved in and let him go live with his dad when he was ten. He's been back and forth between us since then."

Barbara sighs. "We've tried so many things." She tells me about the family counseling, the rules, the agreements—and how all of that fell away when crank took over Mike's life. "We had him in private rehab at the ReTreat. Good thing his dad's insurance covered it—that place cost ten thousand dollars, and twenty-eight days wasn't nearly long enough.

"Then he went to Vista Village and left after three hours. I'm still getting bills from them. I owe Juvenile Hall seven hundred fifty dollars. And now I have the Center Point bills to look forward to. Five grand a month for a year."

Barbara laughs ironically. "I know women whose husbands don't pay child support and the county can't get it for them. But they're sure good at getting *my* money to pay for locking my kid up.

"Mike turns eighteen in seven months. Center Point might be our last chance." Barbara's voice is choked again. "I go through days, Meredith, where I sit and cry. I'm so disconnected from my son right now. Last week he used somebody's phone card; I couldn't see him that weekend. Now they tell me he used somebody's hair gel, so I can't see him this weekend.

"I'm glad Mike's getting the help I've wanted him to get for so long. But the state has control over my child. I can't call and talk to him. I can't get in my car and go see him. It's like being dismissed. And that's really hard."

She blows her nose. "If it works, though," Barbara says, "it'll all be worth it."

As Mike begins to trust me, he invites me to sit in on his Tuesday-night therapy sessions with Tess, his primary counselor. A twenty-four-year-old psychotherapist-in-training, Tess plays a difficult, dual role with Mike. As his individual therapist, she is his chief ally in the community, the one who calls his parents for him when he's not allowed to, helps him write petitions to regain lost privileges, hears his frequent complaints about other clients and staff.

But unlike the other individual therapists, who drop in to Center Point a few times a week for sessions with their clients, Tess is also a staff counselor who works shifts in the house, earning hours for her internship. This makes her the enforcer of rules, the purveyor of punishment. During times of conflict (of which, as Mike's stay at Center Point unfolds, there are many), it makes her Mike's worst enemy.

"I want to start out with an incident that happened today," Mike begins one Tuesday night. "I was playing basketball. Out of nowhere Hakim grabs me, pushes me out of the way." Mike leans forward in his chair. "You tell me to identify my anger so I won't blow up. But I wanted to slap him. I *shoulda* slapped him."

"You had the feeling of wanting to slap Hakim. And you didn't," Tess says, leaning forward in hers. "That's a big step for you, Mike. Do you feel comfortable with your decision?"

"To be honest, no," Mike answers. "Hakim's only fifteen years old. On the street, little kids don't usually talk to big kids like that. I'm not saying he should respect me as an elder, but . . ."

"It's true that two adolescent years make a big difference," Tess confirms. "That's why it makes sense that you'd be the more mature one."

Her ruse seems transparent to me, but it has the desired effect on Mike. In an instant he goes from blustering and angry to thoughtful and . . . mature. "I understand Hakim's in a changing time of his life," Mike allows. "They just told him he can't go home when he leaves here, 'cause his family's a bunch of crackheads."

"You could identify that Hakim had an issue, and you noticed his patterns of behavior," Tess exclaims. "That's wonderful, Mike! If that happens again tomorrow, what are you going to do?"

"I'm gonna tell him 'You better knock that shit off.'"

"Do you see that as promoting your success here, Mike?"

"It's better than letting some little kid fuck with me. That would be *hella* gay." Although Tess usually challenges her young clients' prejudices, their regular use of the word "gay" as a synonym for "weak and stupid" seems to slip under her radar.

"If you don't find a better way to let your feelings out, what's going to happen, Mike?"

"They're gonna go ka-boom."

"Exactly! I'm very proud of you, Mike. That's a very big lesson you've learned."

"I'm in the process of learning it," Mike corrects her. "I obviously haven't quite learned it yet." He smiles beguilingly at his therapist. "I still wanna hit him," he concludes.

After the session Tess and I sit together in her office and she tells me about Mike's first few weeks at Center Point. "As soon as I met Mike I asked Danny, 'What's up with this kid? He's saying all the right things already,'" Tess recalls. "Most kids come in here saying they hate it, they want out—especially the first month when they can't have visits or use the phone. They can't wear jewelry or hair gel. They can't read magazines. They can't talk to other clients without supervision. They can send letters, but they can't get them.

"It's all about breaking their old image, submerging them in the therapeutic community. We're saying to them, 'You're in treatment now. This is not Juvenile Hall. This is not the streets.' Most of them don't want to hear it," Tess says. "But right from the start Mike was like, 'Bring it on!' He's been ultraresponsible, playing by every rule. He's just imitating what we want to see." She muses, then brightens. "His perfect behavior is starting to break down. That should give us something to work with."

I too have sensed a change in Mike lately. He complains about the rules, the other clients, the staff. There's a theme to his grievances. He's being disrespected, misjudged, misunderstood. And Center Point, he's been saying, is "a straight-up money-making scheme. I know for a fact they make up issues just to keep people here. They're smoking crack if they think they're gonna hold me here for a whole year."

I feel a familiar flutter of panic. This kid's about to do something dangerous. And there's nothing I can do.

I've felt that panic before, those awful nights when Jesse summoned his older brother to his room and closed the door. Crouching outside, straining at once to hear and not to, I'd catch snippets of Jesse's latest scheme: cashing the checks he'd stolen from someone's locker at the Y, selling the ten-sack of weed he'd taken off a kid at school, planning retaliation against some *real* thug who'd talked shit to him on some basketball court. I'd pray that this time Peter would talk him out of it, avert the catastrophe that always erupted within hours of these brotherly heart-to-hearts. But night after night Peter came out of Jesse's room mute with despair as I charged in, demanding to know what Jesse was up to, threatening to—what? Deny him telephone, television, allowance? (As if he needed *my* money.) Send him to yet another therapist? (So he could spend one more hour scowling in hundred-dollar silence?) Lock him in the house forever? *What?*

Maybe this time, with this boy, there is something I can do. "Do you think you're ready to leave here?" I ask.

"I have some issues to work on, sure," Mike answers. "But I know what to do to stay clean."

Is this Mike's voice I hear, or Jesse's? "It's under control, Mom. Chill *out*, Mom." Holding my breath, hoping that just this once I've heard wrong, that just this once I *am* being paranoid, not trusting him enough. And then the phone call from the school, the police, the probation officer, confirming that I've trusted him too much.

"My new fucking PO says he's leaving it up to Danny how long I stay," Mike goes on, his cheeks blotched with anger. "I'll be here a fucking *year* if they do that. My parents should be the ones to decide when to let me go."

The agreement I've made with Mike is, I'll only snitch on him—tell Center Point or his parents a secret that he's divulged to me—if I believe he's going to hurt himself or someone else. I know that this revelation doesn't qualify. I know that Mike is not my son, that I can't undo all the times I covered for Jesse by breaking Mike's confidentiality now.

And I can't quite let it go either.

"Promise me you'll talk to me first if you're thinking about running," I say, hearing the foolishness of my words as I say them. Even if Mike had phone privileges, which he doesn't—would he really stop to call me if the urge to flee overtook him?

"I'm not gonna run. I'm just telling you how I feel," Mike answers, his eyes darting around the room. "Don't play me," I want to warn him. "I've been played like a Stradivarius by someone at least as skilled as you."

"Right. You're not gonna run," I say, turning off the tape recorder. "Because you know better than to do that again."

Normally Mike prolongs our time together, reluctant to return to the tedium of the Center Point routine. Today he's out the door and down the hall before I can say good-bye.

Sobriety High

Many of the stereotypes about Marin County prove true: the hot tubs, yes, and the BMWs, the Buddhist CEOs and aura therapists, the artful arrangements of organic arugula served at prime-rib prices on hand-painted plates.

Life is supposed to be perfect here. But it isn't, of course. Not for everyone; maybe not for anyone. There is poverty in Marin County—contained, for the most part, within tightly zipped pockets: the all-black projects of Marin City, the Canal barrio of San Rafael. There is illness here; Marin's affluent white women suffer the highest incidence of breast cancer in the world. There is spiritual suffering, most famously that of John Walker Lindh, Marin's own teenage "American Taliban." Many who are old here wish to be young and free; many who are young here wish to be old and free. And so, of course, there are drugs, and there are kids who do drugs, and there is trouble because of that.

And so there is Phoenix Academy, where Marin County sends just a few of the drug-ravaged teenagers who have had too much, or too little, of the good life it promises. Formerly known as Sobriety High (the irony of the moniker proved intolerable, even in this province of endless ironies), Phoenix is two institutions in one: a public high school that's more like a small, nurturing private school and that rare treasure, a publicly funded drug rehab program designed exclusively for teens.

A half mile off Highway 101, hidden behind the Church of the Blessed Sacrament, the Phoenix campus shares a modest one-acre site with "County"—Marin County Community School, another "alternative" public high school for Marin kids who sink in the mainstream. For both schools' troubled teenagers, the consequence of failure is always within view. The campus sits one block from the Marin County jail and courthouse, a Frank Lloyd Wright–designed complex that houses the county seat of San Rafael—or "San Raf-Hell," as its townspeople grumble every August, when they're baked and bored by its flawless blue skies, its relentless summer sun.

Set between lush, oak-studded hills, surrounded by million-dollar, redwood-decked homes, the Phoenix/County campus contrasts sharply with the opulence of its environs. Lacking many amenities of a "regular" high school, it has no football field, no cafeteria, no library, no gym—just a row of six classrooms connected by a cement walkway, a paved basketball court at the County end (where most of the African American and Latino kids are), an administrative office and counseling office in the middle, and a small vegetable garden at the (mostly white) Phoenix end. To accommodate both schools' growing numbers (yes, even in Marin there are far more drug- and crime-involved teens than there are resources to care for them), a soundproof portable now hosts staff meetings, counseling sessions, and one of the few activities the students of both schools engage in together: detention.

The walkway is lined with wooden benches so hard against the hill that the kids sometimes lean against the daffodils, sitting there eating their free-lunch McNuggets, having a cry with a therapist, a fight with a boyfriend, a heart-to-heart with a friend. When the POs come to meet with their kids or the sheriffs come to arrest them, they park their county cars behind the portable, beside the teachers' Jeeps and Ford Fiestas and the principal's BMW sports coupe.

Nor surprisingly, given its population and purpose, the Phoenix campus is a drama-intensive place. Kids who fled from car wrecks, party brawls, or their parents over the weekend are taken away in handcuffs on Mondays. Girls who might be pregnant, or whose parents are getting divorced, or whose drug tests are about to come back dirty take time-outs from class to sob in each other's arms. Boys are led to the (locked) bathroom for emergency drug tests; parents are led into the counseling office for emergency meetings. High school is hard enough. High school for kids with POs and therapists and drug habits is harder still.

One unseasonably blustery autumn morning a chill wind chases summer into fall; the sky has gone prematurely gray. At the bus stop between the Civic Center and the campus, the Phoenix kids flip their sweatshirt hoods up as they saunter across the street toward school, a slow-moving herd of magenta buzz cuts, ripped denim bellbottoms, graffiti-covered backpacks, and silver eyebrow studs. The girls cuddle and whisper as they walk; the boys stub out their cigarettes at the porcelain feet of the St. Augustine statue standing sentry on the hill.

"Good morning, Kelsey. Good morning, Julia." Clara MacNamee, Ph.D., Phoenix Academy's own matron saint, awaits her students at her classroom door. The founder of Phoenix and one of its two teachers, Clara not so surreptitiously scrutinizes each student upon arrival, checking for eyes reddened by tears or drugs, for knuckles bruised in a fight, for skin scarred or scarified by a blade. She hugs the kids she hasn't seen for a while—those returning from a stint in residential treatment or Juvenile Hall, a family vacation in Paris or Nogales, a week-long cocaine or alcohol binge. The kids stop to pet the two button-eyed Tibetan terriers who are Clara's constant companions, and her students', for the half day they spend studying math and science in her room. Clara won't tell anyone how old she is—"*hella* old" is the kids' consensus—but her hair is a fine white cloud that matches her dogs' fluff; her skin is translucent and deeply furrowed. Five feet tall, barely a hundred pounds, she's often the smallest person in the school.

The kids divide themselves into the two Phoenix Academy classrooms—Group A to Mike's room for English, Group B to Clara's for math. The eight students in Clara's class toss their backpacks onto the multicolored Ikea rug and jostle for position on the two chartreuse velvet couches, or grab the most comfortable of the padded blue plastic chairs.

Even absent the sunlight that normally floods its wall of windows, the room has an upbeat energy of it own. Like a trendy live-work space, it's divided into function areas, arranged around ten individual cubicles designed to give these easily distractible kids, many of them "diagnosed" with ADHD, a shot at concentration. Next to the computers, two station- ary bikes stand at the ready for a quick burn-off of calories, or rage. The walls are papered with students' artwork (a framed painting is inscribed, "For Clara and Sober Classroom with Love and Gratitude, Anne Slater, 1995") and snapshot collages of grinning Phoenix students.

In the back of the room, in cages and terrariums and planters, frogs and snakes and plants hop and coil and grow. "Even when these kids can't love themselves or anyone else," Clara tells me, "they can love the dogs and the snakes." And they do. There's often a pierced-and-studded pothead tenderly petting a snake, a bulimic E-freak sneaking an M&M to a rat.

"Good morning, ladies and gentlemen," Clara begins the school day at the uncommonly civilized start time of nine-twenty. "We're having a weather front moving in. That has a definite effect on your physiology. Who can tell us why?"

A dark-haired girl in lime green flannel pajama bottoms—once a run- away heroin addict, now the school's stellar student—raises her hand. "The change in the barometric pressure?" Sabrina offers.

Clara beams. "Good, Sabrina! Changes in the atmosphere actually cause changes to your nerve endings. So if you're having a lot of negative interactions today, be aware that it's the weather—not you, not the people around you." A former UC Berkeley molecular biology professor with a Ph.D. in oceanography, Clara never misses a chance to use science to teach sobriety, or vice versa.

Her point made, Clara moves on to the first activity of this and every day, the morning sobriety group. She opens a thick, palm-sized paperback, *Our Best Days: A Daily Meditation Book for Adolescents*. "Today's reading is about laziness," Clara says. "Tomás, would you like to start?" She passes the book to the Benjamin Bratt look-alike beside her—a sixteen-year-old Chilean boy who was sentenced to Phoenix after a girl he sold Ecstasy to was rushed to the hospital in a coma.

"Laziness is usually a symptom of depression or anger or impending relapse," Tomás reads aloud. "Today help me use the tools of recovery to overcome my laziness." He ponders this for a moment. "I'm so lazy, even

when I know I have something to do, I'd rather watch TV and get yelled at."
He passes the book to Julia, who's half-asleep with her head on his shoulder.

A veteran of, and runaway from, every treatment program in northern California, Julia is what the counselors call a "garbage-pail kid." Her drug of choice is, well, every drug. "I didn't even go to work yesterday 'cause I was too lazy to get up," she mumbles. Tomás pats her affectionately on the head.

Like the boys at Center Point, these kids would clearly prefer to be somewhere else. Unlike the Center Point clients, though, the Phoenix kids seem to feel free to show it. The next speaker, in fact, dispenses with the formula entirely.

"I had an odd experience last night I need to talk about," says Kelsey, a tightly muscled fifteen-year-old alcoholic—like many of his classmates, the child of hippie parents.

Clara nods encouragingly. Kelsey continues. "I got a month sober on Saturday." Everyone claps, unsurprised. The Phoenix students know each other's "sobriety dates"—the last time each of them got high, or admitted to getting high, or got caught getting high—the way kids on a varsity softball team know each other's batting averages. Just in case they need reminding, those dates are posted and updated daily in the counseling office next door.

"A buddy of mine came over last night. He had a really fine bottle of Italian wine," Kelsey continues. Now the kids look interested. "I held it for a minute. My mouth started salivating. My whole body felt like I needed it right then. It was the weirdest feeling in the world."

"That's your addiction, Kelsey," Clara says.

"I just looked at that bottle," he ignores her. "And then I realized, now is not the time or the place."

"It may never be," Clara intones.

"I'm sure it will be someday," Kelsey replies with equal certainty.

Where, I wonder, is the robotic obeisance of the Center Point clients? The ritualized "soul baring" and "support" that seem to yield their precise opposites? Two freeway exits south, not here. These kids might be concealing some—or all—of their deepest sentiments, but at least they're not being herded into an enforced twelve-step lockstep. The Phoenix kids who aren't on probation, at least, seem unafraid to reject the whole recovery concept loudly and often.

"One day at a time," Clara gets in the last word.

Kelsey shakes his head and passes the book to Tristan, who slipped in late while Kelsey was talking. "Did you get a tardy slip, Tristan?" Clara asks—clearly not for the first time. Tristan nods and hands it to her.

"Today help me use the tools of recovery to overcome my laziness," he reads. He falls silent, staring at his battered running shoes. After a month at Phoenix, Tristan still hates talking in groups, because he can't trust anyone in them. The kids lie about their sobriety the same way the kids did at Journeys and Cragmont, use all kinds of tricks to make their drug tests come back clean, make fun of the staff behind their backs. Tristan doesn't want to play those games.

"I'm feeling lazy right now," he says, the closest thing to an honest statement he can make. He returns the book to Clara.

Everyone gathers in the center of the circle, their arms around each other. "Kelsey?" Clara nudges.

"God," Kelsey begins, and the others' voices take up the prayer. "Grant me the serenity to accept the things I cannot change, the courage to change the things I can, and the wisdom to know the difference."

"Keep coming back! It's better than crack!" Sabrina adds gaily, and the students move to their individual cubicles to begin their individualized math lessons—for some, grade-school fractions; for others, college-level trigonometry.

Clara moves among them, leaning over one student's shoulder, then the next, as they work. "Very good, Tristan," she says, looking over the sheet of fractions he's been struggling with all week. "You know, all those drugs you did cause a total loss of math acuity. So you can be really proud of this work." She pats him on the shoulder. "What a nice, soft sweater."

"I got it at Goodwill," Tristan tells her proudly. "And these too." He shows off his worn-out shoes.

"You're a good shopper. As your math skills improve, you'll be able to calculate discounts in your head," promises Clara, who dresses for school each day in a tailored skirt suit, silk blouse, and matching leather pumps.

Five minutes into class, most of the students have already lost interest, drifting over to each other's cubicles, calling to each other across the room. But Clara never lets the group erupt into the full-on chaos of an out-of-control high-school classroom, modeling and enforcing the calm, contained self-discipline she is here to teach. Certainly it helps that she has eight, not thirty-eight, students to contain, and that her goal is not just to educate them, but to love and save them. "Stay focused, please," she reminds one, then the next, walking around stroking the terrier in her arms.

When the bell rings, Group B shuffles next door for forty-five minutes of English. After a discussion of *The Scarlet Letter,* they're back to Clara's room for science. "What's the universe made of? Two things," she asks from the front of the room.

"Ions and molecules," Tristan calls out.

"No . . ."

"Matter and energy," Sabrina offers.

"Yes!" Clara says. "And who's the genius who came up with the formula describing energy, $E = mc^2$?"

"Clara!" Tristan shouts.

"No," Clara smiles at him tenderly. "That genius was Albert Einstein." She points at the poster of the periodic table of the elements taped to the wall. "Who knows how many naturally occurring elements there are?"

"Three," Kelsey says authoritatively. Clara shakes her head.

"A hundred?" Tristan guesses.

The mission of Phoenix Academy is "to provide, for adolescents who have abused alcohol and/or other drugs, an innovative academic and therapeutic environment, in partnership with their families and the community, in order to support their ability to make a long-term commitment to sobriety and to be a contributing member of society." The school evolved from Marin County's first adolescent drug-treatment program, a residential unit that opened in 1981 inside Marin General Hospital. Clara MacNamee, formerly the science teacher at San Quentin prison, was the program's first teacher.

Six years later, funding problems forced the unit's closure. After a second program was set up and abruptly shut down, Clara decided to roll her own. "I went to Mary Jane Burke, Marin's superintendent of schools, and proposed the idea of a sober classroom within a public high school. Bless her heart: Mary Jane looked at me and said, 'Isn't every classroom sober?'" Clara laughs. "At that time such a thing had never been done. Now I hear there are sober high schools in quite a few places."

Quite a few, but not nearly enough. Because what's wrong with most models of adolescent drug treatment is what's right about the sober high school. Instead of yanking kids out of their homes, sealing them off in an artificial world, imposing cultish rules and rituals that offer scant preparation for real life, sober or otherwise (think: never going to the bathroom alone), recovery high schools allow their students to live "normal" lives while learning to use, or not, the recovery tools that work best for them.

Yes, some kids need to be locked up to protect themselves and others. And even among those who don't, there are some teenagers who, for one reason or another, just can't live with their parents. (I left home at seventeen; my son barely made it to his eighteenth birthday living with me.) But before more drastic—and often less effective and more destructive—action is taken, shouldn't we give every kid who needs drug treatment a chance to get it in a therapeutic, real-world setting like Phoenix Academy?

Indeed we should, but we don't. This opportunity is currently available to less than one thousand kids nationwide. As I write there are twenty recovery high schools in the United States, nine of them in Minneapolis–St. Paul— where the success of the first one led, logically enough, to the establishment of others. The remaining eleven schools are in Arizona (Unity High serves Native American teenagers exclusively), Michigan, Washington, Tennessee, Texas, Colorado, Washington, D.C., and California. Some are private nonprofits; a few are public. Most are tuition-free, understaffed shoestring operations kept alive by the sheer determination of their founders.

Jim Cazarniecki, CEO of St. Paul's Sobriety High, tallies and disseminates data he hopes will help bring the recovery high school the attention and replication it deserves. "We estimate that around 2,000 of Minnesota's 23,000 chemically dependent teens get treatment," he tells me. "So even with nine schools, we're barely reaching 15 percent of those, and only 1.3 percent of all addicted high-school students." His frustration is tempered by his pride: 60 percent of Sobriety High students make it to senior year. Of those who do, 95 percent graduate. Almost 70 percent of graduates go on to college.

Phoenix Academy boasts equally impressive results. Of the 380 students who have been through the program since Clara opened it in 1991, about 75 percent have completed it, either by returning to mainstream high school or by graduating from Phoenix. This success rate is achieved at a cost of $10,500 per student per year (this covers the therapeutic component alone; the school district picks up the academic tab). That's quite a bargain compared to the $60,000-per-client cost of a residential therapeutic community like Center Point, not to mention the even costlier alternatives that many Phoenix students, including Tristan, have already tried.

Until recently, recovery high schools around the country operated in isolation, unaware of each other's existence. To remedy that, and to refine and propagate the model, the Association of Recovery Schools convened its first national conference in July 2002. Funded by SAMHSA's Center for Substance Abuse Treatment, the conference gathered counselors, administrators, and students from nineteen schools across the country for two poignant days in Washington, D.C. The conference established a think tank and outreach committees and allowed for much sharing of war stories and best practices. Should recovery-high-school students be required to attend AA meetings? Complete a residential treatment program before admission? Stay sober? Pay for their own drug tests? Tell the truth? In the closing circle, one school's principal/teacher/counselor summed it up. "We're the bleeding edge," she said.

When I started hanging out at Phoenix Academy—fascinated by the concept of a "sober high school," eager to see whether one school could really support kids' academic and personal growth, when most public high schools can't seem to pull off either task—what struck me first was the relationships between the kids. Their easy banter, mutual caretaking, and steady tolerance of each other's quirks and outbursts made them feel to me more like a high-school clique than a student body thrown together by fate.

As I spent more time there I began to understand why. Despite significant differences of racial, class, legal, family, academic, and pharmacological backgrounds, the Phoenix students have what is currently the main thing in their lives in common. Someone—their parents, their therapist, a judge, a school expulsion committee—decided that they needed a year or more in drug treatment and sent them here to get it.

This too bonds them: the assembly-line conditions that alienate "regular" public-high-school kids from their school, their teachers, and each other do not exist here—or in any recovery high school. Phoenix Academy has twenty students, not two thousand. Its classes have ten students, not thirty-five. (Most recovery high schools have fewer than forty students total, and fewer than fifteen students per class.) Its teachers know—really know—every student and every student's family. Each counselor—and they're real counselors—is responsible for five students, not five hundred. Ironic, but true. By screwing up their lives, recovery-high-school kids have been granted what all high-school students need: a tight-knit school community, a custom-designed individual education plan, and a staff of trained professionals on hand to help them take advantage of it.

They'd *better* like each other. The students at Phoenix Academy spend most of their waking hours together. Each weekday they sit through math, science, history, and English classes; a few days a week they take a computer course with Jeremy in his room full of brand-new iMacs. Interspersed with academics are daily therapy groups: Day by Day, pre- and post-weekend check-ins, Twelve-Step Study, Gender Group, Relapse Recovery.

At "normal" high schools, lunch is a time for kids to huddle within their cliques. At Phoenix, the whole student body is a clique. They all eat together on the benches, sharing free-lunch PB&J's and seven-dollar deli sandwiches, making after-school plans to go to an AA meeting or the mall or to fill out job applications. The girls braid each other's hair; the boys compare notes about their POs, their parents, their cars. When there's news of a former classmate sent off to a wilderness program, to the Hall, on the run, in the hospital, they pass that around with the cookies, string cheese, and Snapples.

"Mommy brought me sushi." A blonde girl holds out a plastic-wrapped tray for her classmates' inspection.

"I'll trade you my Doritos for one piece of California roll," Sabrina offers.

"Thank *God* it's pizza today, not that nasty-ass mystery meat," says Marisol, a Latina coke addict and self-identified drama queen, peering into the bag lunch that she and the other poor-side-of-the-tracks Phoenix kids pick up from a window on the County end of the campus each day.

I visit Phoenix several times a week, often spending mornings at Center Point with Mike, afternoons in the parallel universe of Phoenix. As I watch kids come and go, I am dizzied by the turnover—there seem to be as many who last a day or a week as those who dig in for the long haul—and awed by the unflagging perseverance of the teachers and counselors, who come to work each day ready to have their hearts broken all over again. Unlike at Center Point, where the clients are forced into "program sobriety" by the fishbowl supervision of residential placement, for many Phoenix students, sobriety is just a resting point between relapses. Even the criterion for AA membership—the desire to stay sober—is too stringent a requirement here. Still, the Phoenix staff sends only the most out-of-control kids to residential treatment or the Hall and takes many of them back later for second or third tries.

"Recovery's a lifelong process," head counselor Dana Leigh tells me, when I ask how she keeps going in the face of the self-sabotage and setbacks. "I'm in recovery myself, and I've been at it for thirteen years. So I know this is what it looks like. No one gets there easily."

Listening in, Floyd Jackson, a former addict from the Marin City ghetto, now a counselor who splits his time between County and Phoenix, adds, "You have to join with these kids. When the kid drives you crazy enough, some adults back away from them. To me, that's just the moment when you move toward them, prove you'll hang with them. If you can join with them, you can save them."

As the weeks go by, I interview kids who aren't right for the book, and kids who sign up with me but then disappear or decide the last thing they need is the scrutiny of yet another nosy adult. As I listen to their stories, their drug abuse seems self-explanatory. A white boy who eats LSD and Ecstasy like candy bounces between the mansions of his coke-and-work-addicted dad and his needy, alcoholic mom. A girl from the Marin City ghetto has been high on weed since her mom, then her dad, was diagnosed with cancer. A Salvadoran coke fiend joined a gang because she yearns for her mother, who's too overwhelmed by immigrant life to care for her six children. The hippie mom of a fifteen-year-old whose liver is already failing stashes her pot in her daughter's room.

I shake my head at these parents' failings. And then I wonder, if I'd interviewed Jesse at Phoenix, how he would have answered a journalist's probing questions.

During a lunch break one day in September, I notice a boy sitting at the edge of the crowd, engaging only intermittently in his classmates' conversation, eating only his own food. The other kids glance his way now and then, ask what he's eating, recoiling in horror when he shows them the Portobello mushroom, wild rice, and raw spinach he's brought from home. No Hilfiger or Nikes for this tall, lanky, baby-faced boy—his thrift-store jeans and purple Wildflowers of California T-shirt are as unfashionable as his food; his look is androgynous, verging on feminine.

I introduce myself and ask what he's in for. Tristan rattles off his drug résumé, a tale told to many people many times, speaking slowly and clearly, without a trace of the Ebonic inflection that thickens the tongues of so many of his peers.

"I did a lot of pills. Vicodin, Xanax, Valium, codeine. I stole cars. I stole money. I was smoking pot all day every day. I was using it to numb my brain from feelings."

"What feelings?" I wonder, but it seems too soon to ask. "And now?" I ask instead.

"I still have a beer every once in a while, but I don't like the feeling of cloudedness in my brain. I talk like an idiot, say things I don't actually think. Pot doesn't do much for me anymore, either. But I got into mushrooms this summer. It's a sacred thing, The natives did 'shrooms as a vision quest, a ritual when they were coming of age. I got a lot out of it. And I still wanna try peyote."

My journalistic heart skips a beat. Could it be: a kid in a drug program who's honest about still being into drugs? "How's Phoenix working for you?" I ask.

Tristan stares off into the distance, then turns his laser blue eyes on me. "I really like this place. I like the small classes. I like Clara, and my counselor, Eric, and my family therapist, Floyd," he says. "But I'm not sure I want to be sober. And if I did, I could handle not using on my own. I don't need a program to be sober."

"What an amazing kid," Eric says when I ask him about Tristan. I can see from the way his fresh-scrubbed face goes all soft and open that this boy has caught his heart. I can see too why Tristan likes his therapist. Thirty years old, with a B.A. in psychology and a certificate in Drug and Alcohol Studies, Eric Olson is one of five counselors on the Phoenix staff. Three of them are licensed therapists; Floyd and Eric were schooled by their years of experience with troubled kids.

"Tristan's a turtle without a shell. So open, so trusting, so childlike and good-hearted. The thing is, to survive in this world you gotta have a shell." Eric flips through Tristan's file, bulging with evaluations by psychologists, psychiatrists, and academic consultants—just as Mike's (and Jesse's) bulge with reports by school suspension committees, arresting officers, juvenile probation departments.

"I don't know if it's all the marijuana he smoked, or if he used some drugs he hasn't told us about, but Tristan has a pretty intense history in special ed." Eric shows me Tristan's standardized test scores, which put him in the 98th percentile in reading, the 6th percentile in math. "We all love Tristan to pieces. But between his academic issues, his minimizing of his addiction, and his . . . floatyness, we're just not sure how he's gonna make it in this program, or in the world."

Tristan, Eric tells me, defies the label "addict." Rejects the twelve-step recipe. Refuses to abide by the program's rules. Won't attend the three weekly AA meetings that Phoenix Academy requires. Argues that his pot smoking and 'shrooming is his spiritual path.

Because he articulates what so many kids in recovery programs feel and act on but don't say, Eric says, Tristan would be a great addition to my book—if I can get his mom to agree. Tristan is the grandson of a famous San Francisco artist; his mom is fiercely protective of the family name. Like her son, Eric tells me, she's resistant to the program's rigors, often canceling family therapy sessions with Floyd, missing or coming late to Multifamily Group on Wednesday nights.

"I hope she says yes," Eric says. "The extra attention will be good for him. Tristan's kind of a lost child in that big family of his. Plus, they all drink and smoke pot at his house. He could use your support for his sobriety."

Support his sobriety? Heretical as it sounds, I'm not sure that I do. The more I hang out with Tristan, the more I wonder. If his sobriety means abstaining not only from the pills, stealing, and lying that did him harm, but from the psychedelically enhanced spiritual adventures that he believes have done him good—should abstinence from all drugs be a requisite of Tristan's "recovery"? And, in the bigger picture, are all drugs bad for all teenagers all the time? Or can some teenagers use some drugs in some situations with negligible or even valuable effects?

So don't elect me president: I did that. Between the ages of fifteen and twenty I smoked pot regularly, dropped the occasional tab of LSD, chewed a few peyote buttons, and swallowed some unidentified pills. I had a lot of laughs, more than a few insights, and a couple of freak-outs—nothing worth funding a study or sending a kid to rehab over. The same, more or less, is true of many of the middle-aged people I know. Should we deny our kids the experiences that we defied our parents to deny us?

True, our kids' hybridized THC-boosted pot, not to mention the myriad new drugs available on every school campus, isn't the benign "dope" of our day. And it's certainly easier to banish all drugs from all teens than to try to figure out which substances and which teenagers might be okay for each other.

Still, as clearly as my son Jesse showed me how much damage drugs can do to a teenager in trouble, my own drug use, and my son Peter's, convinced me that recreational drug use can be a blip on the developmental screen for a teenager who isn't. Peter started smoking pot occasionally at age thirteen, worried me when he escalated to smoking several times a week at fifteen, tried mushrooms and Ecstasy later in his teenage years, and pretty much gave the whole thing up by age twenty. He got mostly B's in high school, mostly A's in college, and if his drug use then or now has gotten in his way, I sure can't see it.

But if we parents don't insist—however unrealistically, ineffectually, and/or hypocritically—that our teenagers abstain from all drugs all the time, how can we impart and negotiate the far trickier notion that some drugs are okay for some kids under some circumstances some of the time?

The same way we make our best, most complex, and most difficult judgment calls about our kids' well-being in other areas of their lives: from the gut, and with great difficulty. We don't *just* rely on report cards to tell us how our kids are doing in school or otherwise; we can't *just* decide that occasional pot use is okay, but mushrooms aren't, or that sixteen is old enough to experiment with drugs but fourteen isn't, or that the rules we make for one child will work just as well for another. The kid who can smoke pot harmlessly one week might be using it self-destructively the next. The kid who can get falling-down drunk once and never do it again might have a brother who plummets into alcoholism with his first sip of beer.

It's hard to trust our instincts, update them hourly, and then trust them again. It's hard to wrestle our own denial (and our kids') to the ground. It's hard to believe in our own ability to know what's right for each of our children, each day of the year, each year of their lives—harder than it is to make a set of rules and stick to them, come hell or high teenagers. But considering the alternative, the hard way may be what's best—for our kids and for our relationships with them.

Few "experts" share my perspective. Whether their motives derive from puritanical moralizing, scientific curiosity, pharmaceutical kickbacks, or a genuine concern for the physical, developmental, psychological, spiritual, and academic well-being of adolescents, a wide array of researchers has come up with a wide array of reasons why teenagers shouldn't do illicit drugs, period.

Most research focuses on pot, since that's the most commonly used illegal substance—and since its potency has increased 200 percent over the past decade. In a 2002 Canadian study, "participants who smoked five or more marijuana cigarettes a week had a decline in their IQ scores compared to the test results taken in their preteen years," although "the IQ of those who smoked heavily and quit was not affected."

An international study that year found that "heavy, chronic marijuana use causes memory loss and attention problems [as well as] impaired learning, retention, and retrieval [with] the potential to impact academic achievements, occupational proficiency, interpersonal relationships, and daily functioning." A Harvard researcher argued in response, "The jury is still out on the question of whether long-term marijuana use causes lasting impairment in brain function."

The issue of marijuana's long-term effects is highly relevant to the debate, given the short-term nature of many kids' pot use. "Marijuana users are most actively involved with the drug in their early 20s, but use begins to decline by age 23," a Columbia University study found. "For many drug users, the process of growing up—marrying, working, or having children—puts a brake on drug use."

The Drug Enforcement Agency (DEA) claims that pot is a "gateway drug" whose users experience "the same health problems as tobacco smokers, such as bronchitis, emphysema and bronchial asthma." A 2001 study funded by SAMHSA—the federal government's Substance Abuse and Mental Health Services Administration—found that pot "has been reported to be involved in as many as 30 percent of adolescent motor vehicle crashes, 20 percent of adolescent homicides, 13 percent of adolescent suicides, and 10 percent of other unintentional injuries among adolescents."

On the other side of the debate, a 2001 AlterNet story reports that "Despite an exhaustive search for harm, marijuana has not proved to be particularly dangerous. Driving stoned is safer than driving drunk, according to several studies. Marijuana addiction is rare. . . . Marijuana isn't a 'gateway' to harder drugs, according to the National Academy of Sciences."

Are my sons' IQs lower, their occupational proficiency and interpersonal relationships impaired, because they both smoked marijuana regularly throughout their teenage years? Is mine? Will Tristan's be?

Q: How will we ever know?

A: We won't.

A similar controversy rages about Ecstasy. Created in 1914 by Merck Pharmaceuticals and used by therapists during the 1970s to loosen their clients' inhibitions, Ecstasy became the first "club drug" in the 1980s. X's proponents swear that it's harmless and therapeutic; its opponents point to one hundred Ecstasy-related deaths and nearly three thousand "rollers" admitted to hospitals in 1999, most of them with dehydration or heatstroke suffered during all-night dancing at raves.

Less controversial and far more lethal is the damage done by the first drug many children use: household inhalants. More than a hundred "huffers" die each year from "sudden sniffing death syndrome," their central nervous systems shut down by a single hit of White-Out, lighter fluid, or aerosol fumes.

Then there's Mike's drug of choice: the fastest growing drug in America. Methamphetamine-related deaths in the United States rose 145 percent between 1992 and 1994; hospital admissions rose nearly 2,000 percent between 1986 and 1996. Like crack cocaine, meth—also known as speed, ice, crystal, and crank, among other pet names—produces paranoia, depression, hallucinations, and violent rages. Our kids' speed isn't their father's Oldsmobile (or their mother's diet pills). It's stronger, more addictive, and more damaging to their bodies than the stuff that kept us up all night cramming for finals.

There are experts, including some Phoenix counselors, who concede that since most teenagers aren't addicts, most teenagers can indulge in some amount of recreational drug use without spinning out of control. One expert disagrees.

"When I started doing this work seventeen years ago," Clara MacNamee says, "the average onset of drug use was between fourteen and sixteen years old. Now it's between eight and ten. Even when they're 'just' smoking marijuana, what we're seeing in these kids is nothing less than interference with their neurological development."

Tristan, Clara says, is a prime example. "Tristan has severe brain damage," she declares categorically. "I'm teaching him, but not much. He has no retention. The short-term memory is impaired. The retrieval system is damaged. With a lot of practice and repetition it can come back. But with chronic drug users like Tristan, there are episodes in their lives they won't ever remember. It's simply not reparable."

I tell Clara that some studies disagree. She shakes her head impatiently. "We don't know what the long-term damage is," she insists. "I do know this: I have to do remedial work with every student who comes in here. In math, they lose their times tables. Some of them don't have any sequencing in their brains. With most of my students, it takes four to six months of retooling before we begin to see any progress at all.

"I explain to them that they've lost this part of their memory," Clara says. "I don't want them to feel it as a put-down. So I tell them that there's still something to work with in the cells, but they have to do remedial work to rebuild the connectors they've lost."

Like most drug rehab programs, Phoenix is based on the twelve-step model and requires its clients to attend several AA (Alcoholics Anonymous) or

NA (Narcotics Anonymous) meetings a week. Like most teenagers in drug rehab, the Phoenix kids, for the most part, don't want to go to meetings. So they show up early, get their cards signed as proof they've been there, and sneak out. Or go and don't participate. Or don't go at all.

Their ambivalence is addressed every Tuesday at 2:05, when they're required to attend their least favorite group of the week: Twelve-Step Study.

"Does anyone know why we have you go to AA and NA?" Susan—one of many Phoenix counselors who credit their own recovery to AA—opens the session.

"To make friends," guesses Marisol, her thick pancake makeup failing to conceal the black eye her gang-banger boyfriend gave her last night.

"I've made no friends in those stupid meetings," sputters Kelsey.

"When you leave Phoenix Academy, you can go to twelve-step meetings anywhere in the world," Susan asserts. "It's a valuable connection for you to have."

As usual, the topic of AA divides the kids into two camps: those who support Phoenix's three-meetings-a-week rule (because they're currently using and they're brown-nosing the counselors, or because they're currently clean and honeymooning with sobriety) versus the majority, who are vehemently opposed.

"There's a hella tight Wednesday meeting in San Rafael," offers Emily, a seventeen-year-old "garbage-pail kid" now approaching her one-year sobriety birthday.

Her classmates roll their eyes, snort, or ignore her altogether.

"I know there are a number of you who don't care to go to meetings," Susan acknowledges. "But that's what we're endorsing. Tristan, you're someone who's not thrilled with the steps."

"It's not the steps. It's the obligation to do them," Tristan replies. "It should be your own free will."

"Which step are you on?" Susan asks him.

"The steps, or the levels at school? I don't know the difference."

Patiently Susan explains. "We have four levels at Phoenix. Level One is where you are. Level Four is where you'll be when you graduate from here. The twelve steps are just about your recovery."

"It's interesting. But I don't want to be forced into it," Tristan repeats.

"We're not trying to force it on you," says Bill, the former tweaker who drives the kids to meetings at night, watches the boys pee into their UA cups by day, and makes frequent judgment calls about which of the tidbits of information he overhears in the car or the bathroom to convey to their teachers, counselors, and parents. "But the twelve steps are a wonderful guide for how to live your life."

"My sponsor says it's like baking a cake," says Marisol, one week out from her latest coke relapse. "If you don't focus on each step, you're gonna have a fucked-up cake."

The kids burst into laughter.

"Is it the word 'God' that gets in your way?'" Bill asks the group. "Because everyone gets to choose their own concept of a higher power."

"I definitely believe there's a higher power that's greater than I am," Tristan says. He doesn't add what he's told me: this revelation came to him on his last mushroom trip, when he was visited by a shamanic warrior. "It's not a he or she, just a good thing to talk to. It helps me out."

"Do you know why the twelve steps suggest that there's a power outside yourself?" Susan asks.

"'Cause we're not God," Tristan answers.

"There's a saying in AA: your best thinking got you here," Susan replies. She glances at the clock on the wall. "We're out of time. Let's close."

The kids form a circle, throw their arms around each other, and dully recite the Serenity Prayer—sounding, suddenly, as lifeless as the boys at Center Point do when they mumble the same mantra.

Most drug-treatment programs are built on the foundation laid by the network of support groups called Alcoholics Anonymous. As it describes itself, AA is "A fellowship of men and women who share their experience, strength and hope with each other that they may solve their common problem and help others to recover from alcoholism."

Founded in 1935 by an Ohio surgeon and alcoholic who first described alcoholism as a "malady of mind, emotions, and body," AA spread quickly around the world and now claims more than two million alcoholics and drug addicts saved.

As you're reading this, odds are good that somewhere (or at several locations) in your town, twenty (or two hundred) addicts are gathering in church basements and storefronts for meetings of AA or one of its many spin-offs: NA, Narcotics or Nicotine Anonymous; SA, Sex and Love Addicts Anonymous; CA, Cocaine Anonymous; MA, Marijuana Anonymous; and so on.

AA's only membership requirement is the desire (or imitation of same, to satisfy a nagging spouse, parent, or probation officer) to get sober. New AA members are encouraged to find a "sponsor": a member who's been sober long enough to serve as a mentor, and who's willing to be on call twenty-four seven for support by phone or in person. AA charges no dues or fees; the organization supports itself with donations. Unlike every other mode of addiction treatment, except for sales of AA-published materials, no money ever changes hands.

At each meeting an addict stands up, introduces him- or herself ("Hi. I'm John, and I'm a cocaine addict." "Hi, John!"), tells his or her story of debasement and recovery, and invites attendees to respond with their own stories. After an hour or so everyone joins hands and recites the Serenity Prayer, drinks a cup of coffee from the urn, eats a few cookies from the package, smokes a few cigarettes, and goes home—or on to another meeting. It's not uncommon for devotees to attend two or more meetings in a day, and doing "ninety in ninety"—ninety meetings in ninety days—is an oft-prescribed relapse remedy.

AA's list of guiding precepts is the Twelve Steps of Recovery. Step One requires admitting powerlessness over addiction; Steps Two and Three vow submission to a higher power (whether only the Bible's God, or a personal god or goddess will do, is a matter of ongoing controversy). Step Four calls for taking "fearless moral inventory." Steps Five through Nine entail admitting all wrongs, asking God to remove the character faults responsible, and making amends to anyone who's been harmed. Ten and Eleven refer to continued personal inventory taking and "improved conscious contact with God." The Twelfth Step commits to practicing and promulgating the message of AA.

Whether they're required to attend a set number of meetings, work the twelve steps, or just recite the Serenity Prayer a few times a day, teenagers in rehab are bound to encounter AA in one form or another. As Phoenix does, many day treatment programs drive their kids to meetings—some of them for teens only, although the formula is the same—as part of their weekly activities. Some programs also require kids to work with a sponsor and attend additional meetings on their own. Residential programs either conduct meetings on-site (if their wards are confined to the premises) or do what Center Point does: have the counselors escort the clients on field trips to the nearest outside meeting once or twice a week. Even within programs like Center Point, which stresses behavior modification over the twelve-step protocol, AA's methods are incorporated and its effectiveness unquestioned. After all, it's worked for millions of adults (including most drug counselors); it's accessible, it's safe, and—most appealing of all to underfunded treatment programs—it's free.

A June 2002 editorial in the on-line recovery newsletter JoinTogether.org offers a minority opinion about the effectiveness of AA. "The twelve-step model has always been rife with contradiction," JTO says. "Its adherents recognize, for example, that addiction is a disease, not a sin. But their treatment isn't medical; it's praying, confession and meeting. . . . If a physician told you the only cure for your condition was to join a support group that involves 'turning your will and your life' over to God (AA's Third Step), you'd seek a second opinion." The story concludes, "The view that one can only recover via the moral improvement of the twelve steps is doing more harm than good."

How well-suited to adolescents the AA model is, how well adolescents take to it, and how much good, if any, it does them are the questions that adolescent programs like Phoenix Academy are just beginning to ask. Can a remedy that relies on the epiphany triggered by "bottoming out"—losing a job, family, house, or car to addiction—work on teenagers too young to have acquired these things, let alone to have lost them?

Not as well as it works for adults. And not until AA is adapted to meet teens' unique needs. A study presented at the Research Society on Alcoholism in July 2002 found that "Adolescents who participate in twelve-step addiction recovery meetings have better outcomes when the programs include others in their own age group" because "sharing of experiences by older members may not be perceived by youth as helpful or relevant in dealing with their own life-stage recovery issues."

Over the next few weeks, Tristan and I spend many of his lunch breaks sequestered on the slipcovered couch in the therapy room, talking about his past, his present, and whether he'd like me to follow him everywhere he goes for the next year. I'm struck by how different this process is from my "recruitment" of (by) Mike. Tristan doesn't leap at the opportunity, unconvinced that it is one. He's not bored and looking for distraction, as Mike is. He's into downers, not speed; he's slow to react, methodical in his decisions. Mike is all flash and fire. Tristan is glowing embers; it takes effort to spark his flame. Most of Mike's choices are made for him by his keepers. Tristan is a Marin County boy, raised in a family and a community that are all about choices.

Finally Tristan makes one. And he's sure his mom will approve. "She'll say I can do it if I tell her it'll help me," he says. "She totally trusts my judgment."

I find this hard to believe, given the years that passed between Jesse's last lie and the first time I fully trusted him. But I take Tristan at his word, call his mom, and ask if I can come by their house some evening soon. She tells me she's working eighty hours a week on a big project, and asks me to meet her at her office instead.

Tristan has told me that his mom used to be a hippie. "You guys have a lot in common," he said. "I know you'll really like each other."

"Not a hippie now," I think, waiting for Marian in the lobby of the San Francisco skyscraper where she's the marketing manager of a multinational brokerage firm. "Let's talk in the cafeteria," she greets me, speed-walking toward the bank of elevators, bent forward at the waist in her hurry to get there. Seeing her in her beige blouse, gray skirt, and neutral nylons, it's hard to believe that she and her free-spirit son once occupied the same body.

In the corporate cafeteria Marian perches on the edge of her chair, opens a file folder, briskly reads me a list of questions, and takes notes as I answer. Will I reveal Tristan's name, take photographs of him, interfere with his schoolwork, or give him a big ego? I say that I will not and sign a form to that effect. I give her a waiver to sign, should she decide to let him participate.

"I'll talk to Tristan's stepdad and tell you what we decide," she says, hustling me back to the elevators. I ask if I'll need Tristan's father's approval as well. "Absolutely not," she says emphatically. "He has very little to do with his sons. And no authority. It's up to Rob and me." She shakes my hand, gets off on the twenty-second floor.

The good news, I think, as the elevator spits me back into the lobby, is that beneath her brusque busyness, I can feel Marian's protectiveness of her son. The bad news is, I'm sure she'll refuse to expose him and their family to public scrutiny.

Two nail-biting weeks later I get an e-mail from Marian.

> Hi Meredith—
>
> Thanks for your patience. I read the addendum of your Berkeley High book and was impressed with your love of the three students you observed. I'm willing to sign the approval sheets you sent. There can be no photos, though, even two years from now when the book becomes a best-seller. Can you redo the approval sheet to specify this and fax to me at 399–3995?
>
> —Look forward to working with you, Marian

Surprised and delighted, I e-mail Marian to ask when we can meet for our first interview. She writes back that she can spend fifteen minutes on the phone with me, a week from Tuesday at nine in the morning.

She calls at the appointed time. Thirteen minutes into our interview she says, "Time's up. But this is fun! Let's do it again tomorrow." And so we do. In twelve-, fourteen-, and fifteen-minute sessions, every morning beginning at nine, Marian tells me about being Tristan's mother.

"He was an alert, handsome baby," she begins. "His Apgar score was ten—perfect. I nursed him till he was three. He wanted to be fed fifteen times a day." The trouble started, Marian says, the day she went back to work. Tristan cried for her all day. Baby-sitter after baby-sitter, he never stopped.

When Rob and his two kids moved in with Marian and her two kids, Marian tells me, "Tristan walked around the house with a brown paper bag over his head. He wouldn't take it off, and he wouldn't talk to Rob. Rob called him the 'bag man.'

"He didn't learn to read till third grade. He was feeling desperate. He couldn't do it. He had huge temper tantrums and stomachaches. He missed a lot of school. I let him stay home too much. Finally we put him in a school for the deaf that accepted some hearing kids. He did a little better there—at least it was quiet, so he didn't get distracted. Homework time was hard—I was working part-time, I had dinner to cook, and Tristan couldn't do math at all. I basically gave him the answers."

In fifth grade, Marian tells me, Tristan's problems escalated. "A therapist told him to empower himself, so he brought a knife to school. He got mad at his teacher so he ran away; we didn't find him for six hours. He got into fights. There were constant phone calls home . . .

"I kept seeing his sweet side. My coping mechanism was to make excuses, which I did for a million years." Marian hesitates, an indicator, I've learned, of distress. "When you have a kid with severe learning disabilities, you learn to make excuses. I'm sure I made everything much worse."

"You, me, and every other mother of a difficult kid," I say, noting how much easier that is to believe of Mike's mom and Tristan's mom than it is of Peter and Jesse's.

Tristan and I are beginning to feel more like friends than biographer and subject when war breaks out—in Afghanistan and in his family. During our lunches together at Phoenix, after school at Jamba Juice sharing pumpkin smoothies, in the basement bedroom of his family's sprawling home on the south flank of Mt. Tamalpais, Tristan has shared with me the empathy and loyalty he feels for his mom and his lifelong ambivalence about his stepfather. The post-9/11 bombing of Afghanistan brings their differences to a rapid boil.

"My stepdad's with Bush!" Tristan tells me, horrified, a few days after the bombing begins. We're sitting on the benches at lunch, just out of earshot of the other kids. He shows me a sticker he bought at a Fairfax head shop, the word "THEM" in a circle with a red line through it, and tells me he gave the same sticker to Rob.

"Rob's academically smart. Before the war started, he knew a lot more than I did about what was going on. I was America-centered, basically clueless," Tristan allows. "But he says they attacked us, so we should attack them back. I asked him, what if Bin Laden has a little brother? He'll live his whole life waiting to bomb us twenty years later, when I'm an adult!

"I know Rob's scared for himself and his family. But doesn't he know that no war's ever won?" Tristan screws his face into a caricature of a stern adult—Bush, perhaps, or Rob. "What a great country. We won the war!" he blusters sarcastically. "Now let's wait for the next one!"

It's not just the war that Tristan's been arguing about at home, and it's not just Rob he's been arguing with. On Saturday night Tristan went camping at the beach with his "old using buddies." His friends smoked pot. He didn't, but he overslept and missed his Sunday morning curfew. "Marian and Rob told me, your trust is blown till you build it back. Now I have to ask them before I go anyplace."

His cheeks flush with anger. "They hold the past against me too much. If I do the smallest thing wrong—don't do my chores, forget to call to check in—they're like, this is the old Tristan. They say I'm going backwards. It makes me really angry 'cause I've been doing hella well."

It's they who are going backward, I think, straight back into the grief and worry they once breathed like polluted air. I know this because I still fall backward into mine. Jesse's a man now, a counselor of troubled youth—a Baptist minister, for Christ's sake! But still: if he doesn't call me back for a couple of days, if there are hang-ups on my message machine, if I find him at home in the middle of a workday—instantly it's then, not now. He hears the fear in my voice; he calls me on it, and rightly so. Just last week I got a call from the Oakland police. By the time I realized they were calling for a donation, I was near tears, pawing through my Rolodex for Jesse's lawyer.

"Of course I'm gonna screw up again," Tristan is saying. "Who doesn't? One thing I know, though: I don't have evil in me anymore."

I ask when the evil left him, and Tristan gives me the exact date. "Earth Day 2001," he says. "It was the day after 4/20." He looks at me questioningly to see if I get the reference. I do: April 20 is unofficial international pot-smoking day. High schools record huge absences, colleges have smoke-ins; marijuana-leaf T-shirts are worn from sea to toking sea.

"I went to the Earth Day festival in Berkeley with some friends. I didn't care about the environment then, but I was pretending I did, so they'd think I was cool.

"I started listening to the music. The last song was about love. We all sang along, like five hundred voices singing love, love, love." Tristan glows with the memory. "My brain was still a little clouded from all the pot I'd smoked the day before. But all of a sudden everything just *lifted*. I realized how much I love everybody and every single thing. I realized that I used to be filled with hatred, but now I wasn't anymore. I started hugging people, meeting people, dancing. It was amazing."

His Earth Day turnaround opened Tristan to the option his mom had long been lobbying for: applying to Phoenix Academy. After leaving Journeys the second time, he'd tried a stint at his dad's, who'd promised to home-school him. But home schooling turned into snowboarding, pot smoking, and vodka drinking. By the time Tristan came back to live with his mom and Rob, he hadn't been in a classroom in over a year.

Tristan remembers his first interview with Eric. "He was like, 'You smoke pot?' I said, 'Yeah.' He said, 'You drink?' I said, 'Yeah.' He said, 'That's a drug too.' I said, 'You won't let me drink, either?' When I left there I *hella* didn't want to go to Phoenix. I figured if the interview pissed me off that much, the school was gonna piss me off more."

But Marian issued an ultimatum. Go to Phoenix, she said, or go back to your dad's. Tristan had had enough of fighting with his dad, of boring country life, of missing his friends. He chose the lesser of two evils, telling himself and everyone else that he'd stay at Phoenix for one semester, then transfer to Marin Pacific High. His first week at Phoenix almost changed his mind. "It was hella weird," he remembers. "They kept talking about God. I was like, 'Fuck God, there is no God, you can't push this on me.' I was pissed. And shy. I didn't have any friends.

"Now I'm getting to know people in the program," Tristan says, "so it's starting to be kinda fun."

He forks a spear of broccoli into his mouth. "It's so strange to look back on myself. I used to eat junk food, get expelled, get sent to rehabs, make fun of people, all this mindless belligerent crap. I'm the same person. But now I'm eating broccoli, being nice to people, being honest. That's why I don't agree with the way they talk about recovery here. I'm in recovery from a lot of things, not just drugs."

Floyd walks by, waving a piece of fried chicken. "You want this, T?" he asks. "It's *good!* Believe that." This is an ongoing routine between the two of them: six-foot-four, 200-pound, confirmed carnivore Floyd trying to tempt five-foot-eleven, 160-pound, vegetarian Tristan to eat meat; Tristan trying to convert Floyd to vegetarianism.

"Dude—try this," Tristan counters, offering him a chunk of banana bread. "My mom made it."

A compromise is struck. Floyd chews, swallows. "That *is* good," he admits.

"B'lee dat," Tristan replies, the rich white kid in perfect mimicry of his African American counselor. The two of them exchange a high-five and a grin.

If it weren't for the fact that Tristan's doing no homework, attending no meetings, hanging out with stoners, and refusing to take a vow of sobriety, I think, he'd be a big success here at Phoenix Academy. As it is, he's on shaky ground.

Are Clara and Eric right? Is Tristan an addict whose substance use will always be substance abuse? Does Tristan need to abstain from drugs to be healthy and happy now, and in the decades of his life that stretch unpredictably before him?

Or is Tristan right? Can his life, now and in the future, incorporate some pot smoking, the occasional 'shroom or peyote trip, a few beers on a Saturday night without plummeting him into the abyss of addiction?

If left untreated, would his drug use taper off or stop as he enters adulthood? Can he—can any kid in rehab—pull off the unthinkable: in AA parlance, "run his own program"?

Or will Tristan run himself out of Phoenix and back into trouble in the process of trying?

Juvenile Drug Court

Every adolescent drug-rehab program has its share of tough kids; these pro-grams aren't designed for the easy ones. Along with teenagers like Mike and Tristan, challenging to treat but tethered firmly to earth, Center Point and Phoenix have their gang-bangers, their hard-core thieves, their deeply depressed and self-destructive kids whose ties to their families, the world, their own uncertain futures—if any—dangle by frayed threads.

The Richmond Drug Court has nothing but. Toting rap sheets that belie their short tenures on this planet, the Drug Court clients are the teenagers you're afraid of, the ones you cross the street to avoid, the ones who have nothing much, so they have nothing much to lose. These are the children of the crack epidemic, the scourge of ghetto gangs, the demolition of family life by the wrecking balls of racism, poverty, despair. These are the kids we turn our heads from, because they show us what life is like for the poorest of the urban poor, living proof of the worst America has to offer: parents who can't take care of their children; children who don't care if they live or die.

Trying to save these kids is not an easy job, nor a glorious one. Few people care if it gets done, so there's not nearly enough money or people power allo-cated to do it. Still, every Tuesday afternoon from twelve-thirty to four, the

Richmond Drug Court Team gathers in a courtroom in the Contra Costa County courthouse and bends to the task.

The team encompasses those now responsible for supplanting—or replacing—their clients' parents, many of whom aren't able to feed their children, let alone show up for their court appearances. Kevin Charles, the Drug Court Coordinator, goes to Juvenile Hall, screens kids for admission, and acts as liaison between the county, the program, and the kids' families. Tom Fleming is every Drug Court client's public defender, Pam Collinshill their PO. Commissioner Steve Easton, a kindly-faced grandfather, is the Drug Court judge.

There are two distinct but coordinated components of the Drug Court program: the legal process of monitoring each client's probation and—when it works—releasing him or her from it; and the therapeutic process that aspires to send each graduate into the world a more whole and self-aware as well as sober person. So, also present in the courtroom every Tuesday are counselors from Choices, the treatment program where every Drug Court kid goes—is supposed to go—after school each weekday for drug testing, team sports, and individual, group, and family sessions. The kids make their court appearances each Tuesday at two; the team spends the hours before then reviewing their cases one by one.

"Wen Ho made another suicide attempt last night," Kevin Charles announces. The team is gathered around the defense table, sharing a plate of biscotti supplied by Judge Easton. "He sliced himself fifteen times. We need to order a psych eval."

"Do we know what Wen Ho smokes or injects?" Judge Easton asks.

"Wen Ho's a traditionalist, Your Honor," Kevin replies in his sardonic style. "He denies all but weed and drink."

"Guess he forgot to mention that little bit of crank he shoots." Judge Easton rolls up his shirtsleeves, squinting into the laptop in front of him. "We're horrified they let him out of the hospital when they did. You know how they decided that? They asked him if he was gonna kill himself."

"His parents don't speak English. They're not here legally," says Tom, a thirty-eight-year-old Eurasian man in a blue suit and Jerry Garcia tie. "They're totally intimidated by the system."

"Let's leave him on JEM," says Kevin. "If he goes off the radar, we'll go roll him up."

Although much of what's been discussed here in the past two hours has been in a language unintelligible to me—legalese mixed with the shorthand of people who have been doing this together for the past seventy-five Tuesdays—this acronym, at least, I understand. Jesse was on JEM—Juvenile Electronic Monitoring—when he was Wen Ho's age. The ankle bracelet didn't serve its intended purpose: to corral his movement from home to school and back. But it did give Jesse's PO a way to find him and take him to Juvenile Hall ("roll him up") when he violated those parameters ("went off the radar"), as he regularly did.

"I have a problem with that," Tom interjects. "What if the monitor gives us a false reading?"

"Wen Ho can't come to court if he's dead," Kevin says flatly. "We're doing this for his safety. Agreed?"

Tom nods reluctantly. Kevin flips to the next kid's file. "Mr. Albert Alves," he says.

"Al had a good week," says Leo Kidd, Choices program director. "Perfect attendance, good participation in group, four clean tests."

"See how he turned around when we stopped accepting his excuses?" asks Stacy, a young African American woman who's Albert's counselor. "I especially liked the one about him kissing a girl with cocaine in her mouth."

"But then yesterday he turned awful," Leo adds. "Whiny, defiant. He does have two impacted wisdom teeth . . ."

"So he scored his Vicodin," Kevin says knowingly. "Addicts love their Vicodin. Let's make sure Al doesn't test dirty for opiates two weeks from now."

"Cookie or lunch for Albert?" asks Judge Easton.

"I'd say cookie and lunch, but no prize," suggests Leo. The others nod their agreement; Judge Easton types that ruling into his laptop.

Cookies? Lunch? Prizes? In a court of law? Kevin explained this strange menu to me when we met in his office this morning. "We take on kids who've been in the system for years. Our clients are extremely troubled. Many of them have serious mental-health issues on top of their addictions. But they're also children. They need immediate rewards for good behavior." Sure enough: on the judge's bench there's a pink bakery box exuding the perfume of warm chocolate. Beside Tom's chair there's a Target shopping bag full of sports T-shirts, Frisbees, and journals. Lunch, Kevin told me, happens after court each week, when he takes the kids who've earned it to the restaurant of their collective choice—most often, "Mickey D's."

The team works their way through the twenty kids on the docket, discussing the feedback they've gathered during the week: drug tests, JEM reports, parents' and teachers' comments, and obstetricians' reports. The boys cried discrimination, Stacy informs the group, when they found out that one girl is being graduated from the program early so she'll get out before her baby's born. "The boys asked me what I'd do if they picket," Stacy says, grinning. "I said, 'Lock the door and turn up the music.'"

When the report on a kid is good, the team members radiate satisfaction. When the report is bad—Diamond had a full-blown coke relapse; Aaron threatened to stab his mother; Anthony ditched school all week— they "dispo" the kid to Juvenile Hall, to CYA, to placement (at Center Point, Walden House, or another local residential program) only after ruling out every possible option.

"As you and I sit here," Kevin told me this morning, "there are tens of millions of teenagers getting high. I'll never see them.

"Ours is a self-selecting group. When our kids ran into pot, cocaine, meth, alcohol, something went wrong. They failed in school. They committed crimes. They were offered a choice: go to jail, go to placement, or try Drug Court." Kevin glanced around at the teenagers' art that adorns his office walls: drawings of Spiderman and Bart Simpson, poems titled "Somebody Should Have Told Him!" and "Love Yourself Before Anybody Else."

Kevin told me that there isn't a lie that the Drug Court Team hasn't heard, a disillusionment they haven't endured. "When I go to Juvenile Hall to interview a kid, I figure he'll tell me 10 to 15 percent of the story. They're teens. Controlling disclosure is one of the few ways they have to control their existence in the world." Yet the team discusses each child with a nimble balance of respect and skepticism, take-no-prisoners resolve, and tender-hearted compassion. Where else in their world, I ask myself, do these kids get treated with this much care? And why did it take this—drug abuse, multiple criminal acts, multiple arrests—to get them the attention they deserve?

I told Kevin about my book and asked if he'd keep an eye out for a Drug Court client to be part of it. He warned me just how difficult following one of the Drug Court kids might be. "About half the kids we admit to the program stick around," he said. "And 'sticking around' often means doing our program for a few weeks or months, then relapsing, violating probation, going to residential treatment or the Hall, coming back, and running through the whole cycle again."

"I'll take a chance on Drug Court," I said, "if Drug Court will take a chance on me."

Kevin looked pleased. He promised to run the idea by the team, and invited me to start attending court in Richmond once a week, and sessions at Choices (Changing and Healing from the Outside In Creates Enduring Self-respect) on weekday afternoons.

The first adult Drug Court was founded in Dade County, Florida, in 1985. Its guiding concept—instead of incarcerating nonviolent drug offenders (a population with sky-high recidivism rates), offer them a combination of drug rehab, vocational training, and court supervision—was as controversial then as it is now. Lock-'em-up conservatives and prison construction lobbyists argue that this approach is "soft on crime." The evidence proves them wrong. In *Hooked*, Dr. Lonny Shavelson writes, "Drug Courts, in spite of their hug-a-thug reputation, have been more effective at keeping addicts off drugs and away from committing crimes than anything else the criminal justice system has ever thrown at them."

The U.S. Department of Justice agrees and funds Drug Courts accordingly. Since 1995, more than $80 million in federal money has been allocated to the eight hundred Drug Courts that now exist or are being planned nationwide. It's proved a wise investment. Studies cited in *Hooked* show that Drug Courts graduate more than twice as many drug offenders as traditional treatment programs do. Therapeutic communities lose nine out of ten clients before they complete the program; Drug Courts whose clients are in rehab, on the other hand, retain seven out of ten. Repeat crimes among Drug Court graduates are greatly reduced as well.

Can the Drug Court model work this well for kids? Results gathered from the 167 juvenile Drug Courts operating in forty-six states—up from twenty-five in two states in 1997—look promising. The federal Office of Juvenile Justice and Delinquency Prevention (OJJDP) reports that of

12,500 juveniles enrolled in Drug Courts nationwide, 4,000 have graduated and 4,500 are still enrolled, yielding a wildly successful retention rate of 68 percent.

The OJJDP acknowledges that juvenile Drug Courts face "unique challenges not encountered in the adult drug court environment," including the need to "counteract the negative influences of peers, gangs, and family members; address the needs of the family, especially families with substance abuse problems; and motivate juvenile offenders to change, especially given their sense of invulnerability and lack of maturity."

To meet these challenges, the OJJDP recommends that juvenile Drug Courts "focus on the functioning of the juvenile and the family throughout the juvenile court process; coordinate efforts among the court, the treatment community, the school system, and other community agencies, and [impose] immediate sanctions for noncompliance and incentives for progress for both the juvenile and family."

Since the first session of the Richmond Juvenile Drug Court in May 2000, it has confronted these challenges and others. Meagerly paid and overworked (Tom Fleming, for example, volunteers his time, adding his Drug Court clients to his paid caseload), its team members are evangelists for the cause. "Untreated, these kids don't disappear when they turn eighteen," Kevin Charles says. "They become full-time addicts and criminals. The question is, do we want them to wreak havoc on themselves, their families, their communities? Or do we want to do this kind of early intervention instead?"

Compared to other "dispositions" available to Drug Court clients, Kevin says, the program offers not only the best, but also the most cost-effective, results. "Incarcerating a kid at the Boys' Ranch or CYA costs about the same as residential treatment at Walden House or Center Point: $60,000 per kid per year. Our program costs $14,000.

"And when those kids get dumped out of residential programs with no aftercare"—the follow-up treatment that's critical to maintaining sobriety, yet is offered by few programs—"guess who gets 'em? We do!"

In eighteen months, the Richmond Juvenile Drug Court has demonstrated results that look pretty depressing taken on their own, but are positively stellar in the context of the rehab industry's failure rates—especially given the demographics of the kids. Among the current crop of Drug Court clients, 50 percent have prior convictions for auto theft, 20 percent for battery or weapons possession, 8 percent for burglary. "In some Drug Courts," Kevin tells me, "if you sell drugs you're out. Commit battery, you're out. Not ours. I pushed for us to take the hardest kids."

Reading Kevin's latest quarterly report, it's clear just how painstaking this work is; how few and how sweet the triumphs. "Two clients who were not enrolled in school," he wrote, "are now attending regularly, their truancy reduced by the weekly court review of school attendance and performance. Four clients gained employment. Two maintained it."

Of the eighty-one kids admitted to date, twenty-four remain in treatment, five have been transferred to other treatment programs, nine were terminated due to new arrests, twenty-nine dropped out, and fourteen graduated. Not one Drug Court graduate, Kevin tells me, knocking on Formica, has since been arrested.

I start spending my Tuesday afternoons at the Contra Costa County courthouse, passing through the metal detector, climbing the stairs to the Juvenile Drug Courtroom, sitting through Case Review, then hanging with the kids in the hallway, waiting for court to be called into session.

Several afternoons a week I drive two miles down San Pablo Avenue and sit in on groups at Choices, a facility so funky it makes the humble Phoenix campus and sterile Center Point seem downright sumptuous. Just off the commercial strip of San Pablo Avenue, midway between Berkeley and Richmond, Choices shares a cinder-block building with the El Cerrito Police Department. The carpeting is threadbare, the walls scarred, the furniture as distressed as the kids who flop themselves onto it. The thousand-square-foot space is divided into counselors' offices, two bathrooms (the girls, observed by a female staffer, take their daily pee tests in one; the boys, observed by a male staffer, in the other), a hang-out room, and the big room where the groups are held—fittingly, a former courtroom. The walls are decorated with graffiti-lettered Twelve-Step and Serenity Prayer posters, an Emotions Chart (fifty faces manifesting fifty emotions from "aggressive" and "alienated" to "undecided" and "withdrawn"), and the Choices program guidelines:

Cardinal Rules

No fighting or threats of violence

No property damage: writing, cutting, carving

No stealing or taking things w/o permission

No sexual relationships with clients or staff

No harassing behavior of any kind

No possession of mind-altering substances or paraphernalia

Consequences

1. Serenity Prayer
2. Push-ups/sit-ups
3. Time out
4. Clean up a room and/or pick up trash
5. Essay
6. Sent home
7. Suspended

As we hang out together on the sagging couches, or around the corner where they sneak their forbidden cigarettes, or at the taco truck that pulls up each afternoon at the DMV across the street, the Drug Court kids get used to having me around. They don't shower me with the Marin huggyness of the Phoenix kids, or the desperate curiosity of the Center Point boys. But in their own way they take to me, calling me "Book Lady," critiquing my outfits ("Those pants are hella dope, but that top is *old school*"), asking me when I'm gonna pick one of them to write about already. I start down that path with several kids, only to have them vanish, or change their minds, or turn out to be living in such precarious circumstances that I can't find them, let alone interview them. After several months I'm frustrated but determined. The Drug Court story needs telling. Plus, I need the fashion tips.

One morning in November I get an e-mail from Stacy.

Meredith:

   There's a new girl named Zalika you should definitely talk to.
She's a 16 y/o black girl who's been prostituting & stripping since

she was 12–13. Her pimp is now 28 y/o and still in her life. She is bright & articulate with a vocal faith in God (how does she reconcile *that???*). Two-parent home (parents state that Drug Court is her "one more chance") with two younger siblings. Crack possession, summer on the run in San Francisco's Tenderloin, cocaine abuse, PTSD [posttraumatic stress disorder].

Stacy

That afternoon Leo leaves me alone in his office with a five-foot-tall, mocha-complected girl with an intricate braids-and-extensions hairdo, a skintight, glittering Eiffel Tower T-shirt, skintight hip-hugger jeans, matching Nikes, and the telltale bulge of an ankle monitor under her sock. I ask where she got her pretty name. "My daddy's a Muslim," she says, adding, "I'm a writer too. And a reader."

She opens her backpack, pulls out a Toni Morrison novel and rapper Sister Souljah's new book, and tells me she's reading both of them at the same time. She wants to know what my goals for my book are, what participating in it would require of her, and how, exactly, I would conceal her identity. "'Cause I'm 'bout to *make* something of myself," she declares, "once I put all this bullshit behind me."

Zalika proceeds with her interrogation. "What kind of structure did you have in mind? Is each kid's story gonna be like a book inside a book?"

"Maybe you can help me figure that out," I say, a bit taken aback.

"I got my *own* book to write," Zalika replies without missing a beat. "Will you help me with mine if I help you with yours?"

I say I will and ask if she thinks her parents will let her work with me.

"They leave my decisions up to me."

"So they trust you."

"No. They don't. But I been gone more than I been home since I was twelve years old. They let me run my life." Zalika snorts derisively. "What's left of it, anyhow, with me stuck in this damn *pro*-gram."

Leo knocks on the door, tells Zalika it's time for group. "I'll let you know when I make up my mind," she tells me, and we follow Leo into the courtroom for Zalika's first group-therapy session at Choices.

There, she is transformed. While her fellow clients—twelve black, Latino, Asian, biracial, and white boys; five black, Latina, and white girls—rush in and out of the room, yelling and laughing, slurping up the Cups O' Noodles and hot chocolate the program provides for those who can't afford the taco truck, the bright-eyed, incisive girl who interviewed me in Leo's office slouches in a folding metal chair, shimmering with resentment, observing the chaos around her through heavily lidded eyes.

"Chill out, y'all!" Stacy yells, herding the kids into their chairs.

"Your mouth is awful!" Ursula, the newest counselor, tells eight-months-pregnant Audrey, who's cursing out one of the boys. "You gonna talk like that in front of your daughter?"

"Focus up!" barks Mike, the young African American man—the counterpart of Bill at Phoenix Academy—who drives the kids from court to Choices, to AA meetings, from Choices home at night, in the program's dented Chevy van.

"Today our topic is, What is recovery?" Stacy announces. "I need focused participation from all of you, because recovery is the whole foundation of—" She shakes her head at a new boy. "Take the hat off, please, Braydon." Braydon makes a loud sucking noise in response. "Or you can go home," Stacy adds. Without hesitation, he gets up and leaves the room. The other kids look at each other, knowing what Braydon hasn't figured out yet: his escape won't play well before Judge Easton on Tuesday.

"Let's do a quick check-in," Stacy continues. "Your name, what you're feeling."

"I feel fucked up," says Aaron, a chronic car thief whose drug of choice is coke.

"That's not an emotion."

"He's entitled to his opinion," argues Trevor, a seventeen-year-old alcoholic.

"I feel fucking good, man," says Anthony, moving the discussion along.

"I feel aiight," says Akeel, whose Pakistani parents are the only family I've ever seen at Multifamily Group on Tuesday nights.

"I feel boring," says Tiffany, a white girl who is regularly removed from the home of her meth-addicted parents.

"Good, Tiffany! That's the exact correct meaning of the word!" Stacy crows. She tosses Tiffany a piece of chocolate. Noticing the bag of Hershey's Miniatures in Stacy's lap, all the kids—except Zalika—become suddenly attentive.

"Zalika?" Stacy prods her.

"I'm fine," she mutters.

"'Fine' isn't an emotion."

"Damn! I feel happy! Damn!" snaps Zalika, looking anything but.

"I'll take that for now," Stacy says. "Okay, guys. What is recovery?"

"Recovery is for those that want it, not necessarily those that need it," says Trevor.

Stacy tosses a chocolate into his waiting hands.

"Recovery is power and knowledge," Tiffany says.

"We're getting the best definitions we ever got for this topic!" Stacy enthuses.

"Well, look at the candy you got," Trevor explains.

One boy throws a chocolate wrapper at another. Both jump out of their seats. "C'mon, you guys," Mike reprimands them as Stacy presses on.

"Maybe before you were in recovery, you were walking around calling people stupid bitches. Because what are the two emotions we were comfortable expressing in our addiction?" Stacy works the room like a revivalist preacher, pacing the floor, her voice thundering, her hands gesturing wildly.

"Wanting to use, and not wanting to use," guesses Anthony.

"No! If I'm all up in your face, mugging you and shit, how does that make you feel?" Stacy asks.

"Angry," answers Aaron.

"Angry! Yes!" Stacy shouts back. "We don't say our feelings are hurt. We get angry, because that's the safer emotion to feel. Then we get high, and we say we're happy. Zalika! Do you have something to contribute?"

"I ain't got no anger problem," Zalika mutters. "And I ain't got no drug problem neither." The three counselors in the room exchange a meaningful glance. Plenty of kids sit here and believe that; most know better than to say it.

"The purpose of this activity," Stacy goes on, "is to get in touch with our feelings. Because what are we recovering from?"

"Drugs and addiction," Anthony calls out.

"Which one is it—drugs or addiction?" Stacy doesn't wait for an answer. "Because if we say it's just drugs we can leave them alone; then we don't have no problem. But recovering from addiction—that's a lifelong recovery process from a disease that affects every aspect of our lives and who we are."

"My butt hurts," Audrey complains, her hands crossed over her bulging belly.

"I'm 'bout to walk out," warns Trevor. "This is annoying."

Zalika shakes her head in disgust.

"If I'm using, living a criminal lifestyle," Stacy asks the kids, "who am I interacting with?"

"Criminals," says DeAndre, who was last arrested for dealing crack.

"You calling us criminals now?" Trevor glowers at Stacy.

"I need to take a time-out," Tiffany blurts. "I feel like shit."

"Beautiful!" Stacy declares.

Several boys laugh. "That's beautiful?" one asks. "That she feels like shit?"

"What's beautiful," Stacy explains, "is that Tiffany did exactly what I'm talking about. Before, she'd feel like shit and emanate all that ugly funky stuff. Today she realized how she feels. She took a positive step to make herself feel better."

"I need a time-out," Aaron says, and stands up.

"Sit your butt down," Stacy barks at him.

Zalika folds her arms across her chest and closes her eyes.

Over the next couple of weeks Zalika remains undecided about participating in the book, but her feelings about Choices become ever clearer. She hates the program, hates everyone who works there, and hates all the kids in it—with the notable exception of Braydon, a.k.a. Bo, the handsome, ebony-skinned, gold-toothed new boy she flirts with openly, in flagrant violation of the "no sexual relationships" rule.

One day when Ursula calls her from the bathroom to come take her daily drug test, Zalika imitates a person calling a pet—"Here Zalika, good girl, here, girl"—then snaps, "I'm not a dog! Don't call me like one!" The next day she refuses to participate in group, sits sulking in a beanbag chair instead. Later, when Mike drives the kids to the park for team sports, Zalika takes Ursula aside; they sit on adjoining swings, talking and swinging for an hour. Zalika returns to Choices fuming. "These people are prejudiced against me," she tells me when I follow her to the taco truck. "They read my file. They're judging me for my past. I ain't *never* gon' last a whole year in this program."

I offer to buy her a burrito. "I don't like people buying me things," Zalika snaps. As she passes her money through the truck window, I notice a circle of diamonds sparkling on her wrist. "Except my boyfriend." She smiles then, holding the bracelet up for me to admire. "Yep, yep. It's real. I'm embarrassed to tell you how much it cost."

"Your boyfriend or your pimp?" I wonder, but I'm not yet ready to ask.

"I'm gonna tell my PO to switch me to another program," Zalika announces. "I got four years over my head if I get sent to CYA. But maybe I could go to a residential program for a shorter time instead." We discuss her options as we walk back to Choices, where Mike is loading the kids into the van.

"Hugs!" Zalika proclaims, her warm smile and open arms catching me by surprise. "Five minutes ago," I think as I hug her good-bye, "I couldn't buy her a burrito. Now I'm her new best friend." Zalika's constantly switching dialect is one thing: like a lot of black teenagers, she uses one language to talk to other kids, another to talk to older black folks, another to communicate with white people like me. But this girl isn't just multilingual. She's multi-emotional.

On Saturday when I call Zalika on the private line her parents installed in her room, she tells me she's decided to be in my book, then moves right on to her next agenda item. "Leo told me I'm being too 'social,' that I need to stop flirting with the boys. If he says that in court, the judge is gonna get prejudiced against me too. So I'm gonna call a meeting with him on Monday. Will you sit in on it?"

"Sure," I say. Borrowing a page from Zalika's book, I ask for a favor in return. "Can I interview you sometime soon?"

"You can drive me home on Monday," she counteroffers, "after we meet with Leo."

Zalika doesn't show up at Choices on Monday. Bo, I notice, is missing too. When I reach her at home, we agree to meet after program on Friday, the day Mike drives all the kids to an NA meeting in the mostly Latino, working-poor Fruitvale neighborhood of Oakland.

Toto, we're not in Marin anymore, I tell myself as I follow Mike and the kids into a tiny, musty storefront between a pager store and a check-cashing joint. We squeeze ourselves into an airless room along with twenty adults, many of them in tattered clothes reeking of alcohol and sweat. Except for the kids' resigned resentment at being here, this meeting has little in common with the ones Tristan goes to, on lavishly landscaped church campuses and moonlit Pacific beaches. The kids twitch restlessly in their seats as self-described alcoholics and crackheads testify in slurred voices that indicate they're still in the "desire to get sober" phase of recovery.

I remember an AA meeting I went to with Tristan and the Phoenix Academy kids. They spent most of the hour sneaking in and out of the room, smoking cigarettes—except Tristan, whose honesty vow kept him there, and Tomás, who seemed transfixed. "Do you get something out of this?" I asked Tomás as the meeting broke up. "I see my future if I don't stop now," he answered. I wonder if the Drug Court kids are schlepped all the way to Oakland every Friday so they can see *their* futures in these homeless, bottomed-out addicts.

Zalika perches stiffly on her chair, her upper lip curled in disgust. As soon as the closing Serenity Prayer has been said, she makes a beeline for the van. "I thought we were doing an interview today," I remind her as she jockeys for a seat beside Bo.

"I'll go with you," she says after a moment's thought, "if you drive me to my friend's house in Rodeo when we're done."

I don't know exactly where Rodeo is—somewhere within the 733-square-mile sprawl of Contra Costa County—but I agree to her terms. She climbs into my car. "Here's the deal," I tell her as we drive down Fruitvale Avenue. "I'll do anything I can for you, as long as it doesn't involve helping you lie to your parents or the program." I hand her my cell phone, ask her to call her parents and tell them that she's with me. Zalika dials. She gets into an animated conversation. Suspicious, I ask her to pass me the phone. I'm surprised to find that it's actually her mom, June, on the other end.

June gives me permission to drive her daughter to Rodeo, says she'll pick her up there later, and adds that she's glad Zalika decided to participate in the book. "Maybe it'll give her some motivation to do better."

"You didn't believe that was my mom I called, huh?" Zalika asks.

"Nope," I admit. "And you don't trust me yet either, do you?"

"Nope," she says, smiling at me.

We drive fifteen miles north to El Sobrante, the middle-class suburb where Zalika lives, when she has to, with her middle-class family. She directs me into a vast shopping center and chooses Taco Bell for our dinner venue. This time she lets me pay.

"I broke up with my pimp two days ago," Zalika begins, biting into a beef taco. "He called me a bitch. I refuse to be disrespected."

I ask if she normally feels respected by her pimp.

"Oh, Meredith," she giggles, "you really are a square, aren't you?" She explains that aside from an occasional "whupping"—"Every ho' gets *that*. Otherwise how would pimps keep their ho's in line?"—her pimp treated her well.

"Having a crush on Bo helped me leave him," she confides, a gleam in her eye. "You know we'll both get kicked out the program if they find out."

"Yes," I say, "I do know that."

"This is the first time I've ever been with someone my own age," she says dreamily. "I just love bad boys like Bo. I love the danger that we might get caught. I love the drama!" Later, I show her the "Drama Queen" bumper sticker on the visor of my car. She squeals with delight, and invents the names we've used with each other ever since: "DQ1—that's you, Meredith, 'cause you're older. DQ2—that's me."

We talk about her siblings and her parents. "I'm closest to my dad. My mom and I get along as long as I don't touch her clothes." We talk about why she's had so much trouble in her life. "My lawyers, the counselors, the people putting me in programs—they always ask if my dad touched me. That really pisses me off. That doesn't happen in African American families.

"My parents did everything they could. They gave me their support, taught me to make my own decisions, always told me they loved me. Anything from the store, I could get it. My dad was so poor growing up, he tried to give his kids everything. That's what makes him so mad with my situation."

I ask if she's had any therapy.

"The county made me go to this African American lady. How you gon' ask someone how they feel and think they gon' open up to you, just like that? I told her all the time, this is stupid. You're stupid."

And we talk about her history with drugs. "I started smoking weed and drinking when I was thirteen. I just got into the coke recently. I don't like it that much, the whole nose-running thing. Drugs aren't a problem for me," she reiterates. "But being in a drug program is a way for me to get off probation. Me and a lot of other kids. You think 'cause someone smokes *weed* they need to be in *rehab?* They just stick us in programs like Choices 'cause they don't know what else to do with us."

I nod, thinking even when they stick you in programs like Choices, they don't know what to do with you. And if we knew what to do with kids like you (and Mike, and Tristan, and Jesse) in the first place, we wouldn't need programs like Choices.

When we're finished eating and talking, Zalika directs me to Rodeo, a working-class town in the stinking shadows of the oil refineries five miles north of El Sobrante. I deliver her to the porch of a dark apartment in a housing project and wait in my car, watching, until she disappears inside.

Only after I drive away do I realize that I've already broken my own rule, not once but twice. The terms of Zalika's ankle monitor prohibit her from going anywhere besides home, school, AA meetings, and the program, so our stop at Taco Bell was a violation of her probation. And I'm sure I just left her at Bo's house, for which she could be expelled from the Drug Court program and sent to CYA. It occurs to me, also, that her mother must know all of that, and she let me do it.

"That didn't take long," I reflect on the half-hour drive home. Already I'm intrigued by Zalika, attached to Zalika, being manipulated by Zalika— and ready to come back for more.

What's wrong with Zalika?

"She's insane," her father, Asani, says flatly the first time we speak. "We tried everything with her. We sent her to private schools. I home-schooled her for a year. We disciplined her. We gave her freedom. Nothing worked with that child.

"Among other things, she's confused about race and class. At age four-teen she told me, 'You're not black enough.' She thinks being smart and making money means being white. I told her, 'I'm not moving to the 'hood just so you'll know who you are.'"

I notice that Zalika's father speaks of his efforts in the past tense. Never uses his daughter's name. And has only anger in his voice—none of the self-doubt I've heard in Barbara's voice, Marian's, my own.

I tell Asani that I envy his detachment.

"I used to blame myself," he admits. "But then why are all my other kids in college, on the honor roll, doing fine? I'm sick of parents being blamed for their kids' craziness. That's the only way to explain the trouble she's been in since she was twelve: she's nuts."

"I know they come into this world with their own personalities," Zalika's mother says. "But I can't help looking back and asking, what could I have done differently?"

Zalika's mom sounds more familiar. More like . . . a mom. "When Zalika was three I'd say, don't go in the street, and there she'd go," June says. "When she was eleven she tried out for cheerleading. I was working week-ends and I didn't have time to take her, so she couldn't join the team. Now I feel like maybe if she'd done that, if she'd made friends with normal girls . . ." June sighs. "They're all saying Zalika's so bad. I see a little girl who's really smart, beyond her years. I say, get her active in something. Channel that energy constructively. Then maybe she'll be okay."

The professionals weigh in. "This girl's needs are complex," Kevin Charles says. "Some of the most profound teen addicts I've encountered are the brightest. Zalika fits in that category. We recommended residential treatment, but the parents wouldn't go for it. They're upper-middle-class, high-achieving people. They have their own intricate denial systems. She needs therapy for sure, and plenty of it."

"Zalika's special," says Tom Fleming, her lawyer on the many cases she's "caught" in the past two years. "She needs to be in an environment where she can deal with her psychological issues as well as her substance-abuse issues. She's addicted to weed and alcohol; maybe coke, yes—but her main addiction is to men. My guess is, a lot of it goes back to her relationship with her father. She has serious issues with her parents.

"She has the heart and the brain to succeed," Tom concludes, "but it would be very easy for her to fail: to cut off the ankle monitor, take off with a good-looking pimp or a drug dealer." He sighs the familiar sigh of those who love and worry about Zalika. "I hope to God that's not what happens."

There's a phrase that's unsaid but resounding through everything the Drug Court–treatment professionals say about Zalika, a phrase I know they'd be using about her if they were into dropping blanket diagnoses on kids instead of plugging away at the salvation of each one. "Dual diagnosis," as the Office of National Drug Control Policy (ONDCP) defines it, applies to "juvenile and adult offenders who abuse or are dependent on drugs and alcohol [and] also have co-occurring mental disorders." "Many of these individuals self-medicate with illegal drugs," the ONDCP adds, reporting that 60 percent of mentally ill offenders are under the influence of alcohol or drugs when they commit their crimes.

As difficult as it is to define drug dependency or addiction, it's harder still to define "mentally ill"—impossible (and possibly irrelevant) when the "offender" in question is sixteen years old. "The term 'dual diagnosis,'" comments Harvard Medical School psychiatrist Dr. Lance Dodes in his 2001 book *The Heart of Addiction,* "perpetuates the error of viewing addictions as somehow separate and unconnected to the rest of a person's psychology."

The "dual diagnosis" dilemma is particularly poignant against the backdrop of a program like the Richmond Drug Court, whose clients suffer from so many contributing factors—starting with their involuntary membership in society's most unpopular class and racial groups. "Every kid we have meets the criteria for dual diagnosis," Kevin Charles says. "They're getting attention for their criminal behavior, but there's no separating the behavioral issues from the substance abuse."

Juvenile Drug Courts nationwide report the same overlap: clients in 81 percent of programs take medications for mental-health conditions; 79 percent of the programs serve kids taking meds for ADD/ADHD. Indeed, I have yet to meet a "single diagnosis" kid: one with a drug problem and no accompanying emotional or mental-health issues. And in every program I found kids like Zalika, relegated to drug programs because, as she says, no one knew what else to do with (or for) them. Public funds (albeit not enough of them) are available for drug-treatment programs. Public hospitals have psych wards. But aside from high-end wilderness programs and thera-peutic boarding schools, there are no rehab programs for teenagers like Zalika, or Jesse, whose drug abuse is one of many signs that they're too emo-tionally damaged—or too immature, or too bored, or too bright—to keep themselves out of trouble.

Will twelve-step meetings, group therapy, an ankle monitor heal Zalika's wounds, whatever their origins? "We need another program called Life Court," Tom Fleming tells me, "for kids whose issues are not primarily drugs. But we don't spend a whole lot of money in this society on things like that. That's why I pulled Zalika into Drug Court: no other options." Tom reminds me, as he often does, that "There's a zero percent success rate for girls in her situation. Every single girl I've represented who was into prostitution is either in jail, still prostituting, or dead." Tom adds, "I was hoping the combination of counseling at Choices and being monitored in court would help her address her issues—or at least keep her alive till she can address them on her own."

It's a merciful and life-saving thing the Richmond Drug Court and all these adolescent drug programs do: containing kids who need protection from their own frailties, and the world's. It would be more wonderful still, if our families, schools, and communities were given the resources they need to pre-vent (best-case scenario) and treat (when necessary) the spiritual, financial, racial, physical, and psychological wounds that lead to substance abuse, teenage prostitution, and other symptoms of our children's pain.

"I might get sent to the Hall today. I was out till midnight three nights last week," Zalika whispers to me on Tuesday as we wait outside the courtroom. The Drug Court Team is inside, finishing up this week's Case Review; the Drug Court kids are arriving from the various schools they attend (or don't) in clusters of twos and threes. Looking like traveling salespeople, those who hope to get their ankle bracelets removed today tote the black plastic brief-case that holds the monitor, which must be turned in when the bracelet is removed. Those who know they'll be sleeping in a Juvenile Hall cell tonight slump on the wooden benches, mute with resignation, or despair.

Tom Fleming emerges from the courtroom, stands at a lectern beside the door, and starts calling his clients one by one for their weekly precourt consultation, conducted while the other kids borrow each other's cell phones, gossip, or doze a few feet away. "How you doin', Zalika?" he asks, looking her in the eye.

"Am I going in the Hall?" she asks nervously.

"No. You're all right. You had three negative tests, excellent participation in group, and your mom came to Choices for a session with Ursula. That's all great." Tom glances at the notes in his hand. "But you had JEM violations on two nights. You need to work on your out-of-ranges, Zalika."

"I will." Suddenly the nervous delinquent is a sultry vamp, smiling coquettishly at her lawyer. "I promise, Tom," she breathes.

"I've always believed in you, Zalika. You know how I feel about your future." He turns to me. "She wants to be a public defender."

"You're my inspiration, Tom." Zalika screws her face into a pout. "Will they take me off JEM next week if I do good?"

"How come you're going out of range, Zalika? Where were you?"

"I was just . . . gone." She turns away from him.

"Doing what?"

"At my friend's house."

"You're not hooking up with—"

"No!" Zalika shouts. "That's not what I'm doing!"

Tom pulls a card from his breast pocket, writes a number on the back. "I don't give anyone my cell phone number, Zalika. I'm giving it to you. I'm gonna stand by you. And now you have Meredith too. We're gonna be your team. Okay?"

Whether it's okay or not, we *are* her team. Tom and I have been talking and e-mailing each other daily, strategizing about how to get Zalika through the program, off probation, into a sustainable existence. Nearly instantly, my role in Zalika's life has crossed the line from journalistic observer to assistant lifeguard.

She slips Tom's card into her purse. "What should I tell them in court when they ask where I was?"

"Tell them you know you made a mistake."

"I need to get a job so I don't have to do that stuff to get money." Tom and I exchange a worried look. Did Zalika just admit that she's still prostituting?

"I know you've got what it takes to finish this program." Tom's eyes are locked, now, on Zalika's. "You know that, too, right?"

Zalika nods impatiently. Clearly, they've covered this territory before. "There's nothing but sunshine ahead for you, Zalika." He hugs her and calls his next client.

"Looks like there's some good developments this week; some not so good," Judge Easton, wearing his black robe, says as he peers down from the bench. "How do you feel you're doing in the program, Zalika?"

"All right, I guess," she answers from the defense table, where she sits with Tom at her left side, me at her right. Parents are encouraged to attend their kids' court appearances, but few ever do. So whenever a kid is accompanied by anyone—a cousin, a grandmother, a friend, an author—Tom enlists that person to sit in the parents' place.

"What have you been doing well?" the judge asks.

"Attendance, and my ability not to do drugs," Zalika answers.

From the left side of the courtroom, where PO Pam Collinshill, counselors Stacy Harris and Leo Kidd, and Kevin Charles sit—the men now wearing suits and ties—Kevin confirms, "That's right. Zalika's tests have been negative."

"Zalika's had a very good week," Leo adds. "We see her making some real progress."

"What does JEM say?" the judge turns to Pam. He knows the answer, of course; the team discussed it a few minutes ago. It strikes me that Case Review is the rehearsal; this is the show, costumes and all. And although the outcome of Drug Court has a very real and lasting impact on each of these kids' lives—graduating from the program means being released from probation, offering them the possibility of a life outside "the system"—what happens in this courtroom is more about care than punishment, more therapy than adjudication, a living enactment of the "treatment versus incarceration" debate.

"Apparently there were some violations," Pam says.

"Four hours out of range on the tenth, six hours on the fifth, four hours on the eighth. Took five hours to go to an AA meeting." The judge reads from his laptop screen and looks down at Zalika. "I get the feeling you like being on JEM."

"Of course I don't!" Zalika protests.

"We'll hope you do better with that next week. Meanwhile, your progress at Choices gets you a cookie." The judge steps down from the bench bearing a platter piled with dinner plate–sized chocolate chip cookies. He approaches Zalika, proffers the platter like a butler serving champagne. As they do every time this scene is played out, all the kids applaud. Zalika returns to her seat among them; Judge Easton returns to the bench and calls the next client.

"Bo came up dirty for THC," Leo says. "And he didn't show up yesterday. But other than that he did a good job. We're glad to have him in the program."

"Other than that?" What else is there? Sometimes giving these kids positive reinforcement requires some pretty creative flattery—particularly given the unmistakable aroma of pot emanating from where Bo's sitting.

Next up is Diamond, an African American girl with a flaming bruise beneath her eye. Judge Easton asks how her week went. "Crazy," she replies.

"Anything else you'd like to share?"

"I relapsed. On coke," Diamond admits.

"Diamond did a good job of processing her relapse, so she's still on track to graduate in January," Leo interjects. Straight-faced, Judge Easton offers Diamond a choice between getting off JEM and having lunch with Kevin.

"JEM!" she exclaims.

The judge comments dryly, "So far we haven't had anyone take the other option."

Akeel, whose dad is the only parent present, receives a glowing report. "In the last few weeks we've all noticed you making a significant turnaround," Judge Easton comments. "What helped, Akeel?"

"Getting locked up for a long time."

"Oh, that works?" I think. Should I have left Jesse in Juvenile Hall instead of bailing him out all those times?

Judge Easton turns to Akeel's dad. "How do you feel your son's doing?"

"At program he's doing well," he says through a thick accent. "At school he can do a little more."

Leo jumps in. "Our philosophy is, we're looking for progress, not perfection."

"Cookie, lunch, and a prize for Akeel," the judge beams.

Anthony is called next. "We all love Anthony, but he needs to work on his temper," Leo says. "And we'd like to see his mom."

"If she can't come to Multifamily Group tonight," Judge Easton tells Anthony, "she needs to make contact and tell me what the problem is. Did you get a sponsor yet?"

Anthony shakes his head. "I'm trying to find someone good," he says earnestly. "I don't want no drug addict." Anthony looks utterly baffled when the kids erupt into raucous laughter.

Zalika calls me one Saturday in mid-December, as she often does these days. She calls at eight on weekday mornings when she misses her dad's ride to school; she calls at noon to get a ride from Bo's house to Choices when they cut school together. Sometimes, she calls just to talk—about a fight she just had with her parents or Bo; about Tahira, her only friend ("Besides you, DQ1") and fellow ho', a thirteen-year-old who keeps getting shuttled from one group home in San Jose to another in Sacramento.

"How long does it take to get the results of a pregnancy test?" Zalika asks. I swallow hard. I always thought raising girls would be easier. I'm rethinking.

"How late are you?"

"A week or two."

"You don't use condoms?" I struggle to keep the horror from my voice. In exchange for all they give me, all I have to offer Zalika, Mike, and Tristan is one adult who doesn't judge, criticize, or have an agenda for them. I am often challenged to maintain that stance. Right now, for instance.

"Bo's only the second person I've done that with," she says reverently. In her world, apparently, this is a sign of commitment.

I tell her I'll bring her a pregnancy test.

"You *will?*" she sighs, in that way she has of making me feel I'm the only person who's ever done anything for her.

"There's one condition," I add. "If the test is positive, you have to tell your parents right away. If you don't," I warn her, "I will."

An hour later I'm scanning the home-pregnancy section of the El Sobrante Walgreen's, wondering if the eighteen-dollar brand-name test is any more accurate than the nine-dollar Walgreen's version. Unlike Mike, who's in no position to ask anything of me, and Tristan, who won't, Zalika's already showing signs of becoming an expensive habit. I choose the Walgreen's test and drive to Zalika's parents' house for the first time.

The flatlands of residential El Sobrante roll out in all directions, a monotonous grid of single-story ranch houses, rectangular patches of grass, Old Glory waving from porches and car antennas. To get to the Bey home I leave the flats behind, turn up a long, steep hill that reminds me of the one that leads to Tristan's. As in Tristan's neighborhood, Latino men in earmuffs dot the manicured lawns, stooped beneath the roaring leaf-blowers strapped to their backs. I turn right onto Daffodil Lane, park beside the late-model Rolls Royce in the driveway. Zalika's dad, she told me, is in LA on business. Her mom is at Zalika's sister's soccer game. "So her Infiniti won't be out there."

Walking past the seasonal display of white wire reindeer grazing on the lawn and neatly potted poinsettias on the porch, gazing up at the second-story window Zalika used to hurl herself from, escaping to meet her first pimp, I am dumbstruck once again by the contrasts and contradictions in this girl's life. How did this home produce a twelve-year-old crack dealer, a two-hundred-dollar-a-trick teenage prostitute, the possibly pregnant girlfriend of a boy from the Rodeo projects? Which part of "intact, upper-middle-class, college-educated, suburban nuclear family" didn't Zalika understand?

She throws the door open, greets me in a child's flannel pajamas. "My hair's a *mess*. I'm getting it done later," she says, hugging me. "Let's go upstairs and *do it*."

DQ2 indeed, I think. Four urine drops away from a possible pregnancy diagnosis, Zalika seems more turned on by the drama than anxious about its consequences. She thunders up the thickly carpeted stairs; I follow her into her private bathroom. We read the test directions together. Just like the drug tests she takes five days a week, one pink line indicates the test is negative, two lines means she's pregnant. Zalika plops unselfconsciously onto the toilet and pees into the cup.

"I'm so nervous," Zalika says as we stand before the sink, peering at the tiny plastic tray. I put my arm around her. One pink line appears.

"There's only one line," she whispers. I have a terrible thought. What if the cheap Walgreen's test is wrong?

"Let's give it another minute," I say.

Still, one line. "I'm so relieved!" Zalika hugs me exuberantly.

"Me too," I say. "But now I'm gonna have to give you my safe sex lecture. If Bo loved you, he wouldn't—"

"It isn't just up to him. It's my responsibility too," Zalika interrupts me. "We weren't safe the first time. Then we just got in the habit. C'mon. I'll show you the house."

I take in the black leather couches scattered with mud cloth pillows, the African sculptures and masks on the walls, the decorated Christmas tree piled with gaily wrapped gifts; the well-stocked shelves and homemade layer cake in the kitchen, the foosball table, computer graphics station, and family photo display in the family room.

"Nice house," I say, as we settle in at the dining room table with the KFC I've brought at Zalika's request. She jumps up, rummages around in the kitchen, comes back, and spreads out her collection of hot sauces from the Filipino, African, and Mexican grocery stores where she likes to shop.

"Most Americans are so limited in the foods they eat," she comments, dipping an Original Recipe chicken thigh into Filipino banana sauce. And then in the next breath, "I wish I'd grown up in Richmond. Maybe then I wouldn't have gotten into all that trouble."

I look at her questioningly. "I lived in this big, comfortable house," she explains. "My parents were hecka strict. They wanted so bad to keep me away from all the negative stuff, it made me curious. I was like, 'What is there to see out there? What is so serious?'"

My scorecard runneth over. Zalika would have been okay *if* she weren't so bright; *if* she'd joined the cheerleading team; *if* she got along better with her father; *if* she weren't crazy . . . and now *if* she'd lived in a worse neighborhood? What lesson can I take from *this*?

"When I have kids I'm gonna show them everything so they can know they're not missing anything," she vows. "'Cause now I wish I hadn't done none of that stuff I did."

Zalika feels she's made heroic efforts, as yet unappreciated, to stop doing "that stuff she did." "I'm in a drug program, right? And I'm not doing drugs."

"Except getting drunk with Bo every weekend," I think but decide not to mention.

"But I still got this thing on my ankle that I can't take off. And even when I get off JEM, what's my life gonna be? Get up, go to school, go to program, come home? That'll get old. *Fast*."

I suggest that she get a weekend job, remind her that a boy at Choices offered to "hook her up" with a job at Sizzler Steakhouse.

"For six dollars an *hour?*" she says, rolling her eyes at me.

Right. What would convince a girl who's used to earning five thousand dollars a week to take a minimum-wage job? The fact that the better-paying gig has great potential to kill her doesn't carry much weight. Zalika feels as though she's dying of boredom anyway.

The people running Zalika's life disagree with her self-assessment. Knowing that she's "out of range" most nights, not knowing where she's going, they suspect the worst. Determined to save her, whether she wants saving or not, the Drug Court Team imposes the only consequence at their disposal. When Tom meets with Zalika before court the Tuesday before Christmas, he tells her the bad news: she's going to be sent to the Hall till Sunday.

"No!" Zalika yelps like a wounded animal and takes off running down the courthouse stairs.

Predicting that she would do exactly that, Tom and I have a plan in place. I hand him my briefcase and run after her. "Get her, Meredith," the other kids cheer me on.

I find Zalika just outside the courthouse, sitting on a low wall, sobbing. "These people don't care how hard I'm trying," she cries. "I been doing good in school, going to program, going home to sleep every single night! They don't know what I *could* be doing."

Tom runs up to us, panting, with Bo and several boys from the program in tow. "In the spirit of the Drug Court," Tom tells the boys, "I'm asking you to give Zalika some feedback."

"Don't run, man!" Aaron says.

"Just do that little bit 'o time!" Anthony advises.

"You're looking at three years or more in CYA if you get caught," Tom adds.

"I coulda done *been* in LA by now, man," Zalika cries.

"Court's starting. We need to go upstairs." Tom says. "I'm begging you, Zalika: give this program a chance. We all want you to make it." The boys follow him back into the courthouse.

Bo stays behind, standing beside her, shifting from foot to foot. Zalika looks up at him: gauging, imploring. All it'll take for her to stay, I realize, is for Bo to say that he wants her to. Finally he sits down beside her, puts his arm around her. She melts into his embrace. "Quit actin' crazy, dude," he says huskily. He pulls her to her feet, walks her toward the courthouse door. "You be outta there 'fore you know it."

He pushes her into the courthouse. Zalika follows him up the stairs, then turns to me before she walks into the courtroom.

"Promise you'll come see me in the Hall?" she asks.

I say that I will, and she goes in to face the handcuffs.

PART 3

TESTING DIRTY

Does Any of It Work?

Good-bye, Family

At seven o'clock on a September Monday morning, downtown San Rafael is shaking itself from sleep. From the east, the dawn's first sunbeams skitter across the streets. To the west, the shoulders of Mt. Tamalpais are draped in a shawl of lacy coastal fog, separating the city from the sea. San Rafael's posh bistros and antique shops are shuttered, still, but the scone-and-croissant cafés are doing a bustling business, infusing the air with the lusty musk of espresso, the milky hiss of lattés in the making.

Beneath the shadow of the Highway 101 overpass, tanned and coiffed commuters await the express bus to San Francisco, sipping from steaming cardboard cups, flipping through the *New York Times*. Fifteen blocks away on the seedy side of town, men with dirt-encrusted faces and hair dreadlocked by neglect lean against alleyway walls, gulping from bottles clutched in rumpled paper bags. Squinting into the brightening light of day, a few of them drift to the corner of 3rd and B Streets, where Center Point Adult Services will open at eight.

Around the corner from there, Center Point Adolescent is well into its morning routine. Danny Ramirez is at his desk, hunched over the Sausage McMuffin he picked up on his way to work, reading the files of the boys he'll interview at various Juvenile Halls today. Juanita, one of the two staffers who sleep here each night—conducting Good Night Group at eight-thirty, counting the bodies in the beds before lights-out at ten, then recounting and rousting those bodies at seven the next morning—is across the hall at hers, filling out the endless paperwork her job requires. Before she clocks out, she is required to document every client phone call made or received, every harsh word and gesture of support exchanged, every admonishment, Learning Experience, or Contract administered during her ten-hour shift. The next shift's staff will review Juanita's notes when they arrive, then insert them into the appropriate clients' files and start a new set of their own.

Upstairs, the subjects of all this scrutiny are timing each other's five-minute showers, scrubbing their faces with Oxy 5, spraying deodorant into their sprouting armpits, combing salon products through their hair. Their morning ablutions complete, they hang up their towels, make their beds, vacuum their rooms, and straighten the rows of acne ointments, colognes, hair gels, and shaving creams arrayed on their identical dressers. After they leave their rooms they won't be back till bedtime. To keep them from "isolating"—a known trigger of relapses and AWOL planning—the boys must spend their few free moments in public spaces only. Before they leave, some of them pause for a quick glance at the friends, family, and muscle cars whose photos they've tacked to the small bulletin board issued to each Center Point client upon arrival.

Downstairs, Henry and Mike, this week's designated cooks and table setters, are preparing breakfast for the house. The weekly menu posted on the fridge promises toast, cold cereal, and OJ on Mondays, but there is no toast making in evidence. When I ask why, Henry explains that in honor of California's latest power crisis, he and Mike are conserving energy—their own. "Tomorrow's Tuesday. Pancakes," he tells me, setting two Day-Glo orange jugs on the kitchen counter. "That's a lot of work."

"Twelve, thirteen, fourteen," Mike counts, unstacking plastic chairs in the dining room. "We're getting two new people today. This house is getting hella big." He sets out fourteen white plastic bowls, fourteen flimsy metal spoons, and clear plastic tumblers, then folds a paper napkin at each place. Mike yawns, covering his mouth politely. "If someone goes on Contract they have to get down here by six-thirty instead of me," he says, pointing at the "Rules for Clients on Contract Status" tacked to the dining-room wall. "It makes me hope someone gets into trouble." He grins. "As long as it's not me."

By seven-fifteen the boys have dribbled down to the kitchen and poured themselves bowls of cereal and milk. "Generic Fruit Loops," Stanley identifies the impossibly bright red, orange, and yellow morsels floating in his bowl. "Once in a while they bring us Lucky Charms. But the rest of the time it's same old, same old. Gets kind of boring after a while."

At seven forty-five, Henry and Mike restack the chairs, put away the juice and cereal, and wipe down the counters. The other boys scatter throughout the house like a hygienic SWAT team. Blake runs the dishwasher. Ethan sweeps the courtyard. Ricardo mops the floors. Clifford scours the bathroom sink. Walker vacuums the hall. By eight o'clock they've reassembled in the TV room for the morning's next activity: Facilities Check.

"Everyone to your room," commands Hakim, this week's Work Supervisor. The boys disperse again, standing like sentries in their bedroom doorways as Hakim and Ariana, the day-shift staffer who doubles as the Center Point bookkeeper, walk from room to room conducting morning inspection. They pull back bedspreads to make sure the sheets are tightly tucked, open dresser drawers to make sure T-shirts are neatly folded, check closets for pants crisply hung and shoes perfectly aligned. Hakim takes notes on the clipboard he carries, stopping in Henry and Mike's room to examine the new quilt on Henry's bed. An eighteenth-birthday present from Henry's mom, it's a homemade patchwork of car prints with a poem handwritten on its central patch.

FOR MY SON

A son will make you sure and strong
A son is a special and beautiful treasure to love
A son brings sunshine
To brighten your day
A son is a blessing
That comes from above
A son brings joy
Through his loving ways.

As each set of roommates gets the nod from Hakim, they head for the TV room, where they slip into the listless chit-chat of shipmates on a boat cast too long out to sea.

"How long you been away now, man?" Mike asks Ethan.

"Six months, eleven days," Ethan answers without hesitation. "Two months at Vista Village, a month in the Hall, a hundred and two days here."

The boys begin comparing notes on various rehab programs: which ones chase you down if you run; which ones don't; which day (Friday, most agree) is best for going AWOL.

"I'm saying bye." Juanita pokes her head into the room.

"Later, Juanita," the boys reply. Juanita seems to be one of their favorite staffers; she's one of the few who've been here long enough for the kids to safely care about.

Turnover among Center Point employees, and in most therapeutic communities, is as high (50 percent nationally) as their pay is low ($18,000 on average). Classified as "Child Care Workers," most of them unlicensed and lacking formal training, adolescent TC "counselors" earn fast-food salaries that reflect our society's apparent equal regard for children and McNuggets. Juanita and her peers start at $21,000. Tess, a licensed social-worker-to-be, earns $28,000 for forty-plus hours a week, doing double duty as a primary therapist and a counselor in the house.

As the director of UCLA's Integrated Substance Abuse Programs told the *New York Times Magazine* in 2002, "In many places you can work at McDonald's one day and be a drug counselor the next." So therapeutic community clients are tended to, and have their fates largely determined by, paraprofessionals like my son Jesse. When he got his job at the Walden House Adolescent TC at the age of twenty, six months after his last stint in jail, his prime qualification was his own rough adolescence; his rap sheet was his résumé.

I used to pray that, should he survive them, Jesse would someday repay the social debt he'd accrued during his teenage years. Now, like the Center Point Counselors and legions of others, Jesse is doing just that: using every trick his teenage craziness taught him to try to save one, maybe two, of the crazy-acting teenagers he's paid to try to reach each day.

Jesse could as easily have been hired at Center Point, where the "line staff" is an ever changing, dissonant ensemble of earnest young grad students, former probation officers, and take-no-guff ex-cons. White and Latino, young and old, Asian and black, from rich families and poor, these foot soldiers of the drug war have one thing in common. Many of them are sober addicts, in it for the mission, not the money. And most of them rely on a single therapeutic technique, relentlessly regaling their teenage clients with cautionary horror stories from their bottomed-out pasts.

At Center Point, as at Walden House and many therapeutic communities, the "been there, done that" efforts of these well-intentioned folks are loosely supervised and supplemented by grad school–trained psychologists, licensed therapists and social workers, and/or M.D. psychiatrists. At Center Point, for example, Dr. Liss meets briefly with each client once a month, then spends a few minutes with each client's "therapist"—actually an unlicensed counselor like Tess.

Both kinds of "drug counseling," it seems to me, are good and necessary. But neither can work alone. Jesse and Juanita can reach their young clients as no "never been there, never done that," book-taught professional ever could. And there is much to be gained from incorporating proven therapeutic techniques—and proven counselors—into each client's care.

But this is America, where money talks. And in the rehab biz (as in every biz) clients get what they (or in Center Point's case, the county) pay for. So at Phoenix Academy, well funded as it is by Marin County's abundant tax base, the kids get real therapy several times a week from real therapists. But at programs like Center Point and the Richmond Drug Court—the ones that serve poor kids, kids of color, the ones no one much cares about—funding is scarce and staff salaries low. So clients get lots of what costs less ("counseling" by $20,000-a-year interns and Child Care Workers) and far too little of the expert therapy they also need.

The boys' eyes follow Juanita out the front door, until their focus shifts to a teenage girl who's walking by the house. Their jaws slacken, their bodies tense as her curvaceous body, clad in a tank top and short-shorts, is framed in the TV room's picture window.

"Oh man, she's fine," George moans.

"No shit," sighs Ethan, as the girl's platform flip-flops clop-clop against the sidewalk, mere inches from where they sit.

The girl disappears from view. Hakim and Ariana return from inspection. Walker, today's group facilitator, convenes Morning Group.

"I feel good today. The concept I will use today will be integrity. Good morning, family."

"Good morning, Walker."

"I looked at my calendar this morning," says Rafael, the next boy in the circle. "I've been away from home two hundred eighty-five days and counting. That kind of got to me. I have to use some extra effort today to get through the day. Good morning, family."

"Good morning, Rafael."

"I feel good today," contributes Hakim. "The concept I'm gonna use today will be empathy for my brother Rafael. I haven't been home for six hundred days, but I'm glad to have a chance to finish this program. Good morning, family."

"Good morning, Hakim."

"I feel angry today," Mike says—as usual, with more inflection than the others. "I was looking forward to a visit this weekend with my parents. Now it ain't happenin'. The concept I will use today will be initiative. Good morning, family."

"Good morning, Mike."

I can't help but root for Mike, slipping an actual emotion into the clamped-down Morning Group routine. Learning to take care of himself and others is one thing—a good thing. Learning numb submission is another. In my unprofessional opinion, Mike's fighting spirit doesn't need breaking. As Zalika's mom says about her daughter's fierce will, it needs positive redirection instead. Can that happen here?

When the last boy in the circle has "checked in," Walker reads from the Discipline Status Report in his hand. "No Contracts. Learning Experiences: Henry, Shane, and Mike."

As Henry launches into his LE recitation—"My learning experience is, I need to be responsible for my own behaviors . . ."—I shoot a questioning glance across the room at Mike. He didn't tell me that he'd gotten into trouble again. Mike returns my look with an angry grimace that says, "These assholes are fucking with me," as clearly as if he'd spoken.

Dread skids through me. I know all too well what happens when a kid in trouble starts brandishing blame like a shield, repelling everyone and everything that might possibly help him, pointing to the consequences of what he's done as proof that no one understands or loves him. I know what happened to Jesse, and to me, when neither he nor I could stop looking for someone else to blame—just so it wasn't him, just so it wasn't me.

I remember in particular a meeting I begged for with Jesse's coach, the latest in a long succession of coaches who'd kicked Jesse off a basketball team for bad grades and bad attitude, for getting suspended from school, for getting arrested again. This time it was the varsity high-school team—the only tie, I was certain, that bound Jesse, however tenuously, to school, to normal life, to me. The girls screaming his name at halftime, the college scouts taking notes in the stands, the whole NBA hoop dream: this alone kept my son from succumbing to the siren call of the streets. And so I abandoned pride and everything I'd read in books about good parenting and went pleading to this man I barely knew. "You're right, Jesse needs consequences," I beseeched him. "But please understand. This might be my only chance to keep him out of jail and alive."

As we sat shivering in the coach's unheated office, an unrepentant Jesse railed against all the adults who'd mistreated him—his parents, his coaches, his teachers, the police. I, in turn, rattled off a series of desperate promises: "I'll make him come straight home after practice. I'll make him do his homework every night," as if we didn't all have ample proof of my inability to do any such thing. I was shocked to see tears in this hard-boiled coach's eyes. "You're in denial, man," he told Jesse. I knew he meant those words, too, for me.

Now, five years later and twenty miles away, I'm watching another boy I care about careening down the self-destruction highway without any brakes. Even immersed as he is in this year-long baptism, whose very purpose is the deconstruction of denial, the acceptance of responsibility, I can see Mike drowning in recrimination and self-righteousness. He can stay in this program if he keeps getting into trouble. But he can't stay in this program if he keeps blaming everyone else for it—if he can't convince his counselors that he's actually learning something from all these Learning Experiences.

"My Learning Experience is initiative," Mike spits through gritted teeth. "When I put out positive effort and energy to begin an action, that will help me make a constructive change in my life."

"Focus up, family." Walker moves to the next item on the morning agenda. "We have two new kids today. So now we're doing Intake Group."

Ariana escorts today's arrivals into the room. "This is Dylan," she says, nodding at a handsome blonde boy. "And Richard." Ariana introduces a tall, acne-pocked boy with a stringy ponytail and the most frightened face I've ever seen on a teenage boy. The new clients' last names are not divulged; Center Point's confidentiality policy forbids it. When two or more residents share the same first name, as often happens in this house largely populated by white working-class boys named after their fathers, one Mike or Richard is assigned a last initial to distinguish him from the other.

"My name is Walker. I'm eighteen. My drug of choice is alcohol. What I want out of the program is to get out, go home, be normal. Welcome."

"My name is Blake," says the bright-eyed boy to his left. "My drugs of choice were acid, Ecstasy, and marijuana. What I want out of this program is to be clean, get another perspective on life, get another chance. Welcome."

"I'm Clifford," mumbles a scowling white boy whose Ebonics accent is so thick, the other kids—even the ones who speak like gangsters themselves—often ask him to repeat himself. "My drugs of choice are hero-wine and crank. What I want is to learn to be sober and go home. Welcome."

Last Saturday, while some of the other clients visited with their parents on the patio, Clifford sat with me on the steps, telling me what he has to go home to. His mom, who's been on welfare all her life. His two sisters, who both had babies by age fourteen. His dad, paralyzed by a crack overdose, who now smokes it in his wheelchair. And his real family: the Bloods. "I won't do no drugs when I leave outta this place," Clifford told me, "but I'll never get outta the Bloods unless I have a kid. Like, what if I took my son to the park, and someone from the Crips came into our side of the park and I had to shoot him in front of my kid? That would fuck my kid up even worse than I got fucked up." When I asked what he envisions for his future, Clifford told me he wants to be a counselor at CYA, working with teenagers in trouble.

"I'm Lyle. I'm a primary counselor here. I just started last week," says a twenty-eight-year-old, L. L. Bean–outfitted therapist-intern who seems more miserable each time I see him.

Earlier this morning, I overheard Ariana asking him to strip-search the new boys. "I missed that course in grad school," Lyle snapped. "That's not what I got my training for."

"Searches need to be done by male staff," Ariana replied evenly. "Danny's not here. Ron's out sick. That leaves you."

"That's one reason I hate working in treatment programs," Lyle grumbled to me as I followed him to the TV room, where Dylan and Richard sat waiting. "It feels so invasive to go into people's personal belongings." Approaching the boys without introduction, he instructed them to take off their shoes and dutifully rummaged through the single gym bag each boy had brought with him from Juvenile Hall.

"My drugs of choice were cocaine and marijuana," Lyle concludes. "Welcome."

"I'm Mike. My drugs of choice are crank, alcohol, weed, whatever. What I want is to get my life back together, be able to do good, know what I'm sayin', get a good job, all that kind of good shit. Oh, and get back to my mom. I've been here two months. Welcome."

"This is where we go around and say what the rules are," Walker announces.

Hakim speaks up first. "One, thou shalt not touch the TV. Two, thou shalt not touch the VCR. Three, thou shalt not touch the refrigerator. Four, you shall get a big brother. He'll tell you everything you need to know about this program, like if you need to go to the bathroom you need to ask first."

"We got a bunch of rules here," says George. "They might seem stupid . . ." The other clients snap their fingers in the air. "Don't tell nobody shut up. Don't call nobody a bitch. Don't call no one niggah."

"Y'all in gangs?" Rafael asks the new boys. Both of them shake their heads. "The first month here is real hard," Rafael tells them. "The last couple are real hard. In between you're gonna get a little angry and irritated with the program. That's normal. Know what I'm sayin'? Whatever you put into the program you're gonna get out."

"They told me I only have to stay three months," the new boy Richard whispers, his eyes casting wildly around the room.

"They tell you that," George says, "but it'll be longer."

"There are four cardinal rules," Ethan chimes in. "No drugs. No sex. No fighting. Don't break confidentiality."

"You guys been to other placements?" Rafael asks.

"Thunder Road," Richard answers, naming an Oakland residential program.

"Vista Village," says Dylan. Mike nods knowingly.

"The people here be friendly," Rafael offers. "They have to be. It's required. So be free to talk to people, use y'all's support. Y'all be aiight."

"Okay, everybody . . ." Walker feeds the group their cue. In unison they shout, "One, two, three, WELCOME!"

The group ends as they all do. Everyone rises, huddles tightly in the center of the room, their arms draped around each other's shoulders. "Let this circle represent caring for all the addicts suffering outside this circle," Walker intones.

And then, in voices bass, baritone, and barely beyond soprano, the boys recite the Serenity Prayer.

Mike is not feeling serene. "I called home. And just for that I lose all my privileges for a week and phone privileges for a fucking month!" he tells me during class that afternoon, his algebra book open on the table between us. "Now I don't get to see my parents this weekend. I haven't seen my mom in like five *weeks!*"

"You got an LE for calling home?" I keep my voice neutral, trying to convey sympathy without buying into the blame.

"My dad wasn't home, so I talked to his girlfriend Sue for like three minutes. Big fucking deal!"

"You got an LE for talking to Sue?"

"Well . . ." I wait for the rest of the story. "When I got off the phone, Ron asked me how my talk with my dad went. I'm not supposed to talk to anyone except my parents, so I just said it went cool." Mike rakes his fingers through his hair. "How unlucky is *this:* an hour after I supposedly talked to him, my dad calls and asks Ron how I'm doing. Says he hasn't heard from me in a while. My own dad got me an LE."

Mike tosses me a piece of binder paper covered with his scribbly handwriting. "They made me write this stupid fucking essay. I gotta read it to the whole house tomorrow." He seethes while I read.

WHY AM I ALLOWD TO STAY AT C.P.

I feel I am allowed to stay at Center Point because for one I have a severe drug and addiction problem and two I have issues with my anger. I feel that when I return to society after completing this program I will continue to treat my parents and the people I associate with around me with the respect I would want from them.

For right now I am going in and out of my old behavior and it is hard for me to change because the behaviors I am changing have been with me for a very long time ever since I was 4 years old. It's going to take some time but that's OK because I'll use the support from the clients while I am here for my nine to twelve months it may even take a lot longer.

I also strongly believe that this program will greatly help me in going back into society and being normal how I used to be before I started using drugs. Whatever it takes to stay here and graduate I will do because I strongly want my recovery and need it . . .

"Like I fucking *wanna* stay here," Mike growls as I hand back his essay. "Like they'd fucking *want* me here if it wasn't for all that money they're making off me." And he tells me again what he's told me many times before. "This place is nothing but a money-making scheme."

Mike's accusation is understandable, if inaccurate. Looking at Center Point's facilities, food, and staff salaries, it's hard to account for the $5,000 per client per month that the agency charges parents (the few who can pay) and county probation departments (when the parents can't pay, or won't). Although wads of cash change hands in the service of the fifty or so kids per year who are treated at Center Point Adolescent, a not-for-profit corporation, it seems unlikely that anyone here is getting rich.

In the larger sense, though, Mike's assessment is dead-on. Drug rehab is a multibillion-dollar industry in America today, and teen rehab kicks in its fair share of the take. There's no way to tally the total number of teenagers in drug treatment or the amount of money their treatment generates, because statistics are available only for the one-third or fewer of kids in treatment who are in publicly funded versus private-pay programs. (Also uncounted are the many kids in private therapy and other types of non-program interventions.) But here's what we do know.

Nonprofit adolescent treatment centers like Center Point are the exception, not the rule. Two-thirds of the 3,400 residential adolescent programs nationwide are privately owned, with fees ranging from $5,000 to $40,000 a month.

The teenagers in publicly funded programs alone totaled a hundred and fifty thousand in 1998, the most recent year for which data is available—an increase of 53 percent since 1992. (Given that teenage drug use continued rising after 1992, peaking in 1996, we may safely conclude that the number is significantly higher today.)

The typical teenager admitted to public drug treatment is male (70 percent), white (63 percent), between fifteen and seventeen (75 percent), referred by the criminal justice system (41 percent), and being treated for marijuana (77 percent) and/or alcohol use (63 percent).

And then there's the most disheartening statistic of all. Even with all those kids in all those programs, experts agree that nine out of ten children who need drug treatment aren't getting it.

Residential programs like Center Point are but one of many sources that feed the rehab revenue stream. Others include hospitals, day treatment centers, after-school and in-school prevention and treatment programs, private therapists, and educational consultants who refer distraught parents to wilderness programs and "emotional growth" schools—a booming, unlicensed, and unregulated industry. Two dozen emotional growth schools existed a decade ago. There are more than 350 now, each charging $50,000 to $80,000 a year. Several of these "teen boot camps" have been closed after kids in their care have died in such circumstances as forced hikes in 110-degree heat. Then there are the "escorts" who kidnap kids from their beds to get them there.

The industry also generates nontreatment revenue from rehab trade conferences and newsletters, research conducted by institutions and individuals, and the myriad tools of the rehab trade: recovery books, tapes, videos, posters, and drug tests (sold at $50 a pop in neighborhood drugstores, by the caseload to rehab programs, employers, and the military). Most profitable of all, of course, are the pharmaceuticals: the Ritalin and the Paxil, the Adderall and the naltrexone, the methadone and the Antabuse.

The kicker (so to speak) is, much of that money is spent copycatting adult programs and labeling them "adolescent treatment"—with unsurprisingly unimpressive results.

"Very little is known about what type of treatment is appropriate for young people, and very few programs are tailored to address their specific needs," concludes a report from the 2001 conference of the American Society of Addiction Medicine. "There really isn't much knowledge" about treatment matching, medication dosing, stages of change, or other facets of adolescent care, Dr. Marc Fishman of the Johns Hopkins School of Medicine comments, adding that although there are well over a thousand studies on adult addiction treatment, fewer than one hundred studies of adolescent treatment have been published.

Most adolescents enrolled in treatment, the report says, are placed in programs that were designed for adults—despite the fact that "Progression of alcohol and other drug abuse among adolescents is often quite different than among adults." Those differences, Fishman says, include adolescents' "normative" behavior of risk taking and experimentation and the "nonmonolithic" treatment needs of teenagers of different ages.

The federal government's Office of National Drug Control Policy agrees, calling adolescents with alcohol and drug problems "woefully underserved . . . in most existing drug treatment programs designed for adults." And in *The Heart of Addiction,* Dr. Lance Dodes writes, "[Treatment programs that] require a blind faith in precepts, or in the all-knowing wisdom of a counselor—are understandably often difficult for teens. Unfortunately, these difficult factors are commonly present in many addiction treatments, particularly AA-oriented approaches."

One of the few large-scale studies of adolescent drug treatment, conducted by the National Institute of Drug Abuse in 2001, compared residential, outpatient, and short-term inpatient adolescent programs. As all studies of treatment longevity do, NIDA's found that longer stays in treatment provided the best results. And the study's lead researcher concluded that "In order to maximize [adolescent programs'] therapeutic benefits, we need to devise strategies specific to adolescents to improve retention and completion of the programs."

We need to, yes. But with few exceptions—sober high schools and juvenile Drug Courts, to name two steps in the right direction—we haven't yet.

As Mike's resistance to Center Point builds, his dad fuels the fire. One day algebra class is interrupted by a series of horn blasts from the street below. Like a dog leaping to the jingle of his leash, Mike rushes to the window, leans out, and yells, "Wassup, Dad," waving as Michael cruises slowly by in the plumber's truck he drives to work every day. "He's been doing that a couple times a day since I got into trouble," Mike tells me triumphantly. "So much for these assholes not letting me see my parents!"

"Let's get some work done." Stevo guides Mike back to his seat. Mike hands his teacher a completed worksheet. "I got two hours of math done today, Stevo," he says.

"I'd say one point five," Stevo replies amiably.

"Two!"

"One point five."

"Tell you what, Stevo," Mike says. "You grade it. If it's all right, I get two." .

"That's quite a deal," Stevo smiles noncommittally and offers him a world history textbook. "I hate school," Mike announces to no one in particular, opening it to the first chapter. "But I want a diploma, not a GED."

He flips through a few pages, slams the book shut. "I don't miss the drugs so much. But I really want to hit someone." As he so often does, Mike jumps now from mood to mood and topic to topic like a manic hummingbird. Since I met him I've wondered: is Mike like this because all that crank shortened his attention span? Did he medicate himself with speed to compensate for some short-circuit in his brain? Or is he just a slightly flittier than normal seventeen-year-old American boy raised on amphetamine-velocity video games and the adrenaline rush of violent "action" movies?

"You working on your 'Trust' paper?" Mike calls to Miles, his new Little Brother. Miles shrugs, goes back to staring out the window. "Just watch: he's gonna blow off his paper, and I'll get blamed for that too," Mike growls. "It's hella hard for me to stick it through and stay here. I hope I don't run, man. No one should have to deal with this place. Therapeutic fucking community bullshit. It's worse than jail."

On September 11, 2001, the whole world, even Center Point, comes to a standstill. Just this once, the residents and staff of Center Point are doing what everyone else is doing: sitting in a room with their "family," trying to make sense of what they're seeing on TV.

"We oughta bomb the fucking Eye-Rabs back to hell," Clifford snarls, as the image of the jets being swallowed by the towers appears again and again on the screen.

"Goddamn diaper heads," Miles adds.

"They should let us outta here, let us go fight," says George. "We'd know how to take out a fucking terrorist." There are nods around the room. One of the bobbing heads belongs to Mike.

"You may get that chance, whether you want it or not," Tess says, her tone uncharacteristically derisive. It's been a long, hard day at Center Point for a feminist, for a pacifist, for a counselor—and Tess is all three.

"Everybody knows gangs are stupid," Mike opines. "They pull stupid shit, get in other people's business. Well, that's what we do: piss other countries off. We got our nose up someone's ass, or that shit wouldn't have happened."

"You really think they're gonna draft kids like us?" asks Blake, the only client who has demonstrated anything other than warmongering belligerence today.

"I don't know, Blake," Tess answers. "I really can't say what Bush might do."

In a special art therapy session this morning, the boys were encouraged to express their emotions about the bombing. The results flutter now from the walls like Buddhist prayer flags—only different. Clifford's drawing depicts a pilot flying a plane into a building, yelling "DIE AMERICAN PEOPLE," while stick figures jump out the windows crying, "I love America" and "I'm going to die."

One boy simply wrote "My world has no consequences" across the page. Another drew the World Trade Center towers in rainbow stripes, with the single word "GAY"—the ultimate denunciation—above them. Blake's drawing shows Planet Earth in flames. Mike's is a crude pencil rendering of the plane hitting the burning towers. In the pilot's seat, a turban-clad man leers lasciviously beneath the headline "SCARED-HORRIFIED."

Just before dinner Mike and I spend some time alone in "our" office. "I don't want it to, but it freaks me out," he confesses after I've shut the door. "What if this war shit gets worse and they shut down programs, try and put me back in the Hall? POs come down here, start picking people up . . ."

He shakes his head at the thought. "Naww. If anything comes down, my dad'll come get me."

I ask Mike what he'd do if he got drafted.

"I wouldn't go. Straight up," Mike answers. "If they said you go to prison or you go to war, I'd go to war. But I'd try to leave the country first. Go to Canada or some shit. I don't wanna die—fuck! Especially over some stupid-ass shit."

Lest he be mistaken for an anti-imperialist, Mike adds quickly, "The A-rabs are more like gang members than we are. Maybe I'm not up-to-date with all the kinds of A-rabs, but look at the cheap gas stations around here. Who owns 'em? The A-rabs. And where does the gas come from?

"You see where I'm going with this. Maybe they know someone back home, and that's where they get the gas so cheap." He leans back in the orange plastic chair and nods authoritatively. "Like I said: gangsters."

"I know this obnoxious bravado is just their way of expressing their fears," Tess tells me later when I ask what she makes of the boys' responses, "but it disgusts me anyway."

She briefly considers rescheduling Mike's weekly Tuesday night session, but decides against it. "I'm really worried about Mike right now. He's headed in a pretty negative direction." So while the world falls apart and rearranges itself in the TV room, at seven-thirty Tess, Mike, and I sequester ourselves in Tess's little office. For maximum mobility during the hour, Mike takes his usual seat: a swiveling desk chair on wheels.

"I'm gonna petition to get my phone privileges back," Mike begins without preamble.

Tess seems unsurprised that even today's events haven't superseded Mike's battle to wrest control of his life from the institution that currently owns it. "Do you feel it's unfair that you lost your phone privileges?" she asks.

"Come on now, Tess. You of all people know better than to ask me that," Mike answers. "I've grown up a lot since I've been here. How come they don't care about the good stuff I do?"

"You don't get as caught up in your feelings as you used to," Tess says.

"See how much I've changed? All that bad shit was in the past. Doing drugs, having a fucked-up mind, making stupid decisions." Mike suddenly sounds a lot like the Center Point staffers he's so angry at. "If you're trying to be clean, you should have the shit that goes along with that. You should be acting normal."

"You've summed it up perfectly," Tess validates her client. "In order to become clean you have to clean up your actions and your thoughts."

"Tess! I'm doing that! So how come I can't make a phone call for a month?" Mike doesn't wait for her answer. "I feel like I'm going through a test from up above. The biggest test of my whole life," he says. He rocks angrily in his chair. "And I'm passing it. So why can't I go home in nine months instead of being stuck here a whole year? This program is money hungry. Five thousand a month for each kid. Where does the money go, Tess?"

He pauses for dramatic emphasis, then adds sardonically, "We don't get out that much."

"Those extra three months might be what you need," Tess replies. "We wouldn't be doing all this if we didn't think it would save your lives."

"I miss my parents. I haven't seen my mom in a couple months." Is Mike changing the subject because he's realized the pointlessness of his argument? Or is his mind doing one of those sideways speed-freak somersaults?

"It's been a couple of months?" Tess asks.

"Maybe less. I don't know. My mind's still pretty messed up."

"That's one symptom of post–acute withdrawal. What other symptoms are you having, Mike?"

"Things are kind of blurring together. I can't remember if things happened a week ago or a month ago . . ." Mike spaces out, rocking, then continues, "My dad's been driving by, honking his horn, giving me the thumbs-up.

Yesterday I ran downstairs and talked to him real quick. He says he's gonna try and get me out in nine months."

"He's giving you his support," Tess says.

"He's so proud of me, he gets drunk and brags about me to his friends." Is Mike being sarcastic, I wonder, or pulling for sympathy? As he well knows, a family history of addiction goes a long way in a place like Center Point.

"In the Hall they let you see your parents twice a week," Mike adds, spinning in circles in his chair. "When I was on the run I was tweaked for seven months straight. I came down so hard in the Hall. When you go through withdrawal you want to be with your mom."

"You want to be comforted," Tess says. "Is that what you want now, Mike?"

"I'm not fucked up like that now. I can think."

"You can *feel*," Tess says. "You're allowing yourself to feel more, now that your body's recovering from the drugs."

"I've never gone this long in like five years." Mike's brow furrows as he does the math in his head. "Sixty-eight days."

"Sixty-eight days clean and sober! That's wonderful, Mike."

"I still think about it every day. Blowing clouds, making the pipes, blowing the glass. It's like an art. It's not just tweaker shit."

"You daydream about using."

"I've gained fifty pounds since I got to this place." Has Mike noticed what I've figured out: that the Center Point counselors respond positively to kids who acknowledge their yearnings for drugs, but clamp down on those who seem on the verge of relapse?

"Your body must have been depleted from the drugs," Tess says, and I think, what about the starchy, high-fat food these kids are fed five times a day; the absence of exercise in these growing boys' lives? Just about every Center Point kid is pasty-faced, pimply, and overweight. I would be too, if I lived here.

"Can I take metabolism pills in here?" Mike asks.

"No," Tess answers. "They have a lot of caffeine and traces of chemicals that are similar to speed. So Mike—when you have those thoughts about using, how do you rationalize them?"

"I think about the feeling I had in the hospital when I was handcuffed, tweaking in that chair, hella dehydrated, and they wouldn't give me any water. I felt like shit. It's not cool. It's not cool. Crank is the devil's drug." Mike spins to face me, the heretofore invisible reporter. "Put that in the book," he instructs me. "Crank is the devil's drug."

He waits until I get that down, then swivels back toward Tess. "What time is it?"

"Eight-thirty," she says.

"Oh!" Mike mimics Tess's little-girl voice, her determined cheer. "Time to go!" he trills. And he's gone.

Tess's body slumps as the door slams behind him. "I always want to slow him down. He speeds along so fast," she says, pun apparently unintended. "Identifying the relapse triggers was a big breakthrough for Mike. That's the first time he's described it in such a vivid manner."

She muses silently for a moment. "Still, I'm concerned. We all are. Mike's treatment issues are what we call 'sleazy behaviors': lying, sneaking, taking things that don't belong to him. He's obviously going through a lot of turmoil. And the dad isn't helping, driving his truck around the house, reminding Mike of everything he's missing. The dad's an alcoholic. We suspect he might use speed as well."

I note the odd phrasing used regularly by Center Point staffers: Michael isn't "Mike's dad" but "*the* dad." The Phoenix and Drug Court staff have their own corresponding syntax, but it's warmer, not quite as objectifying. "Mom's in denial about Tristan's addiction," they'll say. "Dad's still covering for Zalika."

But Tess is being trained here, not there. "The dad called and asked if Mike could come home for Thanksgiving. I told him I couldn't guarantee it. Then he asked if Mike could come home for New Year's Eve. I told him, 'Mike's just getting into the program. He's been having some issues lately. You need to give him the space to make some progress.'

"His response was, 'Well there better not be any issues when we get to the nine-month point.' I reminded him that Mike's release date will be decided by his PO, Danny, and me—not by his parents. That seemed to enrage him."

I think of the phone call I got from Barbara earlier today. "I can't stand not being able to touch my son right now," she said. "I'm worried about him being in the Bay Area—they're saying that might be the next target. I'm worried that he's scared and there's no one to comfort him."

She told me she'd called Center Point as soon as she heard the news. "Ron wouldn't let me talk to Mike. I asked if they've addressed this situation with the kids. He said, 'The boys are surprised by the attack, but they're fine.' These boys are facing being drafted any minute! How could they be fine with *that*? I had to say to some strange person I've never met, 'Please tell Mike I'm thinking about him and I love him.'

"Do they not understand the enormity of this event?" Barbara went on, her voice choked. "They're using his visitation with his parents as leverage! They say it's behavior modification, but it can't be therapeutic to keep a child from seeing his mom. Especially right now. I told Danny from the start that I don't want to be out of the loop, and now I totally am. It makes me feel like I've been an abject failure as a mother. I'm having to use the system as if I'm a person who's totally inept, totally incapable of parenting my child."

I tell Tess about my conversation with Barbara and ask her what role, if any, Center Point expects parents to play in their sons' treatment. "That starts when we've got the client stabilized and committed to the community," she answers. "Kids need to do this on their own. Staff doesn't need the parents breathing down our necks."

Later that night I ask Danny the same question. He tells me he's going to call a meeting with Mike's PO, Tess, "the mom," and "the dad" to "clarify what's therapeutic for Mike." "If that doesn't improve the situation," he says, "I might have to cut off all contact with the dad."

On the other hand, he says, if Michael seems willing to work with the program, they'll start family therapy. "But not with all of them together. Otherwise it turns into counseling for the parents. That's not what we're here for."

The differences between day treatment and residential treatment go deeper than where their clients sleep at night; they're philosophical and prescriptive as well. "Community-based" programs like Phoenix Academy and the Richmond Drug Court are predicated on the notion that what's most broken in young addicts' lives are their relationships—with themselves, their families, their communities. So those programs do everything they can to keep kids in their parents' homes, to promote and nurture their family relationships, to repair those broken bonds. In group therapy with their peers, individual therapy with their counselors, family sessions with their parents, multifamily groups with the whole program community, the kids and their families—theoretically, at least—are set to work at that task from day one.

Center Point, on the other hand, believes in demolition before reconstruction, in severing unhealthy bonds before building new ones. Rather than supporting the boys' existing relationships, the program positions itself as a replacement family, a replacement community—not permanently, but for one significant year of its clients' lives. The "reunification phase" of the Center Point program, with intensive family therapy and weekend passes home, begins only when a boy is approaching graduation, only after the staff have been satisfied that he's been, in Tess's words, successfully "submerged in the therapeutic community."

It follows, then, that whereas Phoenix and the Drug Court require parent participation—theoretically, at least—Center Point initially prohibits, then tightly controls it. Given the geographical distance between many Center Point clients and their homes (kids are deliberately placed as far from friends and family as possible, on the theory that this will reduce their temptation to run), that severance is easily enforced.

Which approach works better for kids? Where would we go to find out? Statistics about program outcomes are unreliable, although research has consistently shown what a 2002 New York Times Magazine story affirmed: "The single most important factor in a program's success is the length of time an addict stays in it. And 90 days—not the managed care–driven 28 . . . was the minimum for enduring benefits to manifest."

So, keep the kids for three months or a year, if that's what it takes, but keep their families connected to them, with weekly therapy sessions at least. Call me a bleeding-heart mother—I plead guilty; that's exactly what I was—but I can't believe that severing a teenager from the people who love him, even a child who's in trouble with drugs, is ever the best thing to do.

This much I know for sure: if "the mom" had been me instead of Barbara, if the Center Point client had been Jesse instead of Mike, I couldn't have lived his seventeenth year without him. And I wouldn't have wanted him to live the hardest year of his life without me.

Michael isn't taking the separation well, either. "I was told the program was nine months. That's one reason Mike went along with this whole thing. For Danny Ramirez to say twelve months now is *not* what we agreed to."

I decide not to point out that Mike "went along with this whole thing" because he was facing thirty-six months in jail if he didn't—simple math even a seventeen-year-old eighth-grader could do. "It's not right, keeping a kid from his parents. Especially now," Michael tells me. "Our country's about to go to war, and they won't let me see my son because he used some-body's *hair gel*? What kind of crap is that?"

Anger feeding self-righteousness feeding blame: loath as I am to play the easy game of "like parent, like son" (having had that game played on me a few too many times), I can't help noticing how closely Mike's stance resembles his father's.

Michael asks me to relay a message when I see his son tomorrow. "Tell Mike his dad loves him. Tell him I'm gonna buy him a jet ski and bring it up to his mom's new place once he gets out." Center Point has already deter-mined that Mike will be released to his mother when he graduates from the program; his father's penchant for alcohol and persistent rumors of his crank use have ruled him out as custodial parent.

"Last time they let me visit Mike," Michael continues, "he said, 'Dad, if you'll let me, I'll walk out of here right now.'"

I note to myself that Mike hasn't confessed any such conversation to me, despite my constant probing about whether he's feeling tempted to run.

"I told him, 'You wanna get your jet ski I promised you? You wanna get your driver's license? You better finish up here.' He accepted that." Michael pauses for emphasis. "I'm really proud of him. What he's doing is harder than hell. And you and I both know Mike hasn't done anything we didn't do when we were kids. We just didn't get caught, that's all."

Michael's complaints about his son's unjust incarceration are particularly ironic, since he's the one who first had Mike arrested. Although Mike had been in trouble with his parents, his schools, and the local cops for years by then, it was Michael who called the cops when his tweaking, raging, fifteen-year-old son punched a hole in their front door; it was Michael who pressed the charges that put Mike "in the system."

Only two things can stop that process once it begins. Either the kid has parents who can pay lawyers, therapists, and boarding schools to shift their child's troubles from the public realm to the private, or the kid has an epiphany and stops getting into trouble. Mike had neither. And so his life as a convicted criminal began. At Juvenile Hall he was drug-tested and found "dirty" for amphetamines and marijuana. In juvenile court he was sentenced to probation, requiring him to submit to frequent drug tests to be administered by his PO without warning.

Every pee test Mike turned in came back dirty. Every dirty test sent him to the Hall; from the Hall he was sentenced to "diversion." In Mike's case, because his dad's insurance could pay for it, diversion meant twenty-eight days at a private rehab, ReTreat (where he discovered that drinking a quart of jalapeño juice before each pee test made it come back clean every time), with follow-up provided by Sonoma County's Juvenile Drug Court. Mike couldn't hang with the program; Drug Court sent him back to the Hall; the judge sent him to Vista Village. After three hours there, Mike diverted himself to seven months on the run.

Mike's trajectory through "the system" is appalling, but not unusual— not, anyway, for a kid whose parents can't pay his way out of it. Of the nearly two hundred thousand American juveniles arrested for drug abuse violations in 1998, about one-quarter were "placed out of the home": sentenced to Juvenile Hall, residential treatment, or group homes. Sixty percent were allowed to remain at home on probation, threatened with incarceration should they fail their diversion programs, submit dirty drug tests, break their curfews, or violate probation in any other way. Ten percent were sentenced to pay fines and/or restitutions; 7 percent were released with no consequences at all.

Until the recent check-cashing debacle that left him facing two felonies and a misdemeanor, all the warrants issued for Mike's arrest and his many stretches in the Hall resulted not from new crimes, but from probation violations all stemming from that first arrest. In other words, although Mike has spent many of his teenage years on probation, in Juvenile Hall, or hiding from the law, he has never actually been convicted of a crime. I wonder, but don't ask, whether Michael now thinks of that call he made to the police as having ruined his son's life, or saved it.

A few nights later I get a call from Tess, telling me that Mike's been put on Contract. "He had a pretty terrible day. He had an altercation with Lyle, one of the many staff members he doesn't get along with. I told him to take a deep breath, to see if he could get in touch with something to work on. But he was like, 'I've had it. This is ridiculous.'"

I start to ask exactly what being "on Contract" means—I'm still learning Center Point–speak—but instead tell Tess I'll be there first thing tomorrow.

"Mike's dad made three circles around the house yesterday," Tess adds. "Mike can't get detached from his home situation with these daily reminders. I know there's a part of Mike that really wants to be in recovery, but I don't think he can start working till he stops thinking about going home."

I arrive at the Center Point school halfway through Conflict Resolution, the first Friday therapy group of the day. As I often do, I spend a few minutes eavesdropping outside the room's open door, trying to detect any difference in the boys' behavior when there's no reporter taking notes in the corner. Do they divulge more or less, speak in a different language when they think I'm not listening? No, they sound the same as always: the finger-snapping, the lingo, their flat, indifferent voices.

I listen especially for Mike. And especially today. How will being put on Contract affect him? Might this threat to his placement at Center Point have the desired effect: make him want it enough to work at it?

Suddenly I realize there is something different today. I don't hear Mike's voice.

My heart sinks. I walk into the room. I don't need to look around for Mike. The boys' faces tell me he's not there. Some of them smirk at me. Some look expectant. A few, strangely, look scared. Their conversation stops. I look at Tom, the therapist. He shrugs.

Finally Clifford breaks the silence.

"Mike bounced," Clifford says into the thick silence in the room. "He gone, man. Hey! You wanna write a book about *me?*"

TRISTAN

High on Sobriety

"The holidays are coming up, you guys. We'd like you to share what's going on for you." Lisa Ahrens, Phoenix Academy's perennially cheerful staff therapist, opens the Friday Group she's coleading with Eric on this drizzly November afternoon.

Notorious as the time of year that drives long-sober addicts back to the bottle or the pipe, the approaching winter holidays have sparked heightened skittishness among the kids, heightened urgency among the staff.

"We don't just want 'I'm going to my mom's,' 'I'm going to my dad's,'" Lisa prompts the group. "More like, how are you planning to stay sober over Thanksgiving?"

"I'm gonna lock myself in the basement and play computer games till my skin turns pale," Kelsey says.

"I'm pissed off. That's what's up with *me*. My PO's telling me I can't wear blue," says Jesús, a baby-faced, first-generation Mexican-American. "I'm not involved in no gang or nothin', so why not?"

Many youth programs, including Center Point and the Drug Court, prohibit the wearing of the gang colors of blue or red—an attempt to minimize violence that has drastic repercussions for kids whose wardrobe staple is jeans.

At Phoenix Academy, that rule applies only to kids whose court orders specify it, which effectively defines who can't wear "colors" to school (the Latino and African American students, most of whom are on probation) and who can (the more affluent white kids, most of whom aren't).

"I recommend thinking about the Serenity Prayer, Jesús. This is something you cannot change," Lisa advises with a sympathetic shrug.

"I'm pissed off about Thanksgiving," says Nicholas, who was sent to Phoenix, to everyone's amazement, for being caught drunk at a private-school football game. "My mom's going to Barbados with her boyfriend. He's a real asshole—she's just with him 'cause she's scared of being alone. So I guess I'll go to my aunt's in Carmel for the holiday."

"What about your dad?" Lisa asks him.

"Neither of us can cook. If I went there, we'd probably end up at Denny's or something."

"I had Thanksgiving in a psych ward once," Sabrina interjects.

"I had Thanksgiving in Juvenile Hall twice," says Emily.

"It could be pretty funny to learn to cook a turkey with your dad," Lisa suggests. Nicholas shakes his head wordlessly.

"Or you could just have beans, dude," Tristan offers.

Next in the circle is Sabrina. "I'm powerless over poison oak." Sabrina scratches her arm energetically. "My life has become unmanageable."

"I know what we should do to the Taliban," Kelsey chimes in, scratching the matching rash on his neck. "We should drop a poison-oak bomb on them. They'd be itching too much to fight."

Last week the Phoenix students spent a few days hacking brush at Walker Creek Ranch, a seventeen-hundred-acre spread owned by the Marin County school district. Several of the kids came down with poison oak—none as severely as Tristan, who was hospitalized for two days. This morning, still oozing and itching, he had a session with Eric to process the experience, then a session with me to process what he described as his "awesome" session with Eric.

Unlike Mike and Tess, Tristan and Eric decided against inviting me into their weekly (and as needed) sessions. "I'm trying to create a sacred space for him. I don't want to risk blowing that," Eric told me. Tristan said, "I think I might be less honest with Eric if you were there." Instead, they agreed to audiotape the sessions, and to tell me about them afterward.

"Eric asked if they gave me any drugs in the hospital," Tristan reported when we had lunch together. "I told him they gave me all this manmade freaking chemical shit: prednisone, Demerol, morphine. I told him what I really wanted was some medical freaking marijuana. I was like, shit! Just give me some *pot!*" Tristan laughed; then the look on his swollen face turned to wonderment. "I got real honest with Eric. I told him I wanna leave Phoenix because I don't feel part of this place. I'm not all into AA. I wanna get a job. I can't because of the meetings. Phoenix is holding me back.

"I thought he'd be pissed. But he actually understood! He said if I get to Level Three, I can leave Phoenix in January. And he said I can go to meditation class at Spirit Rock on Monday nights and count that as one of my AA meetings." Tristan's eyes glowed; the ambivalence that normally shrouds his face lifted like a veil. "It's so cool! I feel like he's on my side, like we're working together, instead of me working with the finger pointing at me."

Tristan speaks to the group now with no trace of that old ambivalence. Even before his breakthrough session with Eric today, I'd been seeing something different in him. Marian's been telling me that she's been feeling it too. She named it simply, in hushed tones, as if the words might make the truth of it disappear. "Tristan is doing better."

"Why is that?" she and I wondered aloud. Because he's formed a therapeutic bond with Eric? Because (despite his longing for some "medical freaking marijuana") he's been staying sober? Because the moon is in Aquarius, because his hormones have shifted, because he's one day older today than he was yesterday? All we could be sure of, we agreed, is that he seems happier, less conflicted, more grounded—even at school.

"I'm supposed to decide by tonight if I wanna go to Thanksgiving at my dad's, or stay home with my mom and stepdad," Tristan tells the group. "Rob's trying to make me and my brother feel guilty 'cause our dad wants us to come to his place." He contorts his face into what I now recognize as his Rob mask and speaks in his Rob voice. "It would be really nice to have you he-e-e-re," he whines, and all the kids laugh.

"Why do you have to decide by tonight?" Eric asks.

"My dad said he needs to know what size turkey to buy." Tristan delivers the line deadpan, waits for his classmates to get the joke.

"But you're a vegetarian, dude!" Kelsey says.

Tristan nods. "So's my brother," he adds, cracking a smile, and the kids roar with empathetic laughter. Quiet, solitary Tristan, who barely used to speak in group, now confidently captivates the room.

"Your dad uses, right?" Lisa asks him. "Would being around him jeopardize your sobriety?"

"He-e-e-l-l-l, no," Tristan says vehemently, turning on an emotional dime. "It makes me wanna never drink again. But I feel bad for him. He has two sons and nothing to do on Thanksgiving."

"Could he come to your mom's house?" Eric asks.

"He-e-e-l-l-l, no," Tristan says again. "They don't want him there."

"Tell everyone what happened in the ER," Eric says. I can see it in the way he looks at Tristan; I can hear it in his voice: he thinks Tristan's doing better too.

"I was getting hella shots for my poison oak," Tristan recounts obligingly. "My eyes were stuck shut. My brother Max comes up to me and whispers, 'Dude! The nurse is *hella* fine.' I was like, 'You asshole! I can't open my eyes!'"

Once again, he's engulfed in his classmates' laughter.

"How do you think you're doing here, Tristan?" Lisa asks over the uproar.

"Really good right now," he answers, serious again. "I feel like I have a place here—a second home. I have people here to talk to if I'm in trouble. Especially Eric. I feel more connected than I did a while ago.

"It feels really good," he repeats, his eyes locked on Eric's.

Tristan decides to spend Thanksgiving with his dad. "I see Marian and Rob every day," he explains. "But I haven't seen Bruce in like seven months."

When Tristan and Luc arrive after the two-hour train ride, Bruce and his lover, Jim, are welcoming and warm. Tristan feels hopeful; his dad seems happier than usual. But then Bruce goes out and buys "an unhealthy-ass bird—not even organic" and some trout. By the time they sit down to eat, Bruce and Jim have had a few drinks. The TV is on. Tristan, who eats neither poultry nor fish and never watches TV, feels "crappy."

"When my dad cut into the turkey," Tristan tells me, "I said, the white man came over here starving, the natives gave them corn, then we raped them and stole from them. So now we kill a bunch of frigging turkeys. What are we celebrating? Can we at least go around saying one thing we're grateful for?" Despite his resistance to it, I think, all that Phoenix training hasn't gone to waste.

"My dad said he was thankful to have two great sons. It was the first time I've ever heard him say that. All I've ever heard from him is, 'You lied. Remember that time you stole.' It felt really good to hear him be proud of me."

But before the pie is served, Bruce goes upstairs and falls asleep. Instead of staying the weekend, Tristan and Luc take the train home late that night.

"Usually kids complain a lot about their parents, especially around the holidays," Eric tells me. "But even after that crummy Thanksgiving, Tristan says, 'The guy drinks a lot, passes out at dinner. That's just my dad.' I asked him, you being a guy, is it confusing to you that your dad is gay? He says 'Yeah, it's confusing. But that's just my dad.' Unlike a lot of kids with gay parents, Tristan doesn't find it necessary to prove he's straight.

"I'm trying to go with where Tristan's at," Eric goes on. "So I ask myself all the time: Is this kid really well-adjusted and happy or totally in denial? If his dad isn't a big issue for him, what's the point of pushing it? Does a kid always have to have a *problem?*

"This is what I do for a living," Eric says pensively. "I believe in this. But maybe what works for other poeple won't work for Tristan. Some kids are so heady. Tristan is so much in the moment.

"At the same time I want to say to Tristan: Who are you to say what you need? You've already declared your incompetence. You did drugs. Your life was not functioning. Addiction will always be an issue for you."

Despite my skepticism about the addiction diagnosis, especially as applied to adolescents, I'm starting to wonder if Eric's right. Last Monday Tristan told me that he'd been "looking for a rush—climbing trees and stuff, searching for a high"; on Friday he told me he'd become a "coffee junkie." "I've been drinking it for four days straight. I feel smarter, more on top of myself. It gets me seriously high. Maybe it's the feeling of breaking that boundary, swallowing a substance to put me in a different state of mind."

Predictably, his coffee binge precipitated a bout of insomnia, for which I suggested kava-root extract. Silly me: a week later, he'd finished off what should have been a several-month supply and bought himself a few more bottles. "The whole day at school, I'm just waiting till bedtime so I can take it again," he told me sheepishly. "Junkie behavior, huh?"

When I agreed that he'd described his obsessiveness about pot, mushrooms, and pills the same way, Tristan replied, "I'm an addict. It doesn't matter what the drug is. Vicodin, coffee, brushing my teeth. I get addicted to everything I like."

Who and what determines whether Tristan is an addict? Who and what determines the meaning of the word?

"I don't think Tristan's an addict," Marian says. "He used to be, but he's not anymore. He's just really good at sticking to things he likes."

"Tristan is an addict," Floyd declares definitively. When I ask how he can be so sure, Floyd says, "Because he's at Phoenix Academy." No circular logic, this. "Kids who aren't addicts can use drugs without getting into trouble. They have a shut-off point. Tristan can't use without losing control of his life. That's why he's here. He's a wealthy Marin kid who has had a lot afforded to him. It's the drugs that got between where he is and where he could be."

Can Tristan be addicted, really, to kava root? To marijuana? To mushrooms? But these are all physically nonaddictive substances. Is it his mind that's addicted, then, not his body?

"I know I'm an addict," Mike says. "My body was made for crank. Being on it or getting off it never made me sick. That's what scares me. My body can handle it."

"Mike is an addict," Tess says with utter certainty. How does she know? "Addiction runs in his family. And crank is the main theme of his life. It's kept him from functioning in the world."

But how can Mike binge on crank for months and then, with no symptoms of withdrawal, go cold turkey off of methamphetamines—one of the most physically addictive substances on earth?

Is it his body that's addicted? His mind? Both? Neither?

What, then, is addiction? Is it, as many claim, an incurable physiological condition? A character flaw? A genetic trait?

"You are an addict," Lauren Slater wrote in her 1998 memoir *Prozac Diary*, "if you feel compelled to consistently consume something you wish you wouldn't, and if that something exists outside the basic requirements of your central nervous system."

"Addiction is, at its core, a consequence of fundamental changes in brain function," the Office of National Drug Control Policy says in its 2001 Annual Report. "Thus, addiction must be approached like other chronic illnesses."

"Drug use is not the same as addiction," the *New York Times Magazine* reports in a February 2002 cover story by Peggy Orenstein, who names economic disadvantage and family dysfunction as other motivators of "self-medication." "The former is clearly a choice," Orenstein writes. "But over the last decade, scientists have begun to see the latter as something else: a chronic, relapsing brain disease [in which] the neurochemistry and receptor sites of a user's brain change radically, causing drug-seeking to become as biologically driven as hunger, sex or breathing."

"The danger in calling addiction a brain disease is people think that makes you a hapless victim," National Institute on Drug Abuse director Dr. Alan Leshner argues in the same story. "But it doesn't. For one thing, since it begins with a voluntary behavior, you do, in effect, give it to yourself."

"Genes may also explain, at least in part, why some people are at greater risk of drug addiction than others," *Newsweek* magazine reported in February 2001.

In *The Heart of Addiction* Dr. Lance Dodes asserts, "It has become common practice to suggest that alcoholism, or any addiction, is a genetic disorder—and overlook the fact that nobody has ever found a gene for alcoholism . . . or that if one person has alcoholism, his or her identical twin, with exactly the same set of genes, is more likely *not* to have alcoholism than to have it."

While acknowledging the occurrence of physical addiction to physically addictive substances—"drugs to which the body reacts by developing tolerance, and subsequently withdrawal," as Dodes defines them—he asserts that biological theories of brain disease and genetic predisposition are products not of science, but of our culture's unsympathetic treatment of addicts. "The idea that addiction is a physical problem," he says, "may provide some relief from [addicts'] guilt and shame."

Most addictions are simply "psychological compromises," Dodes says, and addictive acts a way to avoid confronting difficult situations. He believes that teenagers are particularly prone to taking that way out. "The special tasks facing a person in adolescence," he writes, "might be expected to lead to excessive behaviors of both nonaddictive and truly addictive sorts."

The debate between those who see addiction as a weakness of will deserving of punishment and those who see it as a disease deserving of treatment is being played out nationally among scientists, treatment professionals—and voters. In November 2000 California passed Proposition 36, a ballot initiative mandating courts to offer treatment with probation, instead of jail time, to nonviolent drug offenders. Several other states are now considering similar measures; Arizona has already passed one. In a 2001 ABC News poll, nearly 70 percent of Americans said they'd support a state law requiring drug treatment over jail time for first and second offenses. Even Florida governor Jeb Bush, who'd been pushing to cut funding for treatment, saw the light after his twenty-four-year-old daughter, Noelle, was arrested—and sentenced to rehab, not jail—for trying to fill a phony Xanax prescription. "I think she's in better shape because of the fact she went through the drug-court system and knows that in spite of whatever the ailment is that afflicts her, she's got to confront it," the suddenly compassionate governor said.

To those responsible for the care, feeding, and sobriety of teenagers, the struggle to define drug use versus drug abuse and drug abuse versus drug addiction—and the meaning of each to adolescents versus adults—is more than an interesting debate. The way a kid's problem is defined and who gets to define it determines what's done, and by whom, to try to solve it.

I wince to hear drug counselors labeling fifteen-year-olds as lifelong addicts (or lifelong anything), telling them that, for the rest of their lives, they can never again drink a beer or smoke a joint. But whether a kid is physically, psychologically, or situationally addicted to pot, crank, or ice cream—or just using drugs as a means to make parents come closer or pain go away—the question we should be asking about a kid in trouble is not whether the kid is an addict and will be for life, but how to get him or her the help he or she needs now.

Better yet, let's give kids what they need *before* they need drug rehab. That's a tall order, and a complex one. But for starters, why don't we try giving every kid a school like Phoenix?

In my years of being a teenager, raising teenagers, and writing about teenagers, I've never met one—drug-using or not—who wouldn't benefit from a teacher like Clara, a counselor like Eric, a program like Phoenix Academy. That's not to say that every adolescent, or even every Phoenix student, needs a counseling group every day, a sobriety date posted on the wall, and three AA meetings a week. But as idealistic, socialistic, or just plain schmaltzy as this may sound, all children need to be tightly held in a web of adults who know, respect, and love them, who closely monitor their progress, successes, and failures. Phoenix does that for fifty kids a year. Every school, beginning with day-care centers, should do that for every kid, every day of the year.

Mothering my own kids; hanging out with Mike, Tristan, and Zalika, I came to see that whether they were using drugs, abusing drugs, or addicted to drugs, drugs weren't the biggest problem they faced. To whatever extent kids find help in drug-treatment programs, it isn't the AA meetings or the focus on their sobriety that makes the difference. At Center Point Mike honed his hustle, but he also learned to speak the language of emotions. At Phoenix Academy Tristan learned new recipes for beating drug tests, but he also formed his first mutually respectful, loving bond with a man. At Choices Zalika learned, as she often ironically says, that she has "issues" and acquired a few tools that she may choose to use, at some time in her life, to address them.

No drug-treatment program can give teenagers what they need most: a foreseeable future that satisfies their hunger for self-expression, self-sufficiency, excitement, adventure, and joy. As adolescents peer into the abyss of adulthood, they need someone to hold the flashlight while they look for a life worth living, a reasonable trade-off for the instant pleasure of the next hit, snort, or shot. To be seventeen years old, inches from the land's end of childhood, the wind of the world blowing in your face with nothing rooting you to earth—now that's a reason to do drugs.

At 6 P.M. on Wednesday evening, when Floyd herds the kids out of the parking lot and into Multifamily Group, the meeting is standing room only. Twenty parents sit in a circle of chairs and lean along the walls; fifteen kids sit cross-legged on the floor between them. Dana Leigh and Floyd lead the group. In precise opposition to Center Point's strategy of keeping young addicts from their families and clients' families from each other, Phoenix demands family involvement—and gets it. Every Wednesday night, the parents greet each other with hugs and handshakes, ask knowing questions about each other's kids. On this night in mid-December, they trade recipes for Christmas cookies and holiday truces. As they always do, the counselors greet each parent and child by name.

Floyd calls the meeting to order. "Before we get started, I have an announcement. Ben made Level Three!"

The kids cheer. The parents applaud, some of them visibly envious. I remember the feeling well. Happy as I was for my friends when their teenagers showed signs of pulling through, I often felt jealous too. I'd be listening to a fellow mom recount her good news—Dinah was off the Paxil, enrolling in art school; Jake was stable on methadone; Amelia had a new, sober boyfriend—all the while wondering what those parents had done right that I'd done so wrong.

"You've been clean and sober six months," Floyd addresses Ben. "You're not just sober—you're actually in recovery. Your teachers say you're on task. You give your peers strong support in groups. Your daddy's smiling at you, so things must be better at home. What do you think, Bob?"

"We're really proud of Ben's accomplishments," his dad says.

"What a different place you're in as a family, compared to a year ago at this time," Dana reflects.

This has got to be the ultimate teenage torture, I think, having your parents brag about you in front of your friends. But I guess the kids are used to it. Sitting in the center of the circle, Ben gazes at Dana impassively.

"Pulling our hair out," Ben's mom agrees. "A lot of crying." A lot of crying, yes, I recall. And a lot of red wine late at night . . .

Floyd looks to the man sitting next to Ben's mom. "Gene, how's Sabrina doing?"

"We're very happy for her," he answers in a thick Middle Eastern accent. "We're very grateful to the staff at the Phoenix Academy that helped her to find herself . . ."

"Sort of," Sabrina corrects him.

"No parent wants their child to be in a school like this," her dad concludes. "But for our children, this might be just the right place to go."

"Thanks, Gene," Floyd says, and turns to Tristan. "Where's your mom, T?"

Tristan glances at the door. Marian often arrives midway through these meetings, racing from her ten-hour-a-day job across the Golden Gate Bridge. "On her way, I guess."

"You want to check in?" Dana asks him.

Instead of shrinking into himself, as he used to do, Tristan speaks up assertively. "I went to Spirit Rock on Monday. I was really focused when I was there." Indeed he was. In the gift shop of the sprawling Buddhist retreat center in the foothills of West Marin County, Tristan bypassed the hundred-dollar pashmina meditation shawls and hand-painted prayer flags, heading straight for the poetry books.

"You don't have to be good," he read aloud to me from Mary Oliver's "Wild Geese." He looked up at me, awestruck. "Can you believe that? You don't have to be anything at all!" He pulled some rumpled bills from his jeans pocket, bought the book as a gift for Rob ("Maybe it'll cheer him up"), then joined the two hundred other supplicants—nearly all of them middle-aged and white—for a dharma talk followed by an hour of meditation and chanting.

"What I love most about meditating," Tristan told me as we walked back to my car, "is watching my thoughts come and go. Tonight I had all these strange memories of my childhood. I looked at them and let them go. I love that!"

As we pulled up in front of Tristan's house, Rob was leaving in the family van. He rolled down the window. "Are you feeling nice and spiritual?" he asked Tristan.

"Yes. Are you?"

"Not one bit," Rob answered grimly. "I'm on my way to pick up your mother, who's coming home from work on the ferry at ten o'clock at night."

"It's probably my fault, but I don't feel as comfortable at AA meetings as I do at Spirit Rock," Tristan tells the Multifamily Group now. "AA is only support on my sobriety, and that's not all I'm recovering from."

"The first meetings I went to I couldn't relate to at all," Dana replies. "Each meeting in this county has a different flavor. Keep trying. You might find some you really like."

"I wonder if you could look at your addiction differently, Tristan," Floyd muses. "You love to commune with nature. When you use, you do things to your body you wouldn't do to a tree. Could you look at your body like the ecology? That might give you a point of reference for your recovery."

"For a while I didn't want to be sober," Tristan says. "Then I had a really good talk with Eric. We talked about how crappy things were for me when I was using. I wasn't learning anything. I decided I can't risk going back there. For the first time I can say I want to be sober and be proud of that."

Floyd and Dana beam. A few parents give their children pained looks, as if to say, "Why isn't that you?" The kids avoid their parents' glances.

"Is that Marian hiding behind you?" Floyd asks. Tristan turns, sees his mom standing in the corner. He scurries to her side.

"Sorry I'm late," she blurts in her staccato way. "I'll echo what Tristan says. Since he's been sober, things are better. Thank you for the program."

"Traditionally holidays are a time when kids get into some slippery places," Floyd closes the meeting. "If you wanna drop a bottle on your kids over the holidays, just let us know. We can hook you up with some UA kits."

"Our Christmas present from Phoenix Academy," Kelsey comments wryly, and the parents gather around Floyd and Dana, arranging to drug-test their children over the holidays.

Of the many differences between adults and teenagers in drug treatment, there are few more significant than this one: kids almost never want it.

Even among adults, the decision to go into rehab is rarely strictly voluntary. Many are sent by the courts; many others are "encouraged" to get sober by a one-foot-out-the-door spouse, a one-more-screw-up-and-you're-fired employer, or other consequences of a bottomed-out adult life. Still, there *are* adults who voluntarily commit to rehab (once, twice, or repeatedly).

And even those who don't are allowed free-will decisions teenagers simply cannot make. Sure, Mike or Zalika could have "chosen" CYA over Center Point or Drug Court; Tristan could have "chosen" living with his dad instead of enrolling in Phoenix. But none of them could have blown the whole thing off: gotten a divorce or a new job, moved to a different city.

Of the hundred or so teenagers in drug treatment I've met this past year, I can count on two busily typing hands the number who wanted to be sober. I can count on one hand the number who'd chosen to be in rehab.

Consider the treatment implications. Every day, in every drug-treatment program, counselors and teachers face "patients" who don't want to be cured, or don't want to be cured by that particular practitioner, or in that particular way. What are the odds of the success of *that*? Getting off drugs is hard enough for people who are desperately determined to do it. For people who aren't, there aren't enough threats in a drug counselor's arsenal to make that miracle happen.

One afternoon at Phoenix I convened a ten-person focus group—half of the student body, including Tristan—and asked these thirteen- to eighteen-year-olds the questions of this book. Why do you do drugs? Has anything ever helped you to stop? What should we be doing to help you?

Obviously guarded, despite my assurances that I wouldn't rat them out to their counselors, the students began by reciting their "rehab résumés." They said they did drugs because their parents did, because their parents didn't; because they were physically or sexually abused, because they were physically or emotionally abandoned. As to what had helped them get off drugs, some kids said they'd been sober and enjoyed life anyway; others said they'd scared themselves straight, waking up in emergency rooms and Juvenile Hall cells, not knowing how they'd gotten there.

As the hour wore on, the conversation got more real. (Tristan provided a post-interview reality check, confirming or refuting each kid's self-disclosures.) In the end, with the exception of two students—both in the honeymoon phase of new sobriety—the kids had this to say.

"We do drugs because it's fun. Since it's fun, we don't want to stop. If it's not fun anymore, we'll stop, but until then there's nothing grown-ups can do to make us. Oh, and aren't parents and counselors and POs ridiculous, the way they think they can?"

As parents, we can tell ourselves that we know better than our kids do (it's in our job description, after all), that they lie to us and themselves, that what doesn't seem to be working for them today will surface in their psyches tomorrow. All of that is true. But here's something else that's true: one-quarter of the teenagers in America are living, and dying, high and wasted. To save them, we've got to fix what's wrong with adolescent drug treatment. More important, we've got to fix what's wrong with the treatment of adolescents.

Tristan's family spends the holiday week at a rented cliff house perched above the Pacific, watching whales, cooking elaborate meals. Despite one blow-up with his mom—Marian accused Tristan of buying pot for his siblings, warning him, "If you ever buy or sell or use drugs again, you can't live in our house"— for Tristan the holiday is a celebration of his newfound sobriety.

"I was rolling joints for Caitlin and Max the whole time," he tells me. "One night I had this big fat fucking joint in my mouth, and the old thoughts flashed through my mind: they're healthy and they're doing it, I haven't done it in so long, it's no big deal. Then I thought about Eric—how disappointed he'd be. And I realized it would just be the same old scene. So I didn't do it."

Tristan isn't just abstaining from drugs; he's reflecting deeply on what "recovery" means to him. "When I was in the hospital with poison oak," he says, "I could push a button and someone would come in and say, 'Aww, poor kid, you have it so rough.' That's the feeling I was looking for my whole life. I wanted that pity so bad. I had these excuses—like ADD, and not having a dad growing up.

"I'd say, 'I'm never gonna make it in life.' My parents would say, 'It's our fault.' Admitting it was my fault wouldn't get me what I wanted. So I chose the pity pit as an alternative to work. Facing life is hard. But it feels hella cool to do it."

When school reconvenes after New Year's, Tristan devotes himself to schoolwork for the first time in his life, with satisfying results. He shows me a vocabulary test marked 93 percent, his best grade ever. Instead of taking notes on my laptop during his classes, now, at Tristan's request, I sit beside him in his cubicle, helping him find the answers to open-book tests.

"My whole life I've been going to the easier math class just 'cause it's easier," he tells me in early January. We're sitting together on Clara's velvet couch at lunchtime, winter rain drumming against the roof. Around us the other kids are playing chess, feeding the snakes, trading food and gossip. "What I'm realizing is that if I keep on the easy path, I'll be stuck in one spot. So now when I start to give up in class 'cause I don't understand something, I tell myself, *you can do this*. Then I get this feeling of incredible gratification 'cause I've put my heart into it instead of doing it half-assed."

The new Tristan pays avid attention in class, does his homework on the bus, skips family dinners to finish pages of fractions—or to go to an AA meeting. "I still don't wanna go, but I get a kind of joy out of it 'cause it's a requirement," he says. He pauses, then laughs. "Hearing myself say that sounds weird. I used to say, 'Fuck requirements!'"

Tristan chews a mouthful of black beans. "Eric says what I'm going through is called a paradigm shift—learning that I can do what I'm supposed to and still be a spiritual being. He gave me this fat quote from Gandhi." Tristan rummages through his backpack, pulls out a leather-bound journal. "Almost everything you do is insignificant," he reads aloud, "but it's very important that you do it."

"At night I think: I did the three AA meetings, I did the homework. I can sleep with a content feeling. I'm part of the world, not just floating through my days."

I ask him what's responsible for the change.

"I owe it to the people who didn't judge me. My mom, mostly," Tristan answers. "She gave me the chance to screw up and learn my own lessons." He tells me about a conversation that he and Marian had just before he started at Phoenix, the turning point, he says, of their relationship.

"I was down from my dad's, visiting for the weekend," he says. "They totally didn't trust me, so Rob said I could only sleep at their house if Marian slept in my room with me. My mom and I ended up talking all night, like friends. I told her about Earth Day. I told her I didn't need to smoke pot anymore. We've been trusting each other much more since then."

Tristan says that being sober has also contributed to his growth. "Life just kinda gave me a second chance to live. And something in me decided to take it."

Marian is ecstatic. "He went to school early today to work on his homework," she tells me on the phone one morning, sounding positively amazed.

"He's listening for the first time. He's questioning what he doesn't understand. The demons in his head are going away."

Liberated from the time- and money-devouring task of wrestling her son back from the brink, Marian takes a bold step of her own. Without knowing how she'll replace it, she quits the good-paying job she's always despised. "This is the first time I've been able to leave a job without panicking, because Tristan's not in trouble," she says. I tell her I understand the ripple effect on a whole family when a teenager's crisis abates. I didn't realize how distracted I'd been from my career until I stopped having to rush out to schools and police stations and court appearances in the middle of my workdays—which grew luxuriantly longer, my concentration deliciously deeper, as the sucking tide of Jesse's crisis receded.

I ask Marian what *she* thinks made the difference for Tristan.

"Everything he's done has helped him along his path," she answers. "He had to earn his merit badges from the dark side." She too mentions their post–Earth Day talk. "That night I told him he didn't need to get stoned anymore, because he was stoned on his new perspective. He was in such a state of accepting new ideas, being curious about life—all the good things marijuana does.

"After that talk, Tristan agreed to go to Phoenix. He couldn't go there and live at his dad's. That's how we got to keep him."

The move almost cost Marian her marriage. "Rob told me it would be the end of our family unless I made Tristan live by our rules. So I told Tristan that we'd drug-test him all the time and that we'd ship him back to Bruce's if there was even one mistake. That was Rob's idea, zero tolerance. It worked.

"Journeys helped. Cragmont helped," Marian continues. "But Phoenix Academy is the best thing that's ever happened to him. It's spiritually based, and Tristan's a spiritual kid. They're letting him go to Spirit Rock. He's finally bought into the twelve-step program, which has a religious belief system we couldn't give him, a structure the schools didn't give him. It's the most holistic school I've ever seen."

Listening to Marian, I reflect on what a mystery the whole thing is: why teenagers get into trouble, how they get themselves out of it. Research dollars and expert theories notwithstanding, the truth is, we know as little about one as we do about the other. When nothing's working we look for a place to lay the blame. We pathologize the parents; medicate the kid; change the school, the therapist, the rules. When the kid gets better we start dishing out the credit. Mom hung in there, the Ritalin calmed him down, the Hall scared him straight.

"How can you take the blame for me," Jesse asked at age fifteen, as I drove him home from yet another school-suspension hearing, the administrators' accusations ringing in my ears, "and not take the credit for Peter?" A gut-wrenching question then, and a relevant one to this day. Instead of analyzing the many ways in which I'd damaged him, nowadays the people in Jesse's life tell me how proud I must be of him (and, it is implied, of myself). Yet, still, I blame myself for Peter's and Jesse's flaws, real and imagined, and attribute their shining glories—their integrity, their strength, their compassion, their wit—to some unknowable miracle.

"Rob always thought there'd be a magic bullet," Marian recalls. "You have to think that, when you don't have another choice." She's silent for a moment. "It's a process for sure. Tristan has seventy more years in it. That's why we're on the planet, as far as I can tell. To work on ourselves."

"Agenda items?" Dana Leigh kicks off the weekly Monday afternoon staff meeting. Passing bags of tortilla chips around the counseling-office table are the two Phoenix teachers, Bill, the five counselors, and the consulting therapist who supervises the counselors, Dr. Meg Sherry.

"We need to define what we mean by 'going to an AA meeting,'" Bill says. "When I take them, the kids stay in the meeting the whole time. When I'm not there, I know they don't."

"To get credit for a meeting," Meg says firmly, "they have to stay from start to finish." The counselors nod; the new policy is duly noted. "Anyone concerned about a kid?" Meg asks.

"Sabrina has decided she wants to leave Phoenix," Dana announces.

"She's separating from her parents, trying to get some control over her life," says Floyd, Sabrina's family therapist.

"I think she's found a way to do that," Dana says pointedly. "Her mom wants Sabrina to be a Ph.D. She's decided to become a Buddhist nun. Also, she's identifying as bisexual."

"Do you think her sexuality is related to this spiritual path she's taking?" Meg asks. Dana considers this thoughtfully.

I reflect upon how gently they talk about this young woman's sexuality. And about how the gay teen suicide rate would plummet if every teenager got this kind of respect.

"The parents want her to go to Marin Pacific High, lead a normal life, have an academic career," Floyd says.

"We care more about what Sabrina wants," Meg says firmly.

"What she wants at seventeen may not be what she'll want when she's twenty-one," Clara interjects. "Academically, she's not ready to go."

"It's the first time she's ever stood up for herself against her parents," Dana argues. "I've never seen her so passionate about anything."

"Let's support her then," Meg says.

Clara purses her lips. This isn't the first time I've witnessed this dynamic. The counselors feel that Clara overemphasizes academics above emotional growth; Clara feels that the counselors make the opposite mistake. The tension seems to me an inevitable side effect of the rare entity that is the sober high school, its staff crossing therapeutic borders that aren't even approached in "normal" high schools.

"Any kids on Contract?" Dana asks.

"Tristan," Eric says.

When Phoenix kids are tardy or mildly disruptive, they serve detention in the portable. When they relapse—as revealed by self-disclosure, a dirty UA, or occasionally a concerned or revengeful classmate—they're put "on Contract." During that two- to four-week period, they promise to "refrain from blaming others," "request positive support of peers and request their feedback in group," and "focus on academic work and sobriety."

Tristan is on a Relapse Contract now, thanks to a glass of champagne he confessed to drinking at his mother's birthday dinner last week.

"Why isn't Tristan applying to Level Two?" Meg asks the group.

"Clara won't sign off on it. She's being mean," Eric says, winking at her. "She says he's still catching up with his math and science homework. Plus he missed Family Group again."

"He's running the show." Dana shakes her head. I remind myself that in a twelve-step program, that's considered a bad thing.

"Mom isn't showing up at Family Group either?" Meg asks.

"Last week the two of them arrived at seven-thirty, giggling and laughing like little kids," Dana reports.

"Mom needs to know that it's not good for her kid to be on Level One indefinitely," Meg says. "We want him to go back to regular school at some point."

"Mom loves him being here," Floyd says. "When I met her she was drowning with that kid. We're her life raft. In spite of her resistance—which exactly mirrors Tristan's, by the way—this is the most consistent academic and behavior time they've had with him. His drug use is way down . . ."

"*Down?*" the counselors chorus.

"She'll give him a glass of wine every now and then," Floyd explains.

"She's the reason he's not on Level Two," Eric adds. "She gave him champagne on her birthday."

"Does she understand what she's doing?" Susan asks.

"She's so airy, I'm not sure she does," says Floyd. "At the potluck I met the stepdad. The guy looked really normal to me. He wears suits. I think I'm gonna latch on to him."

"They were both raving about the program at the potluck," Dana reports.

"So come to group on time then," Eric mutters.

Dana looks at her watch. "Floyd—you'll address these issues with the family?"

"Believe that," Floyd replies.

The next week Marian and Tristan do show up for their family session with Floyd, who does explain their responsibilities to Tristan's progress. They do agree to take those responsibilities more seriously, and Tristan does catch up on his homework and he does serve his detention.

When it's time for his quarterly review—the meeting each Phoenix student has four times a school year with his or her counselor, teachers, parents, and/or PO—Clara raves about his progress, announces that he earned the second-highest grade on the science test (the subject was nutrition, Tristan's favorite), and asks what his goals are.

"My New Year's resolution is to try my hardest in everything I do," Tristan answers. "If I put my soul into what I do, it feels good—in life, not just in school."

When the staff members have reviewed his class work and commented on his participation in groups, praising his honesty and sense of humor, Eric asks if Tristan wants to speak.

"Phoenix Academy has made such a difference for me," he says slowly. "I'm getting the courage to try new things. A year ago if I faced something hard, I would've done some drug. Now if I'm uncomfortable in a situation I know there's nowhere to turn except to myself. It's just Tristan everywhere. Sometimes that's hard, but I'm learning so much so fast because of it."

Scribbling furiously in her notebook, Clara asks Tristan if she can quote him on that. He nods proudly. Although Marian is quiet throughout the meeting, a small smile playing tremulously across her face, later Tristan tells me, "She didn't want me to get an ego about it, but she was superhappy." As was he. "I expected to hear I was doing good in English, good in science, shitty in everything else. That was the best school meeting I ever had!"

A few days later, Tristan achieves his first Phoenix Academy milestone. When his promotion is announced at Multifamily Group, Marian isn't there to hear it. She rushes in at seven, takes her usual seat in the corner, and chokes back tears when Tristan bursts out from across the room, "Mom! I made it to Level Two!"

Sobriety is Tristan's new toy; he takes it with him everywhere to see what it can do. His brother introduces him to Brother Juniper, a street hustler–turned–street minister who runs a needle exchange program in San Francisco. Tristan takes the ten-dollar-an-hour job Brother Juniper offers and starts spending weekend nights, dusk to dawn, handing out needles, condoms, and hard-boiled eggs to homeless male prostitutes in sleeping bags—many of them his own age.

"At first I was hella uncomfortable," Tristan tells me. We're sitting on the futon in his basement room, the picture window framing the darkening torso of Mt. Tam. As we talk, we're addressing thank-you cards to the donors who pay for the eggs and the needles. "I tried not to take it personally, but there were old guys out there on the street looking at me. They come to pick up boy kids. It's a gay thing." It surprises me that, despite his father's sexuality, Tristan seems less disturbed by this aspect of his new job than most sixteen-year-old boys would be.

Learning more than he ever thought he'd know about IV drug use and its paraphernalia—"Long needles are for old heroin addicts whose veins have gone down; micros are for shooting it into your penis when you can't find a vein anywhere else"—Tristan earns his first legal income. He also gains a new appreciation for the soft cushion of his life.

"I can say peace and love over here in Marin, but I don't see the shit those kids see. I eat organic food in Marin—but when I dropped an egg on Polk Street, this kid ran over and picked it up off the ground. There's so much bad in the world I didn't know about."

Inspired by his new job, Tristan writes a poem called "Beyond All This." He reads it to me at lunch.

> Beyond all this there's a field that leads to endless valleys
> Where the oaks grow strong and the ferns hold rallies
> Beyond all this the elk run free
> And the hyenas chuckle 'cause they see what they see
> Beyond all this there are birds without names
> The tones of their voice distinguishes pleasure from pain
> Beyond all this the raccoon shuffles cards on the grass
> An anteater wanders by and decides to laugh
> Beyond all this the grapevines drink their own wine
> And laugh together over the idea of time
> Beyond all this there's a place for you to sit
> Live in the cycle and stay for a bit
> Take your shirt off and go roll in the grass
> Your hands will get callused as fast as you'll laugh
> Your pants will fall apart and
> Your shoes will make no sense
> Your wallet is good nest material
> Your keys may be left for the ants
> You have nothing left so go hang in a tree
> You're naked now so just let yourself be.

———————

A few weeks after Tristan writes the poem, I show up at Phoenix once, then again, and don't find him there. I check in with Marian. She says he's had a cold, a few doctor appointments—but I hear that nervous feeling in her voice.

"What's up, Tristan?" I ask him one day when I leave Phoenix, drive to his house, and find him in his room, drawing.

"I'm not sure," he answers. He looks at me helplessly. His hair is tangled, his eyes are dim. "I'm just not feeling Phoenix right now. All that recovery shit is getting old."

When I leave him I have that nervous feeling too.

ZALIKA

Moving Violations

"You are gonna be *so* mad at me," Zalika tells me. We're holed up in her room a few days after Christmas. Her mom's at work; her dad, brother, and sister are downstairs eating breakfast. She lowers her voice theatrically. "I took another pregnancy test. It's positive."

My first thought is, she's lying. "I went to Planned Parenthood this time, so it's definite," she adds preemptively. "Plus I been throwing up every morning."

Her words pour out in a rush. "Bo wants to keep it. His mom and his grandma are real happy. They said we have to get married. LaShaundra— that's his mom—said, 'We don't kill babies in our family.' She was my age when she had Bo. Her mom was fourteen when she had her."

"How do *you* feel?" I ask.

"First I was happy," she answers. "Then I started thinking about stuff I wanna do, like going to college. Traveling. Having a career. Getting married and having a family and planning it. The regular stuff of life.

"Still, something inside me is saying, 'Don't be a punk. You the one who laid down and did it, every day violatin' probation.'"

"You're going to have a baby to prove you're not a punk?"

"It could be the best thing for me, Meredith. It might keep me from bustin' out the program and goin' crazy."

I ask if her parents know.

"I called my mom when she was in her car so she couldn't get all up in my face. She just asked me what I'm gonna do. That was it. The communications lines aren't really open in our family."

"And your dad?"

"He says I have to have an abortion. But he can't make me." Her voice quavers. "It's not a bad thing to have a baby, is it? I'm here, and I'm not a bad thing."

"No, you're not a bad thing," I reassure her. Needing a breather, I venture downstairs to talk to her father. I find Asani washing the dishes, his waist-length dreadlocks twisted into a ropy knot. "She's not having a baby 'cause I'm not having baby," he tells me angrily. "I've got six kids. I'm not raising an infant."

Asani glances out at the patio where his ten-year-old son is shooting hoops with his thirteen-year-old daughter. "There are no social causes for her behavior. None whatsoever." He yanks the faucets off, paces the floor. "I'm sick of the whole thing. The cops coming to the door. The invasion of our privacy. I had to put one social worker out of my house—she was looking for crack dealers in our closets.

"She is not a good person right now. I don't like her." Once again, I notice, he's not using his daughter's name. "I was in the Black Panthers when I was her age. An activist. Not her. She's superficial. She likes the whole ghetto thing: the fake hair, the clothes, the nails. I don't know where that came from. I don't know where *she* came from. All my other kids have real hair. She's alien to me.

"She's a user," Asani adds. "I have dope fiends in my family, so I know what that's about. They make you feel special and they rip you off. Like addicts do."

I tell Asani how bad I felt when Jesse was Zalika's age, knowing that he was doing so much harm. And how good it feels now to know . . .

Asani cuts me off. "She doesn't have to go that far. She can pick up trash. She can be a nuclear physicist. She just has to be a decent human being. But she's not.

"I'm just watching the calendar till she turns eighteen," Asani says, the rhythmic slap of the basketball on concrete, the trilling laughter of his two younger children punctuating his words. "I've got one year and three months to go. Then I'm changing the locks, and I'm done."

Tom's sanguine response to Zalika's pregnancy surprises her and me both. "Maybe this will slow her down and settle her," he e-mails me. "Although the more realistic probability is that she is setting herself up, her baby up, and her family up for a lot of tragedy."

When I call June, she tells me that she's trying to talk Zalika into going to Planned Parenthood, hoping the counselors there will convince her to have an abortion. After a heated three-way phone conversation, June, Zalika, and I make a plan to meet at their house the next morning to caravan to Planned Parenthood in Richmond.

"Has it occurred to you," I ask June, as we sit together in the waiting room while Zalika meets privately with a counselor, "that she might not be pregnant at all?"

"Now that you mention it, she *has* been using tampons," June says slowly. "And her period's always been irregular . . ." I don't tell June about the negative test before Christmas. Planned Parenthood and I have this in common: we're both sworn to keep Zalika's secrets.

Zalika appears. Her mom and I scour her face for clues. "The test is negative," she announces. "I'm *so* relieved."

"What about that positive test last week?" I ask.

"The counselor said the baby must have passed."

As Zalika sweeps out of the clinic ahead of us, June raises her eyebrows at me behind her daughter's back. I shrug. She shrugs. She takes Zalika to school.

I wake up the next morning thinking, she *is* pregnant. The trip to Planned Parenthood was a ploy. And I don't even care. If all this drama is what it takes to keep Zalika entertained enough to hang in at her parents' house, in school, in Drug Court, I'll gladly keep buying tickets.

"You are gonna be *so* mad at me," Zalika says again, when she calls the next day. "I'm pregnant."

"Duh," I say flatly.

"You *knew?*" she gasps. "*Serious?*"

"You didn't want everyone bugging you to get an abortion, right?"

"You are *so* understanding, DQ1! You know I just wanna be free to make my own decision."

I ask if the counselor gave her prenatal vitamins or scheduled her next checkup—half wanting to know, half testing her latest version of the truth.

"She didn't bother," Zalika says. "She's probably seen a thousand girls like me. She knows if a girl comes in with a mother wanting her to have an abortion, that's probably what'll happen."

"What *is* going to happen?"

"Hell if I know. Bo and I broke up today."

The experts say that all teenagers with drug problems have one psychological impairment in common: arrested development. I've heard it again and again from these kids' counselors and teachers. The day a kid starts abusing drugs is the day his or her emotional growth stops. It's as if they hit the "Pause" button on growing up. Instead of pouring all that adolescent energy into "normal" teenage passions—sports, school, music, shopping, a job, even dating—they channel it into a single source of gratification (or self-medication), procuring and doing drugs. Once teenage drug abusers get clean—if they get clean—they start growing again from where they left off. So a nineteen-year-old in early recovery might have the maturity, relationship experience, and life skills of, say, a thirteen-year-old.

You can prove it by me, with a couple of qualifications. One, it's not just using drugs that can slow a kid's maturation. Zalika's childhood was interrupted by selling, not using, drugs (and her body); Jesse's was interrupted by his escalating craving for crime. Two, while troubled kids' acquisition of age-appropriate life skills falters, their expertise in less predictable (and/or savory) arenas is often accelerating apace. Mike, Tristan, Zalika, and Jesse can all do things I'll never be able to do: blow glass, manufacture money, instantly discern the difference between a horny man and a psychopath, hot-wire a car. But Jesse was twenty-one and a sober Christian before he learned to set an alarm clock, open a checking account, keep a calendar, pay a parking ticket.

After I'd known them both a year, it struck me that neither seventeen-year-old Mike nor sixteen-year-old Tristan had been romantically involved during all that time—prime time, normally, for young love. Mike had his one-night stands; Tristan had one brief, unconsummated relationship. I've never heard the word "girlfriend" from either of their mouths. But get Mike talking about "blowing clouds" or Tristan reminiscing about 'shrooms—then their pulses quicken, their eyes sparkle with desire.

In Zalika's case, desire *is* her drug; she manufactures it, uses it, sells it (along with the occasional rock of crack). So I'm actually reassured, somehow, by her drama-laden romance with Bo. He's her age, a major breakthrough. He's a boyfriend, not a pimp. He's not buying what she's offering, and she's offering it for free. Even with the pregnancies that come and go, even if Bo isn't the man I would have chosen for her (and God knows I don't choose men for her; that job's already taken), when Zalika's complaining to me about Bo, I feel as though I'm talking to a sixteen-year-old girl who's doing what she's supposed to be doing, at least in this one corner of her life: being mad at her boyfriend. For a girl who's never known love without money, who needs to learn to separate the two if she's going to live to be an adult, that's progress.

"Zalika showed up wearing all red on Friday," Leo Kidd tells the Drug Court Team in Case Review the next Tuesday. "Other than that, she's doing better in the program. Three out of four on attendance, all clean tests. She still gets negative with staff; she pouts if you get on her for anything. But she's flirting less, participating more in group. And she turned in proof of attendance for two NA meetings."

"She did *not* have a good week on JEM," Judge Easton reports, scanning his laptop screen. "She was out every night. Let's see . . . Last week we went for the story about the monitor being unplugged. The week before that, she said she was out of range for six hours looking for an NA meeting."

"I've heard it can take all night to find a meeting," the DA says dryly.

"I think the kids have discovered the value of meetings," Kevin adds. "Get-out-of-JEM-free cards."

"She's dealing with a lot of issues," Tom says.

"So—custody for Zalika if she shows?" Pam cuts to the chase.

Knowing this was a likely outcome, I've come prepared. I'm wearing my running shoes.

"She's had a pretty rough life," says Judge Easton. "What are we gonna do with her?"

"I think if we can get her into custody, I should interview her in the Hall, ask her what she needs," Kevin suggests. "This ain't working."

I know what that interview will mean. Unless Zalika talks Kevin out of it, she'll be dropped from the Drug Court roster and sent to placement—residential drug treatment or a group home—instead.

"Mom is frustrated that she keeps violating," Pam says. "Of course her parents don't know what time she gets home, since they're never there."

"She's not using drugs, as far as we know," Tom says.

"I bet she's drinking, just to take the edge off," the judge says. "What scares me about kids like this, when prostitution's been a way of life—she takes off, goes back to that life . . . I've had a number of girls like Zalika end up dead."

"So, custody and an interview for Zalika?" Kevin says. "I'll be interviewing Braydon too. So it'll be an afternoon of peace, love, and happiness in the Hall."

"Should we give her a cookie for being good in program?" Judge Easton asks.

"I think that would be taken as sarcasm, Your Honor," Kevin answers. "Also, she might throw it at your head."

Unlike most American social issues, drug abuse is stunningly democratic: no race, class, gender, or age group is immune. The *consequences* of drug abuse, on the other hand—the treatments and penalties that determine just how devastating its effects will be on the addict and on his or her family and community—precisely reflect, and effectively perpetuate, the inequities that bisect our society along the fault lines of class and race.

"If I'm a kid with a drug problem and I'm caught burglarizing someone's home," Kevin Charles tells me, "am I going to Juvenile Hall or am I going to treatment? Am I going to get charged or am I going to see a therapist? If I'm black, brown, or poor, odds are I'm going to the Hall."

National statistics confirm Kevin's observations. As is true for adults, punishment for juvenile drug offenders often fits the criminal, not the crime. For example, African Americans constitute 12 percent of the U.S.

population and an estimated 13 percent of American drug users—but they account for 35 percent of the arrests for drug possession, 55 percent of all convictions for drug possession, and 74 percent of all prison sentences.

Juvenile drug use and convictions mirror this pattern. "Contrary to popular assumption," the National Institute on Drug Abuse (NIDA) reports in its "Monitoring the Future" survey for 2001, "African American youngsters have substantially lower rates of use of most drugs than do Whites." NIDA adds, "Differences in use by socioeconomic classes are very small."

Journalist Tim Wise writes in the March 2001 on-line magazine AlterNet.org, "White high-school students are seven times more likely than blacks to have used cocaine; eight times more likely to have smoked crack; ten times more likely to have used LSD; and seven times more likely to have used heroin.

"There are more white high-school students who have used crystal methamphetamine (the most addictive drug on the streets) than there are black students who smoke cigarettes. White youth ages twelve to seventeen are 34 percent more likely to sell drugs than their black counterparts. White youth are twice as likely to binge drink, and nearly twice as likely as blacks to drive drunk."

Why, then, do kids of color, who make up about one-third of the youth population nationwide, account for nearly 70 percent of juveniles in custody?

Not because they commit more drug crimes. Between 1991 and 1998, when the number of juvenile drug-offense cases more than doubled, the proportion of drug cases involving white youth *increased* from 49 percent to 68 percent, while the proportion of cases involving black juveniles *decreased* from 49 percent to 29 percent. And these numbers reflect only those teens who were arrested and remanded to "the system"—not those, like the never handcuffed Tristan, whose race and class keep them below the radar of the law.

Of all drug cases brought to juvenile court in 1997, 68 percent of defendants were white, 29 percent were black, and 3 percent were (the insultingly undefined) "other."

Compare and contrast. Only 14 percent of the white kids were detained (put into custody), compared to 38 percent of the black kids and 16 percent of the "other."

And 19 percent of the white kids were sentenced to out-of-home placement, compared to 33 percent of the black teenagers and 21 percent of the kids defined as "other."

The Office of Juvenile Justice and Delinquency Prevention (OJJDP) acknowledges that "Delinquency cases involving black juveniles were more likely to be handled formally than were cases involving white youth or youth of other races." In fact, the OJJDP says, "78 percent of drug cases involving black juveniles were handled by formal petition, compared with 56 percent for white juveniles and 55 percent for juveniles of other races."

From those facts come these: a black male born today has a 29 percent chance of going to jail in his lifetime. And there are currently more African American men in jail than in college.

Sitting in group therapy sessions at Choices, sitting through sessions at the Richmond Drug Court, I can almost hear the "ka-ching, ka-ching" of those grim statistics adding up. Tuesday after Tuesday the Drug Court Team struggles to wrest its clients back from the jaws of the monster that would swallow them whole: the increasingly privatized, increasingly profitable penal system in which nearly one out of seven African American men between the ages of twenty-five and twenty-nine is now incarcerated. (In comparison, 2.9 percent of Latino men and 1.2 percent of white men are in prison.)

Every time a Drug Court kid steals another car, relapses, or runs, those jaws snap and drool. Every time a Drug Court kid gets clean and graduates, the monster slinks off in search of new prey. And finds it.

"She's gonna run as soon as I tell her she's going to the Hall," Tom confirms my prediction when we huddle before his precourt consultation with Zalika. "As her lawyer, I can't tell her this, but the best thing for her might be to let her go. If she gets busted, she'll be forced into placement. That could save her life."

"What if she runs and doesn't get caught?" I argue. "She'll just go back to her pimp that much sooner."

Tom shrugs, calls Zalika to his lectern in the hallway, delivers the news. She bursts into tears. Bo comes up to her. "You cryin' 'cause you goin' to jail?"

"I ain't goin' in the Hall. I'm fittin' to run."

"You ain't runnin'," Bo scoffs.

"Jus' watch me."

Bo turns to Tom. "I'm going to placement, huh?" he asks.

"They're considering it," Tom answers. "Too many dirty tests, Braydon."

Bo reaches into his mouth, pulls out his removable gold "grill," wrestles the gold ring off his finger, and hands the tangle of metal to Zalika. I see hurt wash over her face. He's not trying to talk her out of running, not even saying a proper good-bye, just using her as his safe-deposit box.

"I'm *gone*," she says, and heads for the stairs. I hesitate for a moment—who knows what's best for this girl right now?—then follow her. Again. I hear the AA truism ringing in my head. "Doing the same thing but expecting different results—that's the definition of insanity."

"I'm through with these people!" Zalika slams through the courthouse door. I speed-walk beside her as she crosses the street, heading for the bus stop a few blocks away. "I could be out there making *money*. I'm gon' call MC right now."

"See that cute guy?" she says, her voice suddenly low. I follow her glance to the late-model gold Buick driving slowly ahead of us, with a young African American man at the wheel. "He's a pimp. I could be out there for him in an hour."

The car pulls over to the curb ahead of us. The man watches Zalika like a hungry lion eyeing its prey. "You know him?" I ask.

Zalika shakes her head.

"Then why—?" I ask.

"He knows a ho' when he sees one," she says, flouncing past him. The car follows us as we walk.

"I need to call my dad," Zalika says. I hand her my phone, relieved to realize that she wants her father to talk her out of running, even if the other man in her life didn't.

Her dad yells at her till she agrees. We walk back to the courthouse, trailed by the gold Buick. Before she walks into the courtroom, Zalika hands me Bo's jewelry. "Mail this stuff to my house, okay?" she asks. "And you *better* come see me in the Hall."

As we walk into the courtroom the kids burst into laughter, no longer captivated by the drama queen's now predictable performance. Head held high, Zalika takes her place at the defense table.

"Someone told me you were thinking of leaving," Judge Easton says. "I'm glad you decided not to do that. So, Zalika, how have things been going for you this week?"

"So-so, I guess."

"Well, the JEM staff say you've been having some problems. You were gone all day yesterday from six in the morning till five-thirty at night. Where were you?"

"With my friend."

"Mr. Kidd, what about the program?"

"Pretty good. Our main concern is her JEM violations. That's what's interrupting Zalika's progress."

"Okay," the judge turns back to Zalika. "The original thinking was to have you screened for placement. But I'm hoping this is a temporary slip. So we're gonna have you detained now, released on JEM on Sunday, and we'll get a fresh start. You gonna test dirty?"

"No."

"Your little party yesterday didn't involve any drinking or drugs?"

"Of course not. I don't have a drug problem."

A shocked silence falls over the courtroom. Facing the judge, awaiting his decision, Zalika has violated the first rule of Drug Court.

"Pardon me?" the judge says, peering at her over his bifocals.

Tom whispers in Zalika's ear. "I mean I didn't do any drugs or alcohol yesterday," she corrects herself.

"Good. We'll have you tested when you get out to the Hall. Then we'll try again next week. Okay?"

"Hang in there. I'm proud of you," Tom whispers to Zalika. She approaches the bailiff, hands him her purse, earrings, bracelets, and belt, lifts her ankle so he can cut off her JEM bracelet, and holds out her hands. The other kids watch impassively as the bailiff cuffs her and leads her away. Zalika is one of three kids to leave Drug Court out the back door today. Bo is another.

When court is adjourned and the kids are off to Choices, Judge Easton descends the bench and makes a great show of offering me the plate of cookies. "I believe you've earned this," he says.

"I'm not sure I did the right thing," I say around a mouthful of cookie. "I'm not sure *what* she needs."

"I'll never figure out what makes some kids get into trouble and others not," Judge Easton muses, shrugging off his robes. "I've had some kids from great families in terrible trouble, and some kids in unbearable circumstances skate on through. I just thank God my own kids did fine."

Tom and I walk together to his office across the street. I tell him that Zalika threatened to call her pimp today.

"She'll be out on JEM on Sunday. She'll be back in trouble by Tuesday, if not sooner," Tom says wearily. "Her chances of making it in Drug Court are not good. She needs a psychological evaluation. And intense therapy. And a placement far away from here."

I ask if there's any program that could meet those needs. "She's too out-there for Drug Court, not crazy enough for a locked facility," Tom says. "There's a pretty good therapeutic program in LA, but if we sent her there she'd just run. We'd be right back where we are now."

"Can't you just get her locked in up in the Hall, let her serve her thirty-six months close to home?"

"In this county, the Hall is a holding station till kids get placed some-where else. Kids don't do time there."

"So," I press him, "there's no way to keep a girl like Zalika safe, let alone get her the help she needs?"

"Not unless the parents pay for it," Tom says. "Her folks tried that once. They're not about to do it again. Even if they would, can you see Zalika staying put in some teenage boot camp?"

No, I can't. Nor can I see the logic in a system that requires kids to be drug-addicted or psychotic in order to get the therapeutic containment that a kid like Zalika needs.

June calls as I'm driving home. She's relieved to hear that her daughter's back in the Hall. "If she can just stay alive till she's eighteen or twenty, I know she'll be okay," she says. The question hangs heavy between us. Once she's released, in a few days, from the only place she can't run from, how will we keep Zalika safe till she's old enough to do that for herself?

Contra Costa County's Juvenile Hall is less depressing than Alameda County's, where Jesse used to go, but more depressing than Sonoma's, where I go to visit Mike. Contained in one windowless building in a county office complex outside Martinez, this place has a bigger, grungier waiting room than Sonoma's, and a far less friendly "receptionist." Without looking up from his paperwork, he tells me the kids are eating lunch; I'll have to wait an hour to see Zalika.

While we wait together, I strike up a conversation with an African American woman who's here to see her sixteen-year-old son. He's in the Hall, she tells me, because he drove a rental car to Los Angeles without a license. "It's a big industry, putting children in prison," she says. "That's why they're building all those new jails." Still, she says, she's glad her son is here. "I told him, 'You are *not* going to wreak havoc in my house. I'll pray for you while you're out there. But if you can't behave, you *will* be out there.'"

Finally my name booms over the PA system. A guard leads me through several sets of locked doors and past a row of glass-walled interview rooms. Each is occupied by an adult—most of them middle-aged white men in suits and ties—sitting at a small table facing a teenager wearing the Martinez Juvenile Hall uniform: light blue T-shirt, navy blue sweats, canvas sneakers. The guard lets me into the room where Zalika waits. The guard leaves, locking the door behind her.

"These fools is so stupid," Zalika says, flashing me a grin. "They didn't make me take my hair out this time." The Hall has a ban on bobby pins, beads, and barrettes, which normally leads to the disassembling of Zalika's hairdo upon arrival. Sure enough, the chunky wooden beads are still bobbing in her braids.

"Guess who's in here?" she goes on. "My bestest friend, Tahira!" As she names the many other inmates she knows, I'm reminded of the times I'd pick Jesse up from Juvenile Hall, then drive home listening to him talk about all the friends he'd "hooked up with" inside. Being in Juvie offered Jesse so many things he craved and was deprived of at home: baloney sandwiches on white bread, freedom from homework and vegetables, unlimited time with his thuggiest friends. "Bo's here too, you know," Zalika adds coyly. "We was kissin' in the van comin' over."

"You're back together?"

"I guess. They left us in rooms next to each other for like a hour. He kept telling me he loved me through the wall. How am I supposed to say I love him when he don't even know 'bout my past? I don't love myself. That's what my actions show."

I ask if anyone here knows she's pregnant. "I told the nurse, 'cause all the pregnant girls get a special snack at ten o'clock at night. When you first get brought in, the nurse asks you questions about your health—have you ever tried to hurt yourself, is anyone hurting you, stuff like that. If you say yes, they put you on suicide watch."

Struggling to sound like the impartial journalist I'm supposed to be, I ask Zalika to help me understand why she couldn't make it through the week without violating JEM.

"I kept getting drunk with Bo," she answers. "That's one reason I'm thinking to get an abortion. It's hecka bad. We been drinkin' VSOP Hennessey, gin, and orange juice. Once I got drunk, I couldn't go home."

"But didn't you realize—"

Zalika interrupts me, speaks slowly as if to a small child, or an idiot. "I didn't *decide* to stay at Bo's. I just stayed. I don't plan stuff, Meredith. I don't think like an adult yet."

Suddenly she jumps up, presses her face against the glass. "Oh my God! Tahira's leaving!" In the hallway a guard is leading a wisp of a girl past us. When she sees Zalika the two of them frantically blow kisses at each other. "Bye bye, baby! I love you!" Zalika yells.

"She looks so young," I say. "Didn't you tell me she used to . . ."

"She's thirteen," Zalika confirms, still waving. "Same as my little sister. Yep, yep we used to do prostitution together. She was selling weed then. I was dealing dope."

Tahira disappears. Zalika doesn't move. "That is my bestest friend," Zalika repeats.

"And your only friend?" I ask. I've never heard her mention another one.

Zalika nods. "I used to have a best friend in El Sobrante. Our families did everything together when we were kids. We still love each other, but we went in different directions. Jasmine's a normal girl. Totally square. She has a driver's license. She doesn't have issues or nothing. She's doing stuff on time like you supposed to. I haven't seen her in two years." Zalika stares out at the empty hallway. "Jasmine's sixteen. I'm like twenty-seven years old."

She plops down, agitated again. "I need to ask Tom why was they even *thinking* about kicking me out the program. I'm not the one who's comin' up dirty every week like Bo and all those other kids." She looks at me angrily. "I'm relapsing on dick, not drugs. You don't kick someone out a rehab program for *that*. What the fuck is wrong with those people?"

"If you were the judge," I ask, "and you wanted to help Zalika, what would you do?" She considers my question thoughtfully.

"I'd let me be," she answers. "They can't change me. There's nothing they can help me with. They keep putting me on JEM. It doesn't work. They keep putting me in here. It doesn't work. They should just let me do what I'm gonna do, so I can get it over with and grow up. All this in and out of the Hall, it's start to make me not care. Once I get all the way to that point, it's *bad*."

As if he's been summoned, Tom appears in the hallway. He uses his key to let himself in. Zalika turns away from him.

"Where's my hug?" Tom asks.

"I'm mad at you," she pouts.

"You're a couple steps away from being locked up in CYA till you're twenty-one," Tom tells her. "We're not there yet, Zalika, but we're getting close."

Zalika ignores him. "I have other kids to tend to if you don't want to talk," Tom says, and leaves.

"See?" she says as soon as the door clangs shut behind him. "Don't none of those people care 'bout me. Not even Tom."

"I had a miscarriage in the Hall," Zalika tells me the following Monday as I'm driving her to school. I ask her what happened, noticing how jaded I've become, questioning everything she tells me. Is this what's made her parents so detached?

"Bo gave me chlamydia," she explains. "I tested positive for it in the Hall, so they gave me some pills. Soon as I took 'em, I started cramping and bleeding. There was blood everywhere in my bed. I was really sad, looking for my baby in all those clots."

I tell her I'm sorry, wondering if I can get Tom to check out her story. If there really was blood in her bed, someone would have seen that . . .

"But I'm hella relieved too," she adds. "I prayed to God. I put it in His hands and he took care of it. I have to believe this was the best thing that could have happened." The Drug Court Team, she tells me, decided to give Bo one more chance in the program instead of sending him to placement, so at least they can still be together.

We pull up in front of Challenge Academy, the charter school that she and many of the Drug Court kids attend. Zalika has told me stories of kids dealing and doing drugs in the halls, carrying guns, pulling knives on each other in class. These stories become quite believable as we park in front of a borrowed church deep in one of Richmond's poorest neighborhoods, and I follow Zalika past the hefty young black man who's guarding the door.

The entryway is lined with two long benches occupied by a dozen Latino and African American boys and girls, slouching, sleeping, or nodding off. "That's where kids hang out all day if they don't go to class," Zalika says, "including me." She gives me the school tour. The "classrooms" are in the church offices; the "computer lab" is a dim hallway equipped with PCs older than the kids using them. The hallways teem with kids reeking of pot and alcohol, stumbling into each other, picking fights, slipping in and out of the building despite the guard's efforts to keep them inside. I ask Zalika why, in February, so many of the kids are sucking on candy canes. She tells me pointedly, "Some store couldn't get rid of 'em after Christmas, so they dumped 'em on us."

I thought that in my years of reporting on high schools across the country, I'd seen America's worst schools, full of America's least valued teenagers. But what's going on at CA isn't even warehousing—it's Dante's Inferno High. "We're funded for twenty-five kids, not the fifty-five we have," the principal tells me when Zalika introduces us. "If you can call it funding. The staff hasn't been paid in two months; we're all volunteers at this point. We can only feed the kids lunch two days a week."

We watch as some boys slip out the front door while the guard breaks up a fight between two girls. "We're supposed to be a closed campus," the principal says, "but the kids regularly sneak out to buy controlled substances. Then they come back high."

"And you let them be here when they are?"

"We're their last stop, the only safe place they have," she answers. She puts her hand on Zalika's shoulder. "We're happy when Zalika comes to school. We're ecstatic when she goes to class. But we love her even when she doesn't."

As soon as the principal walks away, a girl shoves into Zalika, mutters "Fuckin' ho' bitch" at her, and keeps going. I'm surprised to see Zalika shrug it off.

"I'll walk you to your car," she offers, brushing past the guard at the door. Outside a cluster of kids are gathered around a late-model Lexus idling in the middle of the street. In the driver's seat I see Aaron, who's currently on the run from Drug Court. "Every time Aaron steals a car he brings it by here," Zalika explains. "This place is *so* ghetto." She asks me for a dollar twenty-five so she can buy some cheese fries for lunch.

"What are you *doing* at this school, Zalika?" I ask.

"It's a nice place to relax," she answers.

"The justice system is fundamentally racist," Kevin adds. "So is the juvenile justice system. And so is the War on Drugs."

David Simon, creator of the HBO series *The Wire,* agrees. Commenting on the subject of his show, the War on Drugs, he had this to say to Salon.com. "[The government] created war zones where the only economic engine is the self-perpetuating drug trade. It survives no matter what, and they expect people to walk away from it. The naiveté is just incredible.

"They've spent thirty-four years taking these neighborhoods and basically divesting them from the rest of America. We've embraced a permanent war of attrition against the underclass and it can't work.

"What drugs have not destroyed," Simon concludes, "the war on them has managed to pry apart."

What the War on Drugs has pried apart are the communities, cultures, and families of Zalika's chosen peers: the children of jailed crack addicts who go to court with her every Tuesday; the prison orphans being raised by grandparents, cousins—or no one—who go to school with her at CA. These are those prisoners' children, inheriting their parents' addictions and their street-corner businesses. These are their children on drugs.

Why is it that although more white people than black use drugs, more black people than white people go to jail for buying and selling them? According to the on-line newsletter JoinTogether.org, one reason is the location of the drug marketplaces. Why should wealthy white folks put up with drug dealers in *their* neighborhoods when they can pop in the car, lock the doors and windows, and drive into the ghetto to score?

"Disadvantaged neighborhoods may not have a higher rate of addiction problems than other areas, but do have more visible drug markets," the online newsletter JTO.com reports. In fact, JTO says, "visible drug sales are 6.3 times higher in the 'most disadvantaged neighborhoods' than in the 'least disadvantaged' communities."

So kids like Tristan grow up knowing they can make $100,000 a year doing what their parents do (even if they're convinced they'd die of boredom doing it). Kids in the ghetto look to the corner and see only one way to make that kind of money—two ways, if they're female. Once they've hung enough gold around their necks, drunk enough Courvoisier, driven enough rented Escalades, they're more likely to end up in jail than to give it up for a legal job.

"The War on Drugs has been a resounding failure," said Rowena Young, author of a 2002 report by the Foreign Policy Centre. "Rarely in the history of wars have so many achieved so little at such a high cost." The report attributes the debacle to the government's disregard for the link between poverty and addiction. "The key issue is not the availability of drugs, but rather the problematic drug use caused by social exclusion."

The War on Drugs takes prisoners, among them the Drug Court kids and millions of kids like them. Will another generation of children grow up with their mothers strung out, their fathers serving "three-strike" life sentences, their neighborhoods devastated by gunfire, poverty, and drugs? Or can this one Drug Court interrupt that cycle—in this one county, for this one handful of kids?

"I get choked up, looking at you," Lois Haight, former U.S. Assistant Attorney General, now Contra Costa County's Juvenile Court Presiding Judge, told the four kids graduating from Drug Court in June 2002. "This is not an easy program to get through. It takes a lot of hard work, a lot of self-analysis. You've had the courage to break off bad friendships, the courage to return to school, become employed, reconnect with your families. You've set goals and accomplished them. Congratulations on a job well done."

As he handed them their cookies and Certificates of Graduation, shook their hands, and released them from probation, Judge Steve Easton wore his black robes and an ear-to-ear grin. "These are some of the bravest people I've ever met," he told the parents, county officials, counselors, and kids assembled for the ceremony in the Choices "courtroom." He addressed the graduates. "You weren't on a good course when you came in here, but you're on one now. You'll have healthy, happy kids. You'll be able to serve your fellow man. I'm so proud to be part of your lives."

When I congratulated him at the reception that followed, Kevin Charles said, "It ain't perfect. But it's the only end game we've got." I looked at him questioningly. He explained.

"The government had a problem with the Vietnam war: they had no end game, no way to get out without admitting defeat. They have the same problem now with the War on Drugs."

He gestured at the four graduates in their sagging pants, skintight miniskirts, tattoos, and piercings, chowing down on chicken wings and sugar-frosted graduation cake. "They're it: the end game. The only way out is saving these kids."

By the middle of February Zalika has pretty much stopped going to school. Her disenchantment with Choices too is complete. She skips program once or twice a week and blows off her individual sessions with Ursula, who finally manages to pull Zalika and June into their second "weekly" family session in three months. "Ursula kept asking my mom the same stupid questions: How am I doing, does our family eat dinner together?" Zalika tells me the next day. "We told her, it's best if I eat by myself so I don't get into it with my dad. Ursula said, 'I want you to eat dinner with your family at least three out of seven days.' I wanted to knock her in her *head*. But we said we'd do it, just to shut her up.

"She said I need to pull in closer to her. She got her nerve. *Please.* These people think you can treat every child the same way. Well, you can't. Tom's the only one at the program who's cool to me."

"I thought you were mad at him."

"I just *love* Tom," she corrects me. "Tom do everything he can for us kids. Problem is, it's not too much he can do."

A few nights later, June gets a call from Pam. "She's saying they might put Zalika in the Hall for three months, then send her to placement," June tells me, "because she's not going to school, not taking the program seriously. Maybe some time in the Hall will have a good effect . . ."

I recognize the hopelessness in her voice. "I can't understand why Zalika won't do the things she has to do," June says. "Come home by a certain time like everyone else does. Go to school like everybody else does . . ."

June falls silent. "Just when you get your hopes up that she's going to do better, it's another turnaround," she says then. "I told Pam I think Zalika might have a chemical imbalance. I asked her if the judge could order some psychological tests. Pam said to get her checked out physically first. She said sometimes hormones make a person crazy.

"I'm going to make an appointment with Zalika's doctor. Maybe if I can get her to go, her problems can be corrected."

I don't contradict June's fresh hope. I'm amazed that she still has some. And despite my distaste for drugging drug-abusing kids, I feel a wiggle of optimism myself. Maybe Paxil *would* settle her, or Lithium . . .

"I sat down at my computer and started writing my book," Zalika tells me at eight-thirty Sunday morning—an early call, even for her. "All this stuff started pouring out. You have to promise not to laugh at me when you hear it."

"I promise," I say, and she starts reading.

Over the summer I met Marcus Jackson in San Rafael at a Circle K gas station, and ever since my life changed drastically for better or worse I don't know, I guess it just depends on how you look at it. I was homeless when he came along and put me up on the game of prostitution. I absolutely hated it, but it was so much money involved I just couldn't stop even at my worst moments in the streets.

So how did it all start, you ask? I guess it all started when I was six. My sister used to live here. We have the same dad but different moms. When she was living here she used to touch me in all the wrong sisterly ways.

So there was my second sexual experience 'cause the first was with my cousin who I thought I loved more than any other family member until I was old enough to understand that what he had done to and with me about four times a month was wrong and taking my innocence away at an early age.

This was happening for so long that I can't remember what it was like to not be touched by anyone and to feel clean, fresh, totally untouched. Now I'm trying to figure out if it's the right time to tell people in my life what's been going on with me for the last years I've been fucking up.

My family thinks I'm crazy or some sex maniac or something, but if they knew what I know about my life they would see the logic behind my behavior, if there is any. As of right now I can finally say that my life is going smoother than it's been in a very long time. I'm in a stable relationship with one person for a change. I'm in this program for my probation called Choices, it's for adolescents and juveniles who have had a past of drug use and stuff . . .

"That's how far I got," Zalika says.

"Oh, honey," I say. Whether she's lying now, or always, or never; whatever it is that's hurt her so badly, this much I know is true. Zalika is one wounded child. "Have you told your parents?"

"We don't have the kind of family where you can talk about a thing like that. My dad would freak out."

I tell her I'll be there in an hour, and that I'll bring the name of a good therapist I know. I've suggested therapy to Zalika several times before; for the first time, now, she promises to go.

When I get there, the house is dark. No one answers the doorbell or the phone.

Zalika doesn't show up at school or at Choices the next day. She doesn't answer the phone. That night I call Bo. He says she's not there. Two minutes later, Zalika calls me back from his house.

"I'm sitting here thinking if I should cut my ankle monitor and go," she tells me, her words slurred. "I don't feel like goin' to court tomorrow. I'm tired of the whole thing. Hol' on." I hear her close a door, then pick up the phone again. "I called Marcus," she says. "He's in Texas. He says I can go to Texas next week if I want to. Some track out there someplace."

"Zalika," I begin, but she cuts me off again.

"Funny thing is, I'm just now realizing I need that damn drug program." And I'm just now realizing she's drunk. "I never thought of myself as being like those weed heads. But I am. I need to smoke. I wish I could hit some weed right now.

"The judge was right," she goes on. "I been drinking like a motherfucker every day. I go down to the store and get me a Smirnoff Ice and drink it. Then I go back and get me another one. I been drinking about five a day."

"What do you really want, Zalika?"

"I wanna be left alone," she answers without hesitation. "I need to get my mind together. But I can't do it with all this pressure to do it at a certain time and a certain place with certain people. I don't want people running into me all the time like they God. More than anything I wanna be left alone by probation."

"You know how to do that," I say, "if that's what you really want."

"Maybe I want money even more than I want to get off probation," she admits. "And freedom. Yep, yep. *That's* what I want. Instant freedom."

"Zalika's going on the run." June calls me on Tuesday as I'm on my way to court. "She says she's going to get her GED, work till she's eighteen, wait till her juvenile cases go away."

"They won't," I tell June. She doesn't seem surprised to hear it.

"Did you see the story in the paper about that young prostitute who was killed in San Francisco yesterday?" she asks.

I say yes. I don't tell her what Zalika told me: the dead girl was a former co-worker of hers.

"Killed and left naked," June repeats. "Zalika can't earn her living that way. It's too dangerous. One of those men might kill her." June's voice is flat, as if she's talking about her daughter driving faster than the speed limit or dating an unlikable boy. This is what living with a child in crisis does, I know. It makes the unthinkable mundane.

"She wants me to go get them, give Bo a ride to court," June adds. "She says she'll wait outside in the car. Maybe we can convince her to come in once we get there."

Again, I don't argue, but I know Zalika's ready to run. There's nothing we can do this time to stop her.

As I wait in the courthouse lobby, I exchange pleasantries with Aaron, who's been in the Hall since he got caught stealing yet another car. And Jordan—fourteen months into the program, two weeks away from graduation, he relapsed, ran, and came back to start again. Here's Diamond, looking sober and determined, and Tiffany, smelling of booze.

June appears, beckons me outside. Zalika's sitting on the concrete wall, dressed in her "Fuck you, Drug Court" best: a bright red top and bright blue skintight jeans. Bo's sitting beside her.

"Tell her not to run," Bo begs me. "She 'bout to do somethin' hella stupid."

Zalika smiles at me. I've never seen her look so happy. She jumps up, envelops me in a hug. "You really didn't think I'd go, did you?" she whispers in my ear. "But I'm surprised it took this long."

I ask where she's going to sleep tonight.

"Bo's," she says. "My mom said she'd drive me there. If that don't work out, *you* know where I'm goin'."

I make her promise to call me, even if it's from Texas.

"Every day," she says. "Bo's getting me a cell phone so we can stay in touch."

She looks around at her mother, at Bo, at me. "Look at y'all's faces!" she laughs.

"I'm sad," I say. Will I see her tomorrow? Next week? Never?

"I don't feel too good, neither," Bo says, his eyes glued to Zalika's.

She touches his cheek tenderly, turns to June. "I'm ready to go."

Zalika throws her arms to the sky, her expression euphoric.

"My freedom!" she cries. "I'm gonna be *free!*" Then she runs to the silver Infiniti and waits for her mother to drive her away.

Upstairs, in Drug Court, Judge Easton issues a warrant for Zalika's arrest.

PART 4

GETTING OUT

How Can We Get
Kids Off Drugs?

MIKE

Self-Surrender

Mike's gone. I leave the boys in their Conflict Resolution group, stumble downstairs, stand in the mattress-store doorway staring at the house across the street—as if Mike might come bounding out the front door if I stare at it hard enough.

But no. Mike's gone.

Now what? Do I call his mom? His dad? His therapist? Get in my car and try to find him? Go back upstairs and pick another kid?

Wait. I know how to track down a missing boy. I've had plenty of practice trying to find Jesse. I do now what I used to do then: close my eyes, channel his thoughts. If I were Mike, where would I go?

The bus station, of course. The first thing he'd do is get out of town. There's nothing for Mike here but heat. No parents, no friends, no money; no cigarettes, no beer, no crank. First, though, I need information. Ron, the day-shift supervisor, looks up from his desk. Mike's file is open in front of him as if he's expecting me. I sit down, noticing for the first time a sign on the wall that says, "There are no crises we don't agree to have."

"Hakim came to me before breakfast," Ron begins. "He told me Mike's bed wasn't made. A few of his belongings were missing—enough to make a road trip.

"We started the AWOL procedure: searched the property, counted the clients. I called Danny, the police, the parents, the PO. The police came. We gave them Mike's picture. They'll put him on a flyer listing him as a runaway child and distribute it electronically to other police departments."

"What happens when—if—they find him?"

"They'll ask us if we want him back," Ron says. "That'll be up to Danny. Our inclination is to come from a caring place, to make exceptions, especially with someone as charming as Mike. But this would be the second time he's come here and left."

"What we do here is behavior modification. We don't cave in like an enabling parent would." Translation: if the cops catch him, Mike will go straight to the Hall to serve his three-year sentence. Mike knows all of this, of course. And he knows how to disappear to avoid it. The realization lands in my chest with a thud. I might never see him again.

"Do you know what time he left?"

"Between six-thirty and seven. He could have gone through a window or out the front door."

"Can I see his room?"

Ron walks me through the spotless, silent house. "There may be some good that'll stay with him," he says. "A lot has been brought to Mike's attention, whether he wants to accept it or not."

I step into the room Mike shares—shared—with Henry. If a room could talk, this one would be saying, "Fuck Center Point." Hangers, clothes, and shoes are strewn everywhere. Mike's plaid button-down shirt and black jeans are spread out on the floor, as if Mike were a snowman who melted away in the night. The bed looks as if a battle was fought in it—and maybe indeed one was. Was it a struggle or a reflex, I wonder, this decision of Mike's to run again?

Only Mike's dresser is still up to Center Point standards. His bottles of shampoo, acne soap, and deodorant are turned to the wall, as Mike always left them—ever hungry for a morsel of privacy, a crumb of control. Only one of his toiletries has been turned face-out: a bullet-shaped cylinder of mousse called "Head Games."

As I was trained by my own disappearing son to do, I check the only available indicator of Mike's intentions. Which shoes was he wearing when he left? The brand-new Stacy Adams desert boots his mom just sent him—his favorites, not yet broken in, unsuitable for walking long distances—are still in the closet. His next favorites, a month-old pair of Adidas sneakers, aren't. "Face it," I tell myself. "Mike's not taking a walk around the block to cool off. He's gone."

I ask Ron to call me if he hears anything. I go to my car, leave a message on Barbara's cell phone, then one for Tess at home. I reach Michael in his truck.

"I raised him to where he's pretty self-sufficient," Michael says. "So I'm not really worried about him. There was too much nitpicky bullshit at that place. Mike's all boy, sure. But pushing a kid like they did—it was too much for anybody."

Michael promises to call me if he hears anything. I start cruising the streets of downtown San Rafael, looking for a tall, husky kid in Adidas, just as I used to cruise the streets of Oakland desperate for the sight of a tall, lean kid in Air Jordans. I notice for the first time how many bars there are, and that they're all open at eleven in the morning. Might Mike be drinking his first beer in sixty-eight days? No. Not here, anyway.

My cell phone rings. "He's at his dad's," Barbara says breathlessly. I recognize the terrible relief in her voice; I've heard it so many times in my own. Who cares if the kid's wanted by the law, if he's just screwed up the next three years of his life? He's safe for the moment. He's alive.

"I'm praying he'll go back to Center Point," she says. "But Meredith, he didn't run off. He didn't disappear." We breathe in that information together. "I'll call you later," Barbara says. "I just didn't want you to worry."

The phone rings again in my hand. "What's *up*, Meredith?" Mike exclaims. "How you *doin'*?" He sounds elated, energized. Is this a lively Mike I've never known, outside the Center Point monotone zone? Or is he already . . .

"I'm staying in touch with you because I'm not going back to using. And I'm not going on the run. I'm gonna hang out with my dad for the weekend, go see my mom Sunday. On Monday I'm turning myself in."

"I'm so glad you called," I say. "But Mike—are you sure you don't want to try to go back to Center Point, or some other—"

"No way," he interrupts me. "I'm through with fake-ass Tess and money-grubbing Danny. I'll serve my time in Juvenile Hall, get it over with, get on with my life. You can come visit me in the Hall. Okay?"

"Okay," I say. "What made you decide to run?"

"Lyle gave me two LEs last night," he says. "Then I called Richard a faggot. They put me on Contract. That was *it*."

"Did any of the kids know you were going?"

"I told most of 'em the night before. They didn't rat on me." So much for therapeutic community members "supporting" each other.

"Juanita woke me up at six-thirty. I had my bag packed. I went out my bedroom window, ran downtown, took the bus to Rohnert Park. Two seconds after I got off the bus—I swear!—this dude tried to sell me some crank."

"Where'd you get the money for the bus?" The clients aren't supposed to have any, ever.

"A friend at Center Point," he answers evasively, honoring the boys' own code of confidentiality. "Sue came to the bus stop and picked me up. She's pretty upset with me. Everyone's pretty upset with me. We went to my dad's. He's living in a motor home in my grandma and grandpa's yard. We ate some Mexican food. It tasted *hella* good after all that Center Point crap. I'm gonna go see my mom tomorrow. My dad's gonna bring the jet ski."

Talk about your mixed messages, I think, feeling a flash of anger at Michael. And then I think, no wonder the program people beat up on parents all the time. Look how easy it is to do.

I hear a deep voice yelling in the background. "My dad's mad at me for being on the phone," Mike says. "I'll call you tomorrow."

"Fake-ass Tess" calls me as I'm driving home. Even though Mike was raging at everyone in the house last night, she says, she didn't expect him to run. "Whenever I asked him if he felt like AWOLing, he'd say, 'No, I've already put my parents through enough.' That was part of the problem: he was always doing it for his parents, not himself."

Tess says she got more "emotional" about Mike's AWOL than anyone else on the staff. "Mike's leaving broke my heart. I invested a lot of time in him. But I don't know if he ever really attached to me." Tess is silent for a moment. "Mike's attachments tend to be superficial. He has a real conflict with independence versus dependence."

"Unlike most seventeen-year-olds?" I think, but don't say.

"Also, Mike's drug use is addict use, not recreational use," Tess goes on. "Mike thinks he can drink beer because it's not his drug of choice. I think if he drinks beer he'll relapse on crank.

"Unlike some of the staff, I drink wine with dinner. But I'm not an addict. I'm a doctoral candidate. I've never stolen money to buy alcohol. I've never been arrested. I don't think Mike understands the difference. His dad certainly doesn't.

"To be honest," Tess confides, "I feel very strongly that his parents were a big cause of Mike's problems." I wince, knowing what's coming next. Parent blaming is the hammer in every therapist's toolbox. Tess wields hers like the avid apprentice she is.

"Mike has a great mom. But the dad still uses. His boundaries with Mike are not appropriate; they're friend to friend instead of father and child. The kids who are successful in the program are the ones whose parents realize they haven't been able to do it, so they hand the responsibility over to us. Mike's parents never did that."

No, they didn't. And neither did I when my son was a ward of the court. The day Jesse started getting into trouble was the day I started being blamed for it: for not disciplining him enough—guilty. For not taking enough responsibility for what he said and did—guilty. For raising him in a "broken home," as Mike's mom did. For making excuses for him, as Tristan's mom did. For wanting him to be more like me, or at least more understandable to me, as Zalika's parents did—guilty, guilty, guilty. There weren't enough hours in the day for me to feel as bad as I was supposed to feel about the terrible mom I was being—while continuing, apparently, to be one.

Then, suddenly, the accusations changed. Because Jesse was seventeen, not fifteen? Because his crimes became more serious? Because his new probation officer had memorized a different formula? I never knew. But now, suddenly, I was failing to *relinquish* responsibility, to hold *Jesse* accountable, to "let go and let him grow up." The charges were different, but the culpability was the same. And so were the effects on me. When I wasn't hating myself for screwing up my son, I was hating myself for the relief I felt when a therapist or PO heaped the blame on Jesse's father instead.

Parent blaming has much to recommend it. It's endorsed by the psycho-analytic masters, disseminated by their disciples, and so easy to practice; anyone can do it and pretty much everyone does. We're in a mess with our teenagers—as individuals, as a nation. We need a target for our confusion and our grief. Parents make a good one, or so it seems. They're everywhere, they're fallible, and they'll take whatever anyone's dishing out on the off chance it might help their kids.

The problem is, it doesn't. Our kids do best when we think and expect the best of them. The same is true of their parents. The people who helped me be a better mother to Jesse were the ones who pointed out his strengths, and mine, the ones who reminded me that his path was his to stride or stumble down, the ones who showed me a better way to be with him by stepping in and being that way with him themselves. I was already on my knees with self-recrimination and sorrow. There was nothing to be gained for Jesse by knocking me any flatter.

Yes, parents screw up—just about every day, in just about every way. Yes, kids' problems are a product, in part, of their parents'. But when a kid falls down, the whole family needs a hand up. The institutions and individuals who take care of other people's kids need to be trained and funded and screened to make sure that's what they do. To start with, they need to be expert at ferreting out—and expressing—what parents are doing *right* with their kids, then building an improvement plan from that foundation of mutual respect.

I had the opportunity to do it both ways, so I know this as surely as I know my name. It's challenging to be the great parent of a teenager who's doing well. It's impossible to be the great parent of a teenager who's not.

The real problem with parent blaming is, we have seen the enemy, and it is us.

"As soon as Ron called me, I knew where Mike was going," Danny tells me. "To see mom and dad. That was his fix."

I throw diplomacy to the winds and ask if that's a problem, really: a seventeen-year-old boy who runs away to be *with* his parents.

"The problem," Danny retorts, "is that Mike is an addict. To stay sober he needs to learn new ways of dealing with his issues. And neither his parents nor Juvenile Hall can teach him that. In Juvenile Hall Mike's not gonna turn to the guy he's sharing a cell with and say 'I'm hurting right now.'"

I don't point out that Mike never turned to the guy he was sharing a room with at Center Point and said that either. Nor was he likely to.

Maybe because he's the father of a fourteen-year-old himself, Danny manifests more compassion for "the parents" than most staffers do. "I hear from moms and dads that there's a lack of communication from the system," he says. "They get a call from a PO saying, 'Your kid's going into Center Point. If you have any questions, call Center Point.' It's overwhelming to hear that their kid is this far out of control that the courts have decided to put him into a residential treatment program. The parents feel, 'What did I do, what didn't I do?'"

I ask whether *he* feels that way when clients do what Mike just did— and several others have done in the short time I've been around.

"AWOLs are real typical of programs like ours," Danny says. "But still, when we get a lot of them, I personalize it. I'm the one who does the initial assessments. I pick the clients. What I can't get a handle on is, what makes them say enough is enough?"

Answering his own question, Danny says that kids leave therapeutic communities more than adults do because they want sobriety less. "Kids are fresh into the system. They haven't experienced the losses the adults have. They've lost their freedom, maybe their relationship with their parents—if they ever had one. They haven't hit the kind of bottom that can turn an addict around.

"I used to assess adults inside the jails," he continues. "Everybody wanted treatment because they wanted out of prison. But the kids will sit in the Hall and say 'I'd rather stay here.' At the Hall they can stay in their cell all day. They don't have the stress of people asking them about their feelings."

Danny's efforts are thwarted too, he says, by the diminishing pool of appropriate candidates from which to choose. "There are more and more kids in the Hall who are dual diagnosed," Danny says, "and fewer and fewer programs for them." Center Point is rated Level 9 in the statewide group home–rating system, which goes from Level 14 (facilities authorized to treat

clients needing the most mental-health intervention) to Level 1 (authorized to treat clients who need the least).

"A kid with an arson or rape charge or a recent suicide attempt isn't
coming to Center Point," Danny explains. So there's ever fiercer competition for healthy specimens like Mike. "You want the pick of the litter,"
Danny says flatly. "When I get a packet on a kid I want, I have to turn it
around *fast*. The PO who sent that packet to me sent it to two other programs too. If I say I can't meet the kid till next Thursday, somebody else
will get him.

"I'd like to see the adolescent programs work together to meet the needs
of the kids, instead of competing on the business aspect," Danny muses. But,
as Mike never hesitates to point out, it's the business aspect that makes
Center Point run. "We get paid by the kid by the night. If we have vacan-
cies, that costs. As soon as a kid's head hits the pillow we bill for him. When
a kid leaves, we only get paid for the nights he was here."

Each probation department that places a child at Center Point pays the
program $4,479 a month through Medi-Cal, unless the parents can afford
some or all of the $5,000 private-pay fee. Currently, Danny says, there isn't
one client "paying private."

"There are a whole lot more kids who need help than there are programs to help them," Danny says. "The adult population got Prop 36 [the
state ballot measure passed in 2000 providing treatment instead of incarceration to qualifying addicts]. Supposedly there's something like that in the
works for adolescents. But until that happens, this is what we have. And it
just plain isn't enough."

At six o'clock on the Sunday evening after Mike's escape, I pull into the
parking lot of the Rincon Valley Seven-Eleven, where he's chosen to spend
his last free moments before he goes back to the Hall. Mike and Barbara are
waiting for me in Barbara's bright blue convertible. She unfolds herself from
the car—a tall, well-built woman in an ankle-length black tank dress and
platform sandals, her auburn shoulder-length hair streaked with henna. We
exchange hugs, and I turn to Mike.

I swear his skin looks better already, his eyes more alive. I've never seen
him smoking before—the closest thing the boys managed to smuggle into

Center Point was chewing tobacco—but he's making up for lost nicotine now, puffing hungrily on one Parliament after another. "I'm cool," he answers before I ask. "I'm gonna get this over with. Then I'm never going back."

Barbara tells me to follow her in my car, and tells Mike to go with me. She says the five-mile ride to the Hall will give Mike and me a chance to catch up, but I suspect she needs a little distance right now herself.

"It's a hundred degrees out," Mike says as we pass the McDonald's where he jumped out of Danny's truck less than three months ago. "And they got no air conditioning in the Hall." He stares out the window. "That's aiight. It won't stay hot for too long."

He lights a new Parliament with the ember of the last one. "I'm gonna know a bunch of people in there," he says, exhaling noisily. "That'll be cool."

Mike tells me about his "forty-eight hours of normal life," chilling with his dad and Sue, trying out his new jet ski with his mom. "It's so peaceful out there by the lake," he says, his face as soft as a sated child's. "And I got to spend some time with my grandma too."

He draws deeply on his cigarette. "So Meredith—we're still doing the book, right?"

I tell him we are indeed, and ask why he wants to do it.

"Because I know I'm gonna make it. Because I have a good story that's gonna help people understand. I may not be program material . . ."

"How many of the trained professionals in his life have told him *that*?" I wonder.

". . . but I'm definitely book material."

Ahead of us, Barbara turns left onto Pythian Road. Mike's body tenses. "Damn. Here I am again." The signs for Los Guillicos Juvenile Detention Center appear before us. "I can do this. I can do this," he repeats like a mantra. "I'm gonna make it. I'm gonna make it."

We park our cars and walk slowly past a cinder-block wall crowned with rusty curls of barbed wire, toward the low white stucco building where Mike will surrender to the law.

"Let's sit down and talk for a minute, Mike," Barbara says. She leads us to a picnic table chained to the wall. Barbara looks intently at her son. He busies himself lighting a cigarette. The tension is thick. I look up and see a rough-hewn sign hanging above us, its letters carved into a redwood slab.

ORDER FROM WITHIN

"Wow," I say. "Is that some kind of Zen message? Are they trying to give the kids some spiritual guidance, or what?"

Barbara cocks her head quizzically at the sign, then erupts into peals of laughter. "It's an ad!" she tells me. "The kids make these picnic tables here. If you want to buy one, you . . ."

She's laughing so hard, she can't finish the sentence. "Order from within," I say, and soon we're both hysterical. Mike smokes and ignores us, his eyes on the ground.

Barbara chokes and gasps, wipes her eyes with a Kleenex. She looks at her son, suddenly dead serious. "Are you sure you don't want to go back to Center Point, Mike? Why would you rather do three years in here than—"

"I'll be able to see my parents twice a week," Mike interrupts her. "Anyway, Mom, I'm not gonna do three years. They just say that stuff to scare us."

"Mike." Barbara puts her hand on her son's, strokes it tenderly. "You've already bailed from a couple of programs. They're not just going to give you two weeks and let you out. Even if they do that, if you want to come live with me, you'll have to live up to my standards.

"Dave and I have a really peaceful life now. And we like it like that. I don't want the police coming to my house anymore. I don't want to drive you for drug testing at seven o'clock in the morning or to Drug Court an hour away . . ." Barbara takes a deep breath. "That being said, I'll go a million miles for you if I think you're trying."

"I'll never use speed again," Mike declares. "It's the only way my life's gonna stay together."

"I'm not saying I don't believe you, honey," Barbara says gently, her hand fluttering to her son's cheek. "I'm just saying I have to see it. There's been a lot of times you've told me you weren't using and I found out later it was a lie. Do you understand that?"

"Yeah." Mike stubs out his cigarette. "But I've learned some stuff about myself. For one, I'm a very impatient person. That's part of why I used the drug I did. I might even have ADD."

"Were you self-medicating, you think?" Barbara asks.

Mike can't muster the patience to answer. He jumps to his feet. "I'm ready to do this. Let's go."

Barbara stands too, and pulls her son to her. "I know you're not doing this to hurt me. I know this is your life. I know you're not a baby anymore." She starts to cry. "I'm just so sorry I have to take you in there and leave you."

Mike hugs her quickly, then steps away. "I'll be okay in a couple days. Don't worry about me, Mom."

We walk up to the door marked "Admissions." Mike knocks. A buzzer sounds. The three of us enter a tiny room. Mike steps up to the counter, spreads his arms apart, palms up. "I'm self-surrendering," he says into the vent in the glass partition.

"Hi, Mike. It's Butler, right?" The woman turns away, types into her computer.

"Yeah. How you doin', Melissa?" Mike greets her.

Melissa frowns and turns back to him. "They haven't signed the warrant yet, Mike. The computer won't let me accept you."

Barbara laughs, that hearty, half-hysterical laugh. "I guess you're coming home with me, Pooh," she says.

"Come back tomorrow, Mike," Melissa says. "We'll get you in."

"You'd think we were trying to get him into college," Barbara whispers to me.

Melissa buzzes us out. We stand blinking in the sunset's smoldering glow. Mike is glowing too.

"I never thought I'd be going back out that door!" he crows. He turns to Barbara. "Give me my cigarettes. Give me the cell phone. I gotta call Bobby. He won't believe this!"

As I turn onto Highway 101 for the two-hour drive home, I consider this turn of events from Mike's perspective. According to what he's told me, he's gotten away with ten to twenty crimes, many of them felonies, for every one that he's been accused of. He spent seven months buying and doing speed, driving stolen cars without a license, and drawing a paycheck in the same county where there was a warrant for his arrest. He's run from two drug programs (twice from one of them) and did drugs while he was in two others. And now Mike decides he's ready for a little juvenile justice, but the juvenile justice system isn't ready for him.

Gee, I wonder why kids think they can outsmart the system.

We accuse parents of not being accountable enough for their kids' behavior, but what about the accountability of the system that's supposed to contain and rehabilitate them when they spin out of their parents' control? "Giving kids consequences lets them know you love them," the parenting books say, and they're right. A sloppy, inept system that can't give kids the consequences it threatens sends the same message as a bumbling parent— but without the redeeming factor of love.

Three days later, the bailiff ushers Barbara, her boyfriend, Dave, and me into the Los Guillicos courtroom. It's a small, pleasant room, with windows overlooking a tangled twist of oak limbs and, through them, the grassy Juvenile Hall campus.

An armed guard escorts Mike—in green prison jumpsuit and the infamous beige "Chucks"—into the courtroom. Mike gives Barbara a long, longing look and takes a seat beside his public defender, a middle-aged man in a worn tweed sport coat and scuffed cowboy boots.

"Mike, there's a petition filed stating that you left placement," the judge says from the bench. "You understand you can be committed for thirty-seven months?"

"Yes.

"You left placement on September 28 and no one knew where you were. Do you admit that?"

"Yes, I do."

"My client feels placement isn't necessary," Mike's public defender says. "And Probation isn't optimistic about the chance of him completing a placement. He self-surrendered. He'll be eighteen soon. They've done what they can for him at Center Point. I'd ask the court to give him ninety days in Juvenile Hall."

The DA speaks up. "I don't want to send the message that you run from a one-year placement and you get to come back and do ninety days of Hall time."

"I agree," the judge says angrily. "This county has certainly done everything in its power to help this young man. And I don't see that he's received any benefit from it at all. Mike, do you have any thoughts on the matter?"

"I didn't leave Center Point for seventy-five days. I got out of it what I could," Mike answers crisply, with no trace of his usual drawl.

The judge frowns. "You exhibit all the classic signs of still being an addict," he says. "I wouldn't bet on a positive outcome for you, unless you change your mind about some things. I'm half tempted to send you to the Youth Authority."

Barbara gasps. I want to raise my hand and ask the judge, "Can you do that to a kid who's never actually been convicted of a crime?"

"I'm a firm believer in giving kids chances, Mike," the judge continues, "but enough chances have gone down." Barbara grabs Dave's hand, then mine. Her palm is clammy.

The judge sighs and shakes his head. "I sentence you to ninety to one hundred twenty days in Juvenile Hall."

Mike twists around in his chair and gives us the thumbs-up, grinning.

"I feel very badly about the outcome of this case," the judge concludes. "You're being rewarded for violating the terms of your probation, Mike, and that is very damaging to the credibility we have here. This hearing is adjourned."

"He gambled, and he won. Again." Sitting across from me in a Rincon Valley coffee shop, Barbara lifts her latté glass and clinks it against mine. "It's weird to feel like celebrating that my kid's in Juvenile Hall," she says. "But having him in there is the only way I can relax."

"It's not weird to me." I tell her about the time Jesse was in the Hall, and Jesse's dad and I discovered we were feeling the same thing: "The only time I don't look for Jesse in the back of a cop car," Richard told me, "is when he's in jail."

"Exactly," Barbara says. "God. Am I'm still gonna be doing this when my kid is thirty-five years old—only then it'll be San Quentin?"

She blows on her coffee, puts the glass down. "I can't stop asking myself, where did I fail my son? I know a baby is born with a complete personality. But I also know that environment can shape what happens. And God knows I've made mistakes. I wanted to give Mike this *Leave It to Beaver* life. I didn't.

"I had really bad postpartum depression after Mike was born. He was my salvation, the thing that kept me from saying 'Fuck it, I can't go on.' Then Michael and I divorced. Mike became very sickly, almost like he was mourning and couldn't express it any other way."

Barbara twists a napkin between her fingers. "When Mike was in ninth grade, the school told me he had ADD. They wanted me to put him on Ritalin. I refused. I insisted that they test him. *Then* they found out that Mike has learning disabilities.

"This kid always hated school, always acted out, always refused to do the work. Everyone said he was a brat. Mike developed a lot of insecurities, a real sense of inferiority from not being a whiz-bang student. And it turns out he was struggling all that time."

She pulls a neatly folded sheet of binder paper from her purse. "Mike wrote this in his ninth-grade English class. I brought it to show you," she says. "How could I have read this and not understood?"

"PLEASE DO NOT POST" is penciled in Mike's chicken-scratch penmanship across the top of the page. Below it, this poem:

> I am a short white boy
> I wonder why people wear dog collars
> I hear a ringing in my head
> I want a car
> I am a short white boy.
> I pretend that I fight.
> I feel I have got shot
> I touch the clouds
> I worry that I will get beat up.
> I cry when my grandpa died.
> I am a short white boy
> I understand I go to school
> I say I will get good grades
> I dream I will die
> I try at school

I hope to get good grades
I am a short white boy.

"I try not to buy into that long-held belief that Mom gets the big rose pinned on her for all of her kid's problems," Barbara says. "But it doesn't matter what you believe is the cause of it. When you're dealing with the heartbreak of your child, you have a hole in your heart."

On Thursday nights, now, I drive to Los Guillicos, greet Melissa, sign the Visitors' Log, affix a VISITOR sticker to my shirt, lock my briefcase in a locker, and stand with the parents waiting to see their kids. Most of them are white and Latino. Some have small children in tow. All of them are grim-faced. We stand elbow to elbow in silence until seven twenty-five, when Melissa buzzes us in.

Guards scan each of us with metal detectors, then nod us on to the next set of locked doors. At seven-thirty another guard flings those open and steps aside. We burst through them like racehorses at the starting gate, speed-walking past a playing field and a series of one-story beige stucco buildings, the units where the residents of Los Guillicos sleep, eat, watch TV, and attend school. Each has its cheerful-sounding Spanish name displayed on a plaque: Casa Bonita, Casa La Paz, Casa Felice. A unit supervisor stands in every doorway, checking the parents' passes before ushering them inside. This could be a boarding school on back-to-school night, were it not for the metal mesh covering the windows, the razor-wire warning atop the walls.

As each boy's visitors arrive, his unit supervisor summons him to the day room, its scarred walls plastered with colorful posters of football players, muscle cars, and heavy metal concerts. The boys shuffle in wearing grayed white T-shirts, navy blue nylon shorts—they switch to sweats, as fall cools to winter—grayed white socks, and beige Chucks or rubber flip-flops. The "residents" and their visitors pull beige plastic chairs up to beige plastic tables. Some of them talk intently; some play cards in silence. Sometimes the mothers cry.

Mike makes good on his word. He does better in the Hall than he did at Center Point. "I'm getting thirty points every day," he brags, showing me a behavior chart on the day-room wall. Sure enough, Mike Butler is well on his way from Level One (meals in his eight-by-ten-foot cement "room," no privileges, bedtime at six) to Level Two (day-room privileges, TV and radio, bedtime at eight-thirty). In a few weeks, he tells me, he hopes to make it to Level Four (all that, plus a nine-thirty lights-out and a candy bar every night). Mike Butler is a model prisoner.

If the experts are right—if Mike needs treatment in order to live a sober life, maybe even to stay alive at all—this interlude of enforced sobriety will prove to be just that: a vacation from his addiction, a postponement of the inevitable. We're hoping, of course, that Mike will prove the experts wrong, that his seventy-five crank-free days at Center Point will pile onto his ninety crank-free days here to form the foundation of a new, sober, self-aware life, a new, sober, self-aware Mike. I know too much to believe it. We all do. But in the moment we let ourselves hope. Mike is thriving in Juvenile Hall.

"You look good," I tell him.

He runs his hand across a few pimples on his forehead. "I'm breaking out like crazy. The food's disgusting. Long hairs in the oatmeal. The pastrami's green and shiny," he says. "But I'm doing push-ups in my room. And we get to play football every day. That's one reason I like it so much better here." He laughs, showing me his bruise-blotched arms. "If you got a beef with someone, you just hit 'em on the football field." I think of Danny, worrying that Mike wouldn't have anyone to talk to when he's hurting in the Hall. Mike doesn't need to talk, when he can tackle.

"I got lucky, Meredith." he tells me. "If they'd sent me to CYA or another drug program, I would have had to leave again. I'm so much happier here. You can cuss all you want, say whatever you want. And I get to see my parents."

"Seventy-three more days," Mike greets his dad as Michael walks into the day room. Michael hugs his son, pulls up a chair, gets down to business. "I found you a really cherry RX-7. I'm gonna have it waiting for you at your mom's when you get out."

"Is it a twin turbo?" Mike asks. "You know I really want a Mustang."

"Anything you want to talk about tonight, Mike?" Michael changes the subject.

"I've been freaked out that we're gonna get bombed or something," Mike answers, accommodating the quick switch. "Did you hear about the anthrax in Florida? What if we get bombed and I'm stuck in here? And I can't run? And I can't even be with my parents?"

"The Raiders are doing good," Michael says, as if Mike hasn't spoken. "But the Giants lost. How's school?" Marveling at the speedy maneuvers, I find myself thinking, "Like father, like . . ."

"Perfect," Mike says. "I'm gonna have like thirty-seven units when I get out of here. I'm gonna go for my GED."

"Mike! Do some long-run thinking here, would you? Get your diploma!" Michael lowers his voice. "I want you to be something better than a blue-collar guy. Be a lawyer. A banker! The world's open to you, son."

As I'm trying to picture Mike as a banker, a boy at the next table shouts, "Get me out of here! Just get me out of here!"

Mike ducks his head at the boy, grinning. "He came in here tweakin' yesterday," Mike whispers. "He's still tweakin'."

Michael looks at the clock on the wall. It's eight o'clock, halfway through the allotted hour. "Shit," he says. "I gotta get up at four-thirty tomorrow. Steve got fired. He tested positive for crank too many times."

Michael stands. Father and son embrace, clapping each other on the back. "I love you, son. You know that, right?"

"Yeah, Dad. I know."

"Don't forget what happened in your past," Michael offers a few parting words of advice. "But keep looking forward, son."

What does Mike have to look forward to?

The world may be open to him, but it doesn't feel that way to Mike. He doesn't have a high-school diploma; he's never been able to learn in a classroom. The kids he knows are all strung out, in rehab, or in jail. The men he knows are "blue-collar guys" like his dad and Steve, strung out and working construction—or just strung out.

I've spent hours talking to Mike about what he wants to "be," what moves him, trying to unearth the passions and talents that lie buried beneath his self-doubts and bravado. Driven to distraction by his only love—crank—he has trouble focusing on the question. Pressed and prodded, he says he'd like to own his own car-detailing shop, or build a race car, or drive one. (Somehow being a lawyer or a banker has never come up.)

Standing between Mike and anything he might love to do is a whole bunch of stuff he'd hate: go to school, work a straight job, save money, give up crank. What would motivate him to make that trade-off, to envision and create for himself a life that will sustain, not kill, him?

Despite a loving mom and a well-intentioned dad, Mike feels he is "a short white boy." He hears a ringing in his head. He dreams that he will die.

What could we have done for Mike, what can we do for him now, to keep that nightmare from coming true?

Weeks go by; a month; two. Mike continues to ascend the Juvenile Hall level system, to earn credits in the Juvenile Hall school. Between visits Mike and I correspond by mail. "It doesn't get harder or it doesn't get easier," he writes. "It's always the same."

> I'm confused about whether I want my GED or my diploma because the teachers are couraging me to get my GED but I know how much it means to my dad to get my diploma. . . .
>
> The only thing I miss about Center Point is the chew and a few kids. I do feel I got something out of it, like think before I do something, stuff like that. Even if you fake it you still get a lot out of it because you find out a lot of things about yourself. . . .
>
> I don't really miss crank at all cause the longer I don't do it the easier it is not to even think about it. I don't get tested in the Hall but I would never get spun in here because it sucks and I know that from prior experience and I'll tell u about that some time. I know I can't live a comfortable life if I start to use speed again. . . .
>
> Overall the food still sucks but I've been a Level IV for two weeks now I've got 47 days left. I'm hella happy and I hope to see you soon.
>
> Sincerely
> Mike Butler

Barbara does the math, figures out Mike's release date is New Year's Eve day. "Oh great," she groans. "Send the little junkie home on the rowdiest, stonedest day of the year."

As the countdown to Mike's release begins, his family's stress level escalates. The only definite is that Mike will live with Barbara and Dave—as long as he can abide by their rules. But what, Barbara, Dave, and Michael debate, should those rules be? Should they insist that Mike go to school every day? Get a job? Should they drug-test him once a week? Once a month? Never?

Should Mike be allowed to drink a beer—six beers?—while he's watching a football game with Dave? Smoke a joint while he's working on a car with his dad?

Will he be allowed to stay out overnight? Drive a car? Hang out with his old tweaker friends?

The biggest question, of course, is this. Will Mike go back to crank? And what will any of them do about it if he does?

Mike gets out of the Hall on Christmas Day, six days early. Two hours later he's at a party, drunk. By February, still swearing he'll never touch crank again, he admits to me that he's selling it. I don't tell Barbara. I don't have to. Mike's coming home with new stuff every day: a leather jacket, a stereo, a boat.

Two weeks after his eighteenth birthday in April, Mike is driving to his mom's house with some friends. He sees a sheriff's car in the rearview mirror. He reaches into the backseat to grab the joint they've all been smoking. The car swerves off the road, comes to a stop in a ditch. Mike swallows the joint. The cops pull up behind them, lights flashing. They ask to see Mike's driver's license. He doesn't have one. He says he can't find his wallet.

"What's wrong with you?" The cop shines his flashlight in Mike's eyes, presses his fingers against Mike's wrist. "Your pulse is 110. Been doing a little speed tonight, son?"

Mike tries to think straight. It's not easy; he's been tweaking hard for days. "I smoked a little weed a few hours ago, officer," he says, flashing his winning grin. The cop asks him to take a blood test. Mike refuses. He's not too high to know that driving under the influence of methamphetamines is a felony.

"Mike Butler, you're under arrest for driving under the influence, driving without a license, and lying to a police officer." The sheriff cuffs Mike, folds him into the back of his car, drives him to the Lake County jail.

This time, Mike gambled and lost.

TRISTAN

High Again

Clara pounces on me as I walk through her classroom door. "I need to talk to you about Tristan," she says. "He's going downhill, fast."

"I'm concerned about Tristan," Phoenix principal John Martin tells me later that day. "He's missing school, coming late, being defiant, acting out in class."

"Everybody's worried about Tristan. Including me," Eric says when I find him in the counseling office.

Well prepared by having witnessed Jesse's trajectory, and more recently Mike's, I'm not shocked by the possibility that Tristan's path might include a few detours. He's been warning me himself.

"After this semester, I can't go to Phoenix Academy anymore," he told me last week. "I don't wanna go to AA meetings. I know there'll be rules anywhere I go, but I want new ones. I really want to go to TEAM"—another Marin County alternative program, this one focused on outdoor experiential learning.

Champing at the bit now, he has a blowup with John Martin. "He said my necklace was a marijuana leaf," Tristan fumes. "I showed him it had six points, not five, but he took it from me anyway. What does he think—I'm gonna smoke my necklace?"

I ask John for his version. "We have reason to believe that Tristan's using again." He shows me the cabinet in his office where he stores confiscated beer bongs, crank pipes, marijuana paraphernalia, and now Tristan's necklace.

"Won't his UA tell you that?" I ask.

John shakes his head. "Check out the ads in *High Times* magazine. They'll sell you urine, they'll sell you goldenseal, they'll give you recipes to make your test come out clean. You think the kids don't do that?" In fact, I know they do. Several kids at Phoenix have shared their recipes with me, including some so research-intensive I suggested to Clara (to no avail) that she give them science credit for devising them.

I ask Eric for his thoughts on Tristan's latest shift. "We had a really powerful session the other day," he says. "He sobbed through most of it, talking about how he can't get any support at home for being sober. I think it scared him to get that vulnerable with me."

Eric runs his hand through his hair. "His mom called this morning. She thinks he relapsed at a concert this weekend."

"What does Tristan say?"

Who's crazy here? I wonder. Me, for believing that Tristan wouldn't lie, or the people who said they trusted him and suddenly don't?

"He says he didn't use. I believe him. But no one else does. Including Marian," Eric responds.

Imagining how that must feel to Tristan, I ask where I can find him.

"Detention," Eric says.

I wait for him outside the portable. "I came home from the concert in a hella good mood," he begins as we walk toward "our" bench for lunch. "The first thing Marian and Rob said to me was, 'You should have called.' No hello, nothing—just that whole 'You're only sixteen' thing. They were doing taxes, washing the dishes, having frustrating stress fights. I went to my room to get away from them. Mom came down and asked me if I was high.

"They couldn't believe I'd feel that good without drugs. Maybe that's because Rob's only way to happiness is 'Martini time,'" he speculates bitterly. Or maybe, I think, because it'll take them as long as it took me to trust that the bad times are over.

"How hard was it not to smoke pot at the concert?" I ask.

"*Hella* hard," Tristan answers. "Everyone was high. All this curiosity came up. I wanted to have a really good time."

"What kept you from doing it?"

"It's programmed into me: I go to Phoenix Academy. I'm sober," Tristan answers slowly. "I didn't wanna come back and lie to Eric, Clara, my parents—all these people with all this hope for me. It wasn't worth the consequences. But it wasn't for me that I didn't do it."

He stares off into space. Ringing in the silence are the words Tristan and every person in recovery has heard a thousand times. Do it for yourself or it won't stick.

"I hella wanted to smoke pot," Tristan says finally. He turns to me, his eyes wide. "I hella wanted to get high."

Two days later, Tristan's UA comes back clean. "Everyone thought I was lying," he tells me angrily. "And no one even apologized when they found out I wasn't."

They wouldn't be teenagers if they didn't screw up. They wouldn't be addicts if they didn't relapse. But how can teenagers in recovery "get clean for themselves" when there's a long line of adults they must answer to, even before they answer to themselves? And how can they build enough trust to make those adults back off and let them "do it for themselves," when they keep screwing up and relapsing, as all teenagers and drug abusers must?

Ask any teenager in rehab to name his or her goals, and "Regaining my parents' trust" will be somewhere close to the top. Ask any parent of a teenager in rehab what he or she wants most; "Being able to trust my kid" pretty much says it all. But when a parent, a counselor, the kid himself believes that the sole measure of his trustworthiness is sobriety, trust becomes the impossible—or at least the elusive—dream.

I've seen them all in it; I've been in it myself: the heartbreaking spin cycle of accusations and denials. Because Marian wants so desperately for Tristan to be sober, she accuses him preemptively of smoking pot. Barbara, Michael, and I hoped for as long as we could—longer even—that Mike's self-prescribed cure would make him the one exception to every recovery rule. Zalika's mom described it. "Just when you get your hopes up that she's going to do better, it's another turnaround." But how can parents live, and love our kids, without hope?

We can't, and we shouldn't. So we thrash through the muck of impossible parental paradoxes. Staying detached while struggling for connection. Setting goals and letting go. Loving limitlessly and setting limits. Remembering and naming and heaping praise upon the best qualities of our kids, even when they seem to be acting only out of the worst.

"Welcome back, guys," Eric begins the Monday group. "Let's check in about the weekend. Sierra?"

"My mom hides her pot from her boyfriend," responds a magenta-haired, sixteen-year-old alcoholic pothead. "On Friday night she gave me two huge baggies of pot and told me to keep them in my room."

"I thought your mom quit using," Eric says.

"She did. Last week. I watched her put her whole stash in a paper bag and soak it."

The kids look horrified.

"She put it in *water?*" Tristan asks incredulously.

"She shoulda just sold it," Marisol says, shaking her head in disgust.

"Do you feel like your sobriety's being respected," Eric asks, "when your mom knows that pot is your drug of choice and she puts a bunch of it in your room?"

Sierra shrugs. "I'm thinking hard about going to this party Friday night," she announces.

"Bill's taking people to a meeting that night," Eric responds. "Unless you wanna go to the party more than you wanna go to a meeting . . ."

"Who wouldn't?" Sierra retorts. Several kids roll their eyes at Eric's cluelessness.

"Anyone who's in recovery. That's who." Eric turns to Tristan.

"I'm okay," Tristan mumbles listlessly. "I worked on my new job till three in the morning on Saturday. I stayed sober all weekend."

"How long do you have now, Tristan?" asks Lisa, Eric's cofacilitator.

"Three months."

"What about meetings?"

"I went to two last week. I was gonna go on Saturday, but Bill didn't pick me up."

"How many people went to less than three meetings last week?" Lisa asks.

Hesitantly, Kelsey, Jesús, and Tristan raise their hands. "You guys have to go to four by Friday," Lisa announces.

"*What?*" Tristan bursts out. "That's wack!"

"It's a condition of your being at Phoenix, Tristan. You know that," Lisa replies.

"Maybe I don't belong at Phoenix," Tristan says, looking miserable.

"You know we all want you here," Lisa says. "But the rules apply to you same as everyone." Tristan's eyes seek out Eric's.

"Lisa's right," Eric says gently, and Tristan's eyes drop to the floor.

Yes, the rules apply to Tristan, and that includes the rule about relapse. If you're a person in rehab—teenager or adult, rich or poor, lifelong heroin addict or habitual pot smoker—it's likely to happen to you not once, not twice, but repeatedly.

For teenagers, though, relapse may have a different meaning, and a more positive prognosis. Time, after all, is on their side. As that Columbia University study reported, "For many drug users, the process of growing up—marrying, working, or having children—puts a brake on drug use."

Adolescent rehab programs don't, as far as I can tell, incorporate that possibility into their treatment plans. They show kids all the bad things that will happen if they keep abusing drugs, but they don't much prepare them, practically as well as psychologically, for what will happen if they don't. The focus of rehab, as Tristan keeps complaining, is all on one facet—the most damaged facet—of kids' lives, psyches, and futures.

The problem for parents and drug counselors is that when a kid's in a state of raging drug abuse, no one knows if those brakes will be applied in time, or ever. What are the odds that Mike will give up crank for a wife, a job, kids? It's understandable that Tess and Barbara are less than optimistic. Is Tristan's pot smoking and psychedelic exploration an adolescent phase he'll move on from unharmed, or warning signs of a lifelong addiction that might ultimately destroy him? It's understandable that Eric and Marian pray for the former, while acting on their fear of the latter.

But as Tristan keeps saying, he's in recovery from more than drug abuse; he needs support for more than getting sober. As he says, "You can't just take a shoe away from a puppy. You need to give him a chew toy instead." He needs help finding the vocation, or avocation, that will sustain him economically as well as spiritually. He needs help finding what's right and strong and healthy about him, just the way he is. He needs help seeing the benefits of being sober, not just the dangers of being high—something to chew on that's as much fun as the shoe. Tristan, Mike, Zalika—and every teenager I've met in every drug program—need help moving toward things that are good for them, if we want them to move away from the things that do them harm.

In Monday group a week later, Eric calls on Tristan first. "Were you gonna talk about something?" Eric prompts him.

"A friend blew smoke in my face," Tristan mumbles, his eyes downcast. "I didn't mean to get high. I don't think I relapsed, but the school says I did."

"You're not gonna get in trouble about that, are you?" asks Nicholas.

Tristan nods. "I got put back on Level One. And I have to tell my parents. Otherwise the school's gonna tell them."

"We work with your families to help them support you," Lisa interjects.

"I don't want to bring my sobriety into my house," Tristan says. "It's my problem, not my parents'."

"Do you kids have any feedback?" Eric asks.

"I do. Parents suck," Kelsey says. "I'm not allowed to hang out with my *using friends*, so I'm stuck at home every goddamn weekend. Friday I stayed up all night playing computer games. My mom came down at five in the morning with a UA cup. She told me I must be on drugs to stay up so late. I threw the cup at her."

"Before you peed in it, or after?" Emily asks.

"After!" Kelsey says, and the kids laugh. "The hell of it is," Kelsey goes on, "I know my dad still smokes weed. When I got in the van the other day it smelled like a hotbox."

"What if you brought that up in family therapy?" Lisa asks.

"Fuck that," Kelsey says. "I don't care if he smokes weed. I just wish I could."

Lisa looks around the circle. "Can anyone think of another way Kelsey could have handled the situation?"

"Our parents are so clouded with fear," says a new boy, Zachary, "they can't deal with us in the proper way. Think about it. There's not much reason for them to trust us."

"There's no gray area for addicts," agrees Emily, who's lived in a string of foster homes since her mother's most recent breakdown two years ago. "We do everything to the extreme. We don't go out for the evening, come home, and hang out with our parents. We're like, 'I'm going out. I'll be back next week.'"

Nicholas speaks up over the kids' laughter. "Not everyone's an addict." He turns to Eric. "Is this program about staying sober the rest of your *life?*"

"It's about taking it one day at a time," Eric says.

"I don't wanna be sober the rest of my life," Nicholas shoots back. "I'd like to get to a point where I'm at legal age and I can go out and have a drink or smoke a joint."

"I used to say I wanna smoke a joint once in a while," Jesús says, "but I ended up smoking a quarter ounce."

"We're addicts," Emily agrees. "We can't do that. You can't drink one beer, Kelsey. I can't do a small line of meth."

"It's a struggle," Eric says. "At sixteen or seventeen, looking at twenty-one, that's a long time away. It helps to focus on right now."

"Any more thoughts on the parental trust thing?" Lisa asks.

"Just ignore them, man," Jesús advises.

"Fuck it," Tomás agrees. "Go with the game."

"I know Tristan feels like I came down too hard on him," Eric tells me that afternoon. "My role is so confusing to him. Am I his therapist? His authority figure? His friend? I hope he can see me as all three, but that's a lot to ask. He needed a clear message about what's acceptable and what isn't, and it was my job to give it to him."

Unlike Zalika, who calls me often, Tristan never calls except to make plans. He doesn't need rides to Planned Parenthood; he doesn't need me to call his public defender; he's not having daily crises, and he's got Eric to talk to when he does. So I'm surprised to get a call from Tristan during spring break.

"All hell has broken loose," he says. "I relapsed. Twice."

He tells me about the first time, on a trip to the beach with a "using friend." "Before Logan and I left the house, Luc told Logan not to let me have any pot. I was kinda proud of Luc for saying that.

"But as soon as we got in the car, I asked Logan if he had some. He said he did, but he wasn't gonna give me any. At first I was like, 'You're a real friend.' Then my heart started beating hard. I asked him if we could hit the pipe. He said yeah."

Once again, getting high didn't make Tristan feel good. "I tried to use the high, make it a spiritual experience. Instead we just went to the store. I ate a bunch of food till my stomach hurt, turned around and went home. We never even got to the beach."

This time Tristan told his mom right away. "We had a really good talk. She said she was glad I did it, 'cause she knew it was gonna happen sooner or later. But by the time I went out the next night, she was back to being hella sarcastic, like, 'Are you gonna go have another *spiritual experience?*' I said, 'I don't want to. But I might.'"

He didn't want to. But he did. Two nights later, with Logan and some other friends. Tristan spent the four hours he was high waiting not to be— and the next two days avoiding his mom. Finally he confessed. "I could see her confusion. What role does she play? She could say it's for the school to deal with. Or 'You're a bad boy.' She could ask me if relapsing is a bad thing or is it just part of sobriety—like everyone says, we have fifty years to get clean.

"My parents and my siblings can't coach me with my sobriety 'cause they haven't done it themselves. My dad drinks a bunch, my mom's parents drank every night, same with Rob. How can they be proud of me for being sober? It would be like me having a Republican mom and saying, 'Look mom, I invented a new peace sign.'"

Even more than he dreaded telling Marian, Tristan dreads facing Eric at school. "Our whole relationship has to do with sobriety and trust. I feel like I went behind his back. And I know where this goes. There's no other way. I'm not gonna smoke a little pot and be cool.

"I didn't believe in addiction for a long time," Tristan continues. "But when I observe myself I'm pretty sure I'm an addict. If I wasn't going to

Phoenix, I'd probably be doing mushrooms all the time, smoking pot every day."

The next day in group Tristan doesn't even wait his turn. "I relapsed," he blurts. He forces himself not to turn from Eric's gaze.

"Thanks for admitting that, Tristan," Eric says. "We'll talk later." Tristan feels half relieved, half sick to his stomach. Eric doesn't look mad, he thinks—he looks *disappointed*.

He's not. "Tristan learned from the fact that he relapsed, and that's great," Eric tells me. "He did just what AA teaches addicts to do. If you think you can use, consequence-free, go out and try it and see what happens. The experience that Tristan gave himself speaks so much louder and clearer than anything we can do for him. Instead of 'Eric says this, the school says that,' it's like, 'I tried the old game. It didn't work. I didn't like the way it felt.'"

How will this cluster of relapses affect Tristan's status at Phoenix? "When a kid's coming to us, being straightforward, processing it the way Tristan is, that's the goal. You can't treat chemical dependency punitively and have it work. You need fear of consequences, sure," Eric says, "but it's more important that these kids are seen and heard.

"I don't want Tristan to feel I'd judge him," he goes on. "When he gets a consequence from me he feels like there are conditions on our relationship. I work pretty hard at showing him that it's unconditional."

I can't keep from asking Eric the unanswerable question. "Do you think Tristan's going to make it?"

Like every adolescent drug counselor, Eric has been wrong too many times to answer it. "The odds are against these kids staying sober long-term," he says. "My experience is, the kids who struggle openly and honestly have the best chance at it. The kids who are full of shit, staying under the radar, cleaning their urine, denying, denying, denying—they don't get consequences, and they don't get sober.

"The relationships we have with them are the most healing thing. If they trust us, we can help them see that there are consequences to their *soul*. What else are we gonna do for these kids? Jail? Mental institutions? This is their best shot, right here. Whether they're able to take it or not—that's up to them."

I ask Eric what kind of guidance Tristan needs now. "I want to help him get clear on what he wants out of life," Eric says. "His greatest concern is, how am I gonna live in this world? How am I gonna survive with my values and beliefs and passions? He doesn't want his parents' lives, but he doesn't know how to make one for himself. That's where his work is."

I tell Eric I couldn't agree more, and go off to get Tristan's side of the story.

Tristan is "blown away" by Eric's response. "It was like, 'You relapsed, I'm not mad at you or anything, sounds like you got a lot out of it.' By the end we were joking around, like 'Good job relapsing!' 'Thanks! I'll have to do it more often.'

"I thought there would be a huge scene about it." Tristan shakes his head, perplexed. "I feel like I'm looking at it more seriously than they are."

But not, apparently, seriously enough. As the end of the school year approaches, Tristan keeps blowing off his classes and homework. He gets into arguments with John Martin, Bill, even Clara. He stops talking to his mom, Max, Luc. He transplants ten pot plants from his bathroom to a nearby state park, hikes in often with gallons of water on his back to tend them. He starts wondering if Eric is really his friend. And he starts smoking pot and drinking all weekend, every weekend.

I can't count on seeing Tristan at school now, so we talk on the phone, hang out on weekends. We plant rows of artichokes in the garden outside his bedroom door, march together for peace in San Francisco, eat veggie curry at his favorite Thai restaurant. Lucky me: as the only adult in Tristan's life with no tabs to keep, no consequences to mete out, no messy history to overcome, I get to stay close to him even when he's pushing everyone else away.

I remember a confrontation I had with Jesse—or rather Jesse had with me—when he was early into his "recovery." "You still worry about me," he said accusingly. "The other day, Peter said the best thing anyone ever told me. He said 'I'm not worried about you.' It made me *cry*, Mom. That's how bad I need to hear it."

I didn't quite understand then, but I do now. While everyone in Tristan's life gyrates around his seeming disintegration, I remain confident that he'll emerge from it in fine form. Despite everything he's doing that looks so worrisome, somehow I'm not worried about him.

"John Martin's saying if I keep screwing up they don't want me at Phoenix anymore," Tristan tells me one May afternoon. "Even Clara's bugging me about going to meetings. If they kick me out of Phoenix, I don't get to go to TEAM."

I ask if he's spoken to Eric.

"He came by the house to see me. He's scheduling a meeting between me, my mom, John Martin, and Floyd." Tristan groans. "My mom doesn't know about anything I've been doing. And I don't want her to find out."

"Are you having a good time?" I ask.

"That's the worst part," Tristan answers. "I'm having a *great* time. I'm chasing that high again. I spend like 60 percent of my weekend thinking about how much pot to buy, how much I have to sell to get enough to smoke, where I'm gonna grow it, how I'll get away with it. My head feels foggy all the time. I keep waking up washed and hung over and wanting to do it again."

"You seem pretty well aware of what's going on with you, though."

"I'm working on myself, definitely," Tristan agrees. "I feel like this is gonna be an endless process—not just with drugs, with so many things. I can touch my hand on the burner, feel that it's hot, burn myself, and not do it again. But with drugs I keep on doing it 'cause my mind keeps building up this story that the burner's not gonna be hot anymore.

"It's a scary time. In a month I'm not gonna live in the make-believe fantasyland called Phoenix anymore. I don't trust myself to be out in the world without using. And I don't wanna leave Phoenix Academy, or Eric, on a bad note."

"Pardon my two-bit psychologizing," I say, "but maybe that's what this is all about: trying to keep yourself from leaving Phoenix. Unless you have a better explanation?"

"I think it might be addiction," Tristan says. "I'm doing it over and over and there's no thought process involved. I was smoking with my friend Russell the other day. Before he was even done smoking I was asking him if I could smoke some more. He was like, 'Chill, dude.' I was craving it like a junkie freak. I had that burning desire to get far from reality, to get completely *out*."

I reminisce aloud about how different he sounded a few months ago: in love with schoolwork, with academic success, with sobriety.

"I remember when I loved it," he says slowly, as if he's talking about something that happened five years, not five months, ago. "I was kinda consumed in that. It was like another addiction. Then I realized that it just wasn't who I am. I'm not good at being the perfect student. I didn't feel comfortable being looked at that way.

"Now I'm the exact opposite, and it's just as uncomfortable," he says with a small, humorless laugh. "It's either 'Tristan's doing good' or 'Tristan's doing horrible.' It's always two extremes. That's why I wanna get outta Phoenix. We talk about sobriety too much. I have so many other things I could be turning my energy on."

"What kinds of things?" I ask.

"That's exactly what I need to find out," he answers.

Eric sits in the counseling room, waiting for Marian and Tristan and fuming. They rush in fifteen minutes late, take seats facing each other across the table. "I want to talk to both of you about how we're gonna end Tristan's time here successfully," Eric says. He looks at Tristan. "We've seen you slip, with relapses, tardies, attendance problems. We're not seeing that sense of self-direction you're going to need next year at TEAM.

"Your mom has said this is the best you've done, ever. You've said that. But I don't see the sense in coming here, doing well, then blowing up at the end." He turns to Marian. "And I wanted to remind you, Marian, about Multifamily Group. You've both missed the last two meetings."

"Right, right," Marian says nervously.

"Our goal isn't to punish you or make you feel bad, Tristan. But if you want our blessing for TEAM, you're gonna have to work for it." Eric looks at Marian. "What's your reaction when he comes home and says, 'Mom, I used all weekend?'"

"The first time I was relieved," Marian acknowledges. "It took the pressure off. The second time I was disappointed. Tristan and I talked about it. It's his decision—he chose a path and then he chose not to be on it."

"Tristan says he doesn't want to go back to being the person he was before he came here," Eric says. "I'm asking if the family is supportive of his goal."

"A thousand million percent," Marian declares.

"Then you need to understand that any drug use pushes him closer to that old reality." Eric looks at Tristan. "You're questioning why you have to say you're an addict. You're thinking maybe you could use once in a while. My job is to say that any use at all is jeopardizing your health and safety."

"I want to be sober," Tristan says. "I went out with a friend. I didn't know he had pot . . ."

"You had an opening in your brain," Eric says. "That's all it takes. All you gotta do is crack the door. The three-hundred-pound gorilla will do the rest."

"It's in my house," Tristan says. "It's hard to get support from a parent who uses."

Marian looks as though she's been slapped. And perhaps she has been. "I drink beer," she says defensively.

"Tristan's sixteen," Eric says firmly. "He lives in your house. He's trying to get sober."

"I can't judge him," Marian says.

"I'm not saying judge him," Eric says, gently now. "Kids want to be supported: see me, congratulate me, nurture me. That needs to happen more. Tristan's an amazing boy. We value him greatly here. But we need the family on board as much as the kid."

"My role and my husband's role is to be more supportive of his sobriety," Marian recites.

Eric nods. He hands Tristan a Probationary Contract. "I will phone when I'll be late or absent," Tristan reads. "Do assigned work or complete it as homework. Get a sponsor from NA or AA by 5/22. I will be compliant with the three-meeting weekly requirement. This contract will be reviewed in two weeks during a four-week probationary period."

"It's actually up the day you leave Phoenix," Eric says with a little grin.

Tentatively, Tristan returns the smile. For the first time in weeks, I see the bright flash of the bond between them.

But Tristan doesn't get to Level Two, and he doesn't get to leave Phoenix in June. He doesn't get a sponsor, doesn't do his schoolwork, doesn't accrue the academic credits he needs to complete his sophomore year. So he's forced to stay at Phoenix for the summer-school session, in hopes of being ready for TEAM by September.

The TEAM director comes to Tristan's house and grills Tristan about how he's going to stay sober, what he'll do if he relapses. He warns Tristan that if he tests dirty even once before the start of the new school year, his application will be denied. The interview doesn't go well. "I got the vibe that he doesn't want me to be there," Tristan tells me. "But I'm cool with whatever happens. If I can't go to TEAM, I'll just go somewhere else."

But there *is* nowhere else for Tristan to go. His academic and drug histories disqualify him from "regular" public high school; his parents' debts (the by-product of myriad adolescent interventions) preclude private school. Seeing TEAM as Tristan's only option, Marian and Rob accuse Tristan of sabotaging the interview.

"Rob's pissed 'cause I wouldn't lie and say I have a plan for sobriety," Tristan tells me when I'm driving him home from school. "So his wonderful idea was to tell me that I have to get tested at school tomorrow. He said if I start using ever again, he'll send me to residential treatment."

As Tristan shares his plans for an upcoming camping trip—a week-long psychedelifest at Joshua Tree with his friend Pablo—I'm moved to ask a similar question. Testing dirty at Phoenix will rule out whatever chance he has of being accepted at TEAM. Why would he take that chance?

Tristan shrugs. "I'm hella tired of putting so much thought into my sobriety" is all he'll say. It's as though he had a predetermined sum of time and energy to devote to getting clean, and every penny of it has been spent. Can he keep traveling this new, postsobriety path without a life-threatening collision with addiction?

Certainly Tristan's drug use is careening around the margins. Like kids in day-treatment programs everywhere, he's drinking regularly on weekends. And on the way to a former classmate's graduation, the two of them tried a new high: opium. "I loved it," he tells me. "I felt drunk in the good way, like I could do anything."

"Did you think about the opium showing up on your next UA?" I ask. "Or are you giving up on TEAM?"

"I didn't really think about it," he says, and then he repeats the familiar refrain. "I'm tired of the whole Phoenix Academy thing: 'I feel good 'cause I'm sober, I feel bad because I relapsed.' I want to see how to do the real-life thing. And Phoenix isn't real life."

Since Tristan's known drugs of choice are pot and mushrooms, the "Screen for Opiates" box goes unchecked on his UA lab slip. His opium smoking goes undetected by the Phoenix staff.

Since the day I met them, I've never stopped worrying about Mike and Zalika. Although I haven't always agreed with the methods used by the people who treat them, I've always agreed that their very survival is at stake. Yet even in the face of Tristan's flat-out rebellion, his return to regular drug use, his rejection of all that is holy to the keepers of the sobriety grail, I remain unworried about him. Can I trust the instinct that tells me Tristan will be okay?

Oddly enough, what makes me have so much confidence in Tristan is the very thing that makes others have so little. They worry because he insists on "running his own program"; because he takes from Phoenix only what he wants—the chance to learn in Clara's safe, strict classroom; the chance to love and be loved by a man who admires and respects him; the chance to change and be seen for the new person he is each day—and leaves the rest alone. I see more than denial or entitlement in Tristan's choices. I see the ability to assess available resources, go after what he needs, and get it: a life skill that will serve him well.

I'm confident too because, for Tristan and kids like him, those resources are so abundant. Fair or not (not), white middle-class kids have a better shot at ducking the curve balls that the vicissitudes of life and their own psyches throw in their direction. If Jesse had been black or poor or both when he was an acting-out teenager, he would likely be in jail or dead today. If Zalika were white, if Mike's family were wealthy, I'd have more reason to be optimistic about them too.

How should we evaluate Tristan's success at Phoenix, and Phoenix's success with him? Like Mike and Zalika, Tristan never "bought" the program; unlike Mike and Zalika, he stayed with it nonetheless. As they are, he's still doing what got him sent to there in the first place. Yet everyone concerned (including Tristan, and me) considers his tenure at Phoenix a great success.

If Tristan had surrendered to the program, as some kids do, maybe he'd be leaving Phoenix, reassuringly drug-free. But if he—or Mike or Zalika—had surrendered to the program, they wouldn't be the strong-willed, independent, determined young people they are. What hasn't killed them (yet) has made them stronger. We can only hope that, post-rehab, that equation won't be reversed.

I'm at Tristan's house for dinner when the letter from TEAM arrives. Marian hands it to Tristan to open. "I got in," he says dully.

"Yeah!" Marian cheers.

"I'm not sure I wanna go," Tristan says. The letter outlines the conditions of his acceptance. Besides submitting to drug tests, he'll have to sign a contract promising to keep his math grade above a C. Marian and Rob must commit to hiring tutors as necessary. All of them must promise to attend all TEAM family meetings.

"Of course you're going," Marian says. "This is great news! It's such a wonderful program, Tristan!"

Tristan glares at his mom. I've seen him spacey. I've seen him sad. But I've never seen such a venomous look on his face as this. "*You* go, then," he snarls, and stomps downstairs to his basement room.

Summer school at Phoenix isn't going well. The classrooms are hot and stuffy; the kids resent being there even more than they usually do. They're relapsing so regularly, sobriety is now the aberration. They're lying about it so consistently, even Tristan has abandoned the truth.

Eric refuses to surrender to the morass. "What's your plan when you get out of here?" he asks Tristan during a session in late July.

"I don't have one," Tristan answers. "Whatever happens, happens."

"How are you gonna stay sober?" Eric persists.

Tristan considers his answer carefully. He's been lying in groups all summer, denying his drinking, his opium smoking, his plans for 'shrooming at

Joshua Tree. But he hasn't lied to Eric yet, and he's determined not to start now. Eric is still important to Tristan. Eric is still his friend.

"I might not stay sober," he says, his eyes locked on Eric's. "I'm not disappointed in myself for wanting to smoke some pot with my friends."

"But Tristan—"

Tristan interrupts him. "I know I have a lifetime ahead of me of experiments," he says. "And I know that all of them are gonna be risks."

"But—"

"I have some things now I didn't have a year ago." Tristan speaks slowly, his eyes locked on Eric's. "I know where to come back to if I have a problem."

This time Eric doesn't argue. He returns Tristan's gaze. "I know *who* to come back to," Tristan adds.

Their half hour is up. Tristan gets up to go. "You really helped me," he tells Eric, his voice choked with tears. "Thanks, dude."

The two of them hug long and hard. Then Tristan walks out the door.

On the Run Again

"She'd be safer in CYA than she is on the streets," Tom says. He and I are debriefing in his office an hour after Zalika's escape in her mother's car. "She's street smart. But so are most women who sell their bodies, and a lot of them end up dead. If I could, I'd get her arrested, force her into placement. But I'm her lawyer. I can't sell her out."

"Won't someone—Judge Easton, Pam, the DA—send the cops to do that?" I ask. They've all seen her in the same room with Bo. I'd bet a plate of cookies that their first guess about where to look for her would be correct.

Tom shakes his head. "We don't have an enforcement arm. That's a major weakness of our program. There are Drug Courts like ours all over the country. Same kinds of kids, great staff, same system of rewards and punishment. But they're funded for enforcement. We're not.

"We need officers knocking on doors, doing random Breathalyzers and drug tests, picking up the kids on warrants," Tom goes on. "We know our kids are getting drunk on weekends, testing clean on Mondays. And they know they can run any time it gets too rough, without much risk of getting caught. It comes down to whether the families will snitch them out. And most of these families are too dysfunctional to do that."

"I was too dysfunctional to do that when it was my kid," I say.

Tom nods. "I know it's hard to turn in your own child. But Zalika's mom keeps saying she wants to help her. That doesn't mean covering for her. It means calling her on her shit—telling Zalika's counselors that she's messing with Bo, that she's talking to her pimp. If her family's not cooperating, the cops won't get her."

He looks at me intently. "What about you, Meredith? When Zalika calls you—which she will—are you going to do what's best for her, or what's best for your relationship with her?"

"I'm not convinced that what the system has to offer *is* what's best for her."

"Just so you've thought it through. For her sake, and yours," Tom says. He slips Zalika's file into his desk drawer and locks it. "If you break her confidence, she'll see you as one more person who betrayed her. If you don't, you might end up with her blood on your hands. Are you prepared for that?"

"Zalika wasn't getting the services she needs in this program," Pam Collinshill tells me. "She does have a drug problem. But she needs psychological treatment as well."

I ask Pam if she'll send a sheriff to look for Zalika. "We have a bunch of kids right now with warrants hanging around their parents' homes," Pam answers. "I just left a message about it for my deputy. But it's not a top priority."

"Why not?" I ask.

"When kids run, that's their choice," says Pam. "Do you know how many kids I've got on my caseload?

"I care about Zalika," Pam continues. "She has a lot on the ball. She just needs help. But I've been doing this seventeen years. After the fifth year I got detached." I hear Pam's cell phone ringing. "I'll hold out hope for her," she says, and hangs up.

"The number one reason Zalika failed this program is that we didn't have the cooperation of her parents," Leo Kidd says. We're sitting in his office at Choices, his door locked against the nonstop interruptions of kids who want to take their pee test "right now 'cause I gotta go," begging for Cups O' Noodles, offering to replace Zalika as the subject of my book.

"Every kid does better with parent involvement," Leo says. "But given what Zalika's into, it's crucial to have the parents working with us to control that behavior. Her parents never really connected with anyone here."

"It's not just her parents," I say. I've never seen more than one or two parents in court on Tuesdays or attending Multifamily Group at Choices.

Leo nods. "We tell the parents their attendance is mandatory. Then they get here, see no one else, and stop coming. We get about half of them in for individual sessions with their kids, which is fortunate. If we don't have the parents, we don't have a prayer with the kids."

I wonder aloud why it's so different at Phoenix, where twenty or more parents show up for Multifamily Group each week. Leo guesses, correctly, that the Phoenix parents are mostly white and middle-class. "People like that are more familiar with the group therapy concept. That's not our population. We've got a lot of Asian parents—they're used to dealing with their own community; they're not comfortable talking about their stuff with other people. And Latino parents, who might not speak the language. And black parents, who don't trust Whitey. No matter how many people of color I have on staff here, they still see this as a white establishment because we're tied to the courts.

"I'm considering using the court to get parents more involved. If the judge starts issuing warrants when parents don't come for sessions, maybe then they'll show up."

I ask Leo what he thinks will happen to Zalika now.

"If she chooses to come back," he says, "and if we can enlist the support of her parents, we might give her another shot here." He mulls this over. "A lot of kids disappear; then they pop back up. But my sense is, she has contacts out there. She can stay gone if she wants to."

"Got any advice," I ask, "in case she gets in touch with me?"

"I learned a long time ago that there's only a certain percentage of kids who are gonna turn around in front of me. That doesn't mean they won't turn around someday. I try to do what's best for the kid, not what'll keep the kid liking me. You have love in your heart for Zalika," Leo adds gently. "Trust that. Your heart will guide you to the best decision."

A few days later, having heard nothing, I call Bo's house looking for Zalika. LaShaundra tells me she hasn't seen her. As soon as we hang up

Zalika calls me back. "LaShaundra didn't know if you were a cop or what," she explains.

I ask how she's doing.

"I'm doing good. I can't believe I really am on the run again," she answers breathlessly.

"How are you and Bo getting along?"

"He's a very angry kid. He got *issues*. He really do. When I try to go get me a Smirnoff he gets abusive." She sighs. "Every time I go outside, he yells at me to go back in. Hey—you think they'd tap the phone?"

"Let's keep things in perspective. You're not Zalika Bin Laden," I say.

Zalika laughs uproariously, and I wonder how many sixteen-year-old ho's would appreciate the joke. "I got totally spooked out this morning," she says. "Four cop cars pulled up right in front. I was high on weed, so I was hella paranoid." She laughs again. "Guess what I found out? I can fit in the dryer."

I ask if she'd consider turning herself in. "When I think about twelve months in that program it makes me sick. And Juvenile Hall—I ain't *never* goin' back there."

"Have you talked to your parents?"

"My mom says she'll give me fifty dollars a month. I'll keep twenty, pass the rest to LaShaundra for groceries. I know what my mom's thinking. 'Girl, I'll come over there and whup your butt if you don't turn yourself in.' But she doesn't come out with it like she should.

"My dad—his ass is the one that didn't give me any credit for trying to do better. Well, I'm gone now. So he don't need to worry about it."

Days go by. Weeks. Months. Imposing a somewhat arbitrary boundary, I've told Zalika that I won't risk a felony conviction for harboring a juvenile fugitive by driving her in my car or letting her come to my house. So we fall into a new rhythm, talking on the phone every few days, seeing each other rarely. "DQ2, reporting in," Zalika tells my voice mail on her good days. "Meredith—I really need to talk to you. Call me," she cries on her bad ones.

I keep thinking I'll get a call from Tom, telling me that Zalika's been busted—because Pam's sheriff finally got around to it, because Zalika's mom turned her in, because she tried to buy Smirnoff from the wrong liquor store or weed from the wrong dealer. But no.

Bo's still going off to Choices every afternoon and court every Tuesday—until the day his dirty drug tests move Judge Easton to order him into residential treatment. Bo walks out of the courthouse, cuts off his ankle bracelet, and joins his girlfriend on the run—in his mom's living room. Now he and Zalika are living like a ghetto Bonnie and Clyde, selling weed and smoking it, drinking Smirnoff and Bacardi, going for joyrides in stolen cars, having fights and making up. "We do pee tests on each other just to see how much THC is in our systems," Zalika tells me, laughing. I ask where they get the fifty-dollar tests. "We stole a box from Choices," she says. "I mean, damn!" She pauses for emphasis. "There wasn't nothin' *else* to take from that place."

Bo's family celebrates Zalika's seventeenth birthday with a couple of blunts and a bucket of KFC. "Everyone had Original, 'cause they know that's my favorite," Zalika tells me, sounding quite content. For her gift from me, she asks for a journal. "A little, pretty one. No kittens or anything princessy—a grown-up one, with a lock." She tells me she wants to work on her book, which she hasn't mentioned since she read it to me months ago.

One day Zalika calls me all excited. She's decided to get her GED. First, though, she needs a California ID. She asks me to take her to the Department of Motor Vehicles—half a block from the Choices office—to get it.

"How are you going to do this without getting caught?" I ask.

"If they look at me funny, we'll just leave," she says.

When I pick her up, she hugs me, tells me I sound like I have a cold. "I just want you to know, Meredith," she says somberly, doing her best imitation of a drug counselor, "that I'm there for you in your recovery."

We laugh a lot that day, as we always do. And men of all ages buzz around her, as they always do. At the DMV she fills out the forms, using her real name, and makes an appointment for next week. Then, "spooked out" by a funny look from a security guard as we're leaving, she decides that she won't keep it. On our way back to Bo's, we stop at Kmart to pick up the "personal hygiene items" she needs. After much deliberation, Zalika chooses a Big Bird toothbrush and bubble gum–flavored toothpaste. "Let me be a kid any way I can," she says when I laugh at her selections.

Every few weeks, she has a fight with Bo, or a near miss with a cop on the street, or is simply bored to tears and calls me crying. "I wish I could talk to Marcus, but he got married and moved to Texas," she says. "I'm trying to think, what would Marcus say to do?"

I think of the book I've seen at Jesse's house: *What Would Jesus Do?* In Zalika's life, an ex-pimp plays the role of Jesus.

"Marcus would say, 'Why the fuck is you on the run?'" she answers her own question. "Then I'd say, 'I don't wanna go to the Hall.' And he'd say, 'All right, man, pack yo' shit and come on.'

"Then you know what I be goin' to do," Zalika tells me. "Somethin' I don't wanna do."

"Zalika's been staying in touch," June tells me. "She came and got all of her clothes. She says she's looking for a job, but how's she going to do that without getting arrested?"

I ask June if she worries that her daughter will return to her old career.

"That's why I'm giving her money," she answers. "It's a shame those kids know they won't face any consequences for running away. The JEM people came and picked up the monitor. That's all they care about. They haven't even called here once, looking for her.

"I don't know why those Drug Court people can't put two and two together," June says, "and figure out that she and Bo are sitting up there at his house."

"Have you thought about calling the cops on her yourself?" I suggest.

"I wouldn't do that to another mother," June answers. "LaShaundra's son is having his problems too. I'm not going to turn Zalika in as long as she's not prostituting."

That's what I've been telling myself too. But how will we know if she is?

Each of these programs has the same big problem. The kids don't want to be there, so they run away. And the same solution: none. So, Center Point, Phoenix Academy, Drug Court—each program is a tightly sealed container with a big hole in the bottom.

There are reasons for this, both philosophical and practical. If the programs were to close the hole, chase down kids when they run, who would do the chasing, and who would pay for the chase? Even if programs could afford to hire private detectives to find the kids—not likely, since most of them can't even afford trained therapists—only officers of the law are authorized to make arrests. As Pam Collinshill says, in counties full of murderers, rapists, and armed robbers, why would a sheriff's department go after a pot-smoking kid?

The programs' enforcement capacity suffers from a familiar philosophical flaw as well. In their approach to retention, too, they adopt the adult model without making teen-appropriate modifications. The adult-treatment watchword is "You gotta want it for it to work." No one stops adults at the door when they walk out of rehab. The open-door policy has different implications for kids. Dare an adult to run, and he might have the presence of mind (and the life experience or the awareness of his own mortality) to stay. Dare a teenager to run, and, well, the AWOL stats speak for themselves.

Leaving the door open for escape doesn't make kids want treatment. It just offers them a more attractive way to avoid it, and another opportunity to damage their legal status, futures, and families. It gives them three equally viable options: (1) do the program; (2) blow the program and go to placement or jail; or (3) go on the run.

When kids run, parents like Zalika's are forced to make a choice that makes Sophie's look simple. They can (1) lose track of their kid, (2) harbor a fugitive, or (3) have their kid arrested. Unable to count on their parents' "loyalty," many kids run away from home when they run away from treatment, becoming not only fugitives from the law, but fugitives from their families—the last thing they, or their families, need.

Living with warrants hanging over their heads, even kids like Zalika, whose parents (and boyfriend's parents) offer some measure of shelter, become stuck in a no-exit life of lawlessness. Unable to go to school, get a job, drive legally, or get help for whatever problems sent them into treatment, they do what they can—steal, sell drugs, sell their bodies—to stay alive and "free." As the Drug Court kids do, they hang out together, sharing resources (and food, drugs, and needles) and hatching criminal schemes to get more of them. If this isn't what we want for our kids, for our communities, we need to spend the money, hire the cops, seal the container. We need to let kids know that if they need drug treatment, we're going to make sure that they get it.

———————

"I broke up with Bo," Zalika calls to tell me. "The other news is, I'm with someone else. Let me get this out of the way right now. He's twenty-nine."

"Is he a pimp?"

"Yes. But I swear I haven't even been *near* the track! He deals crack, plus he's on parole. So he wouldn't take a chance on pimping a young girl like me."

"Well, that's reassuring."

Zalika ignores my sarcasm. "Kingsley's a pretty boy. He was shot in the face before he went to prison, but you can hardly see the scar. He drives a Lexus. He's a grown-ass man, not like Bo."

Zalika tells me that Kingsley helped her to move out of Bo's, set her up in his mom's apartment two doors away, paid her rent, bought her some groceries, and gives her money.

"What does he want for all that?"

"Just me, I guess."

"Uh-huh."

Zalika is silent for a moment, a sure sign that she's concocting one of her special blends: truth and lies, stirred with a spoonful of sugar. "Promise you won't get mad. I'm doing in-call and out-call."

"What's that?"

"Escort service. But it's on-line. So it's hecka safe." She gives me the URL and tells me to check it out. "I'm using the name 'Amour,'" she says.

My heart sinks as the home page appears on my screen, flashing with images of lingerie-clad girls who look Zalika's age or younger. And there in the middle of them is "Amour," in a G-string and bra. "Petite and sensual, your high-school sweetheart. If you're looking for a beautiful, intelligent girl who's ready to pamper you and show you a great time, call Amour." There's a phone number I don't recognize.

I call the number. "H-I-I-I-I," a sultry version of Zalika's voice answers. "This is Amour. I'd love to get back to you at my earliest convenience. So *do* leave a message. And have a nice day."

"How'd you get into this?" I ask when she calls me back.

"A friend of mine hooked me up. I met her in that Sun and Moon program I was in before Drug Court. There's hella young girls like us on that Web site. There's like a thousand other Web sites just like it too."

I'm silent, taking this in.

"If I don't do this," Zalika says defensively, "I'm gonna be on the stroll. To me, it's better than standing out there all day. To you, on the other hand . . ."

She waits for my response. I don't know where to begin.

"It's almost all rich-ass guys," she says. "They just want sex. There's only a few stalkers and crazy ones.

"There's hella money involved here, Meredith. And this way I don't have to give none of it to no niggaz like I used to. Just three hundred a month to keep my picture on the Web site. I make that much in one session, easy."

"Easy?"

"I'd get me a legal job if I wasn't on the run," Zalika says. "If I could I'd get my GED, take some classes, find out what I really wanna do. Maybe I'd get a degree in business, start something for myself. But right now this is the only way for me to make money and not get caught."

I hang up, shaken. If I don't turn her in, will Zalika end up dead in a motel room, the victim of one of the "crazy ones"? Will her future be any brighter if I do?

I can't make this decision alone. I call Tom, who encourages me to set up a meeting with Kevin Charles. I call June and convince her to join me at Kevin's office the next day.

Kevin dispels the illusion I've been operating under: that I can turn Zalika in. "Only her parents can do that," he says. "And even if you decide to do it," he tells June, "it won't be easy. The police just aren't that interested in a kid with a warrant." If June decides to have her daughter arrested, he says, she'd have to camp out at a precinct, convince the police that Zalika's worth chasing, then lead them to her. "If I were you," he tells June, "I'd have her kidnapped and taken to a locked treatment program. She'll be eighteen in a year. After that, you won't be able to force her into treatment."

June says she sent away for information about "escorts" and locked programs a few years ago. "I couldn't believe what it cost," she says. "You have to be rich or sacrifice everything to do that."

"What would it cost to plunk her down in Utah? Twenty-five thousand bucks?" Kevin replies, regarding June unblinkingly. "And what do you figure it might cost if you don't?"

When we leave Kevin's office June says she'll talk to her husband. A few days later, she tells me, "We can't afford the kidnappers. Even if we could, she'd find a way to escape. I guess we'll just have to hope she comes to her senses on her own."

Asking questions about Zalika brings me back to those Big Questions about America. How has it come to pass that this bright, precocious, big-hearted girl is living in hiding with a pimp nearly twice her age, selling her body on a Web site for horny men?

The answer comes to me as a laundry list of our nation's ugliest "isms." Racism and sexism. Misogyny and child exploitation. The media's simultaneous idolization ("petite and sensual high-school sweetheart") and demonization ("marauding gang members") of adolescents.

Could it be this simple: the FBI shuts down the hundreds of Web sites trafficking in underage prostitutes, arrests the operators and johns, and fines them enough to pay for the care and treatment ("Life Court," as Tom Fleming envisioned it) that could save these young girls' souls?

Idealistic as it sounds, that, or something like it, is what needs to happen. Zalika couldn't have made many of the "bad decisions" she's been rightly accused of making if we weren't making some worse decisions ourselves. Zalika couldn't sell what she's selling unless her customers—drug addicts, pedophiles—were buying. Let's help Zalika and all the Zalikas make better decisions by giving them therapy that meets their needs, by keeping them safe, at least, until they're adults. But let's also put an end to the circumstances—child prostitution, for starters—that make her bad decisions so dangerous, and so lucrative.

Zalika's crying so hard into the phone, all I can hear is her best friend's name.

"What about Tahira?" I keep asking.

"She's *dead*," Zalika sobs. "She died in a car crash with her boyfriend and some other dude."

I try to comfort her, feeling near tears myself. How much more pain will this child have to bear?

"I'm lonely," she sobs. "I'm used to having someone hugging on me and stuff. Kingsley never comes around. I asked him to spend the day with me today. He said 'Hell no. I can't miss a whole day of money.'

"I'm sick of being on the run," she hiccups. "I'm sick of the whole probation shit. It's making me be so far behind! If they'd just leave me alone, I'd go to school. I'd be fine."

"Maybe it's time to think about turning yourself in," I say. "We could call Tom, see what he thinks . . ."

"Bo's in jail," she says, ignoring me. "The Rodeo police came to his house and took him away. He's going to Byron Boys' Ranch."

"Why him and not you?" I wonder silently. For the hundredth time I imagine calling Pam and leaving Zalika's address on her voice mail. For the hundredth time I play that scenario out, now factoring in Kevin's sobering advice, and decide not to do it.

Zalika bursts into fresh tears. "I can't stop thinking back about all the bad decisions I've made in my life. My dad told me I'd go through this sometime, feeling bad about everything I've done. Now it's happening. I'm so depressed, I think maybe I should go to a doctor, get me some pills."

The next time I hear from Zalika, there are two people's voices on the message. She and Tom are calling from her apartment.

"She called and said she wants back into Drug Court," Tom tells me later. "She asked me to come see her. When I got there she was out of her mind on weed.

"I told her that Drug Court might not take her back. She said as long as it's not CYA, she'll go wherever they send her. I suggested the Chris Adams Center, the residential girls' home right next to Juvenile Hall. She agreed to that. I said I'd put her on the docket for Tuesday if she'd promise to be unintoxicated and ready to turn herself in.

"Can you represent her in court on Tuesday?" Tom asks me. "And can you make sure that Zalika's on call, ready to surrender at two o'clock?"

I express my skepticism—I can't see her showing up for court, let alone doing nine months in the program—but I promise to do what I can.

"What made you call Tom?" I ask Zalika on the phone that night.

"Hella bored," she answers promptly. "Plus I was pissed at Kingsley. No pimp 'sposed to treat his ho' like he treat me."

"His ho'," I think. "If they offer you what you're saying you want," I say, "you'll turn yourself in?"

"As long as they're not sending me to CYA," she replies.

"I'll see you Tuesday then," I say, hoping against all available evidence that I will.

"Zalika contacted me," Tom tells the Drug Court Team when they gather for Case Review on Tuesday. "She wants to be back in Drug Court. If she can't do that, she says she'll do a placement."

"Zalika is not a candidate for Drug Court, in my opinion," Pam says firmly.

"She's a candidate for residential," Kevin agrees. "After she finishes that, we'll welcome her back with a party."

"One reason she hasn't come back earlier is, she's afraid she'll be sent to CYA," Tom says. "Can we send her to Chris Adams?"

"CYA costs more than a placement," Kevin says. "I think Chris Adams is a great idea. It's nearby. Her parents might even show up to visit her."

"I'll dispo her to Chris Adams," Judge Easton says, typing into his laptop.

How many kids on the run, I wonder, get to name their chosen punishment—and then have it offered to them? I've never seen it happen before. But that's Zalika: breaking all the rules, crossing all the boundaries.

"Then she's ready to surrender," Tom answers. I wince to see him stake his credibility on hers.

"Tell Zalika that we're concerned about her," Kevin says. "And tell her it doesn't get any better from here. Hopefully, she'll grab this chance."

Tom gives me the nod. I step outside to call Zalika.

"Hellooooo," she answers the phone in her happy, high voice.

"You ready to go to jail, DQ2?" I ask.

"*Hell*, no!"

"You can go to Chris Adams. They're giving you exactly what you want."

"I ain't goin' to jail today. I'm not mentally ready."

"This is the best offer you're going to get."

"Well, now I know what they're thinking," she says calmly.

"You put us through all this just to find out what they were thinking?" I remember Zalika's dad telling me I'd end up feeling burned by his daughter. I thought I'd stay detached enough to keep that from happening. I thought wrong.

Some kids just don't fit. They're not like the other kids in their families, their classrooms, their neighborhoods, their times. Jesse was one. Zalika is another.

If they have someone who understands them—a loving grandmother who lives nearby, a teacher in a small, nurturing school—that person might find or make a place for them. A calm, wise grandmother, a relaxed, dedicated teacher might sit beside them day after day, praising their drawings and their stories, holding them close when they flail, filling them with the feeling that even though they don't think or act or pray or talk like the other kids, they belong to this world, they're loved and seen and wanted in this world.

Few kids get that kind of attention. Not every kid needs it. Jesse was one. Zalika is another. All of the qualities that should make them shine—their brilliance, their creativity, their rootedness in who they so strongly know themselves to be—make them troublesome in a thirty-eight-kid classroom, an overworked, stressed-out family, or an underfunded drug-treatment program. But that doesn't mean we don't need them. And that doesn't mean they don't need us.

Solutions don't come easy. When Jesse was beating kids up on street corners, when Zalika is slapping away every hand that could help her, it's hard not to go to that cold, barren place—"She's insane. There's no other way to explain it"—where Zalika's dad hides, shivering alone with his grief. But we must resist the temptation to blame, to distance, to pathologize, to reject the kids who aren't easy, fine, white, rich, or cute. As families, as a nation, we've got to offer the toughest kids the same thing we offer the easy ones: exactly what they need. Whatever it costs us, the savings will be immense.

"How's my character coming along?" Zalika calls to ask. We discuss her possible pseudonyms. "Now don't be givin' me some ghetto-ass name," Zalika instructs me. "It has to be something strong that fits me like my real name does."

I hear her pager going off again and again. "I gotta make some call-backs," she says. "I miss you, DQ1. Will you come see me?"

I miss her too, so I drive to the same Rodeo housing project where she used to live with Bo. As I'm parking at her new address a few doors down from the old one, pulling a bag of KFC Original out of my car, Zalika throws her arms around me from behind. "DQ1!" She's wearing her "working wardrobe": a see-through, royal blue lace teddy, blue denim short-shorts, black platform slides.

"You've been smoking weed," I say, sniffing at her. She giggles, nods, changes the subject.

"That's Kingsley's car," she says excitedly, pointing to a freshly painted "tricked out" Buick. "Isn't it *pretty?*"

"It looks like a pimp's car," I reply.

Zalika giggles again. "That's what it *is*."

I follow her into the living room of a ground-floor apartment. The room is small and dark, its walls cinder block, its floor torn linoleum. A TV rests on a stack of cardboard boxes. We sink into black "suede" couches, lay out our lunch on the glass coffee table. This time we eat our KFC without Zalika's collection of international hot sauces.

"Who lives here?" I ask.

She ducks her chin at the concrete stairs. "Kingsley's mom. His sister. His sister's kids." Zalika lowers her voice to a whisper. "His mom works at the post office at night. She be up there in her bedroom doin' drugs all day."

There's a knock on the door. A blonde, middle-aged white woman walks in. "Hi there, honey," she says to Zalika, as if she's a teacher greeting a favorite student.

Zalika leads the woman to the kitchen. I hear the woman ask if Zalika has change for a twenty. I hear the sound of a cabinet door opening, of plastic bags rustling.

"Thanks, honey," the woman says, and walks back through the living room. "Nice to meet you," she says to me, and pulls the door closed behind her.

Zalika sits down on the couch, picks up a biscuit, rummages through the KFC bag. "They never give you enough honey," she complains. When I don't answer, she meets my gaze. "You should be happy. I'm not ho'ing any-more," she says.

"What are you selling?" I ask.

"Crack, coke, crank. But it's not mine. I'm just sitting here. If Kingsley's customers come, I serve 'em."

"You're selling *meth*?"

"White people can't get enough of that shit. That lady you saw? She comes like four times a day. Black folks be gettin' into crank now too." Zalika gestures at the ceiling. "That's what Kingsley's mom be doin' up there." Zalika darts into the kitchen, beckons me to follow. The counters are strewn with dirty dishes; the sink brims with murky water. She pulls open the freezer door. The compartment is crammed with plastic Seven-Eleven Slurpee cups filled with frozen brown liquid. "Frozen Coke: that's all she eats," Zalika says, shaking her head. We go back to our lunch.

I ask if she's tried meth herself.

"*Hell* no! That's dope fiend shit! I'll do coke and weed—they're natural. But I ain't puttin' nothin' in my body you cook in a lab." She shakes her head at me. "I told you. I don't have a drug problem."

Zalika peeks through the blinds. "He's coming!" she exclaims. She stuffs a few bills into her bra, straightens her teddy, sits up expectantly. A stun-ningly handsome man, his smooth face marred by a scarred-over bullet hole, strides into the kitchen with an older Latino man in tow. I hear the familiar cabinet rummaging and bag rustling. As the two men walk back through the living room, Kingsley tosses a twenty at Zalika. He leaves without a word to her. He never even glances at me.

"I made him like three hundred dollars today," Zalika explains, stuffing the money into her bra with the rest of it.

"You're not worried about getting busted?" I ask.

"You know how *small* this dope business is? It ain't like we doin' no drug *traffickin'* or nothin'."

I know I won't get anywhere, trying to convince Zalika of the danger she's in, but I can't help tallying her risk factors in my head.

"Are you having sex with Kingsley?" I ask.

"We've done it, but we don't do it no more. I be too nervous. There could be holes in the condoms and stuff when he does it to other girls." She repeats the sentiment she's expressed to me several times. "If I get that HIV, you can just shoot me. I don't wanna live with that shit."

The door bursts open again. This time, a rail-thin, middle-aged twitching black woman rushes through the door and thumps up the stairs to Kingsley's mother's room.

"Damn dope fiend," Zalika mutters. "See what that crank shit do to people?" She sprinkles salt on her mashed potatoes and gravy. "I want to get a tattoo," she tells me. I ask what she's got in mind.

"I want it to say, 'RIP Tahira.' You know I cry sometimes, missing my best friend." She takes a bite of potatoes, glances nervously out the window. "Is that his car coming?" she asks. We stare out together through a bent slat in the blinds. "Guess not," she says, sounding half relieved, half disappointed. She picks up a chicken leg, puts it down.

"I called my dad for Father's Day," she tells me. "He didn't even care. Doesn't it count for something that I call my parents nearly every day? I mean, *hello!* I'm still here! I'm still your daughter. Can't I get some support or something?"

"What kind of support do you want?" I ask.

"I need a family, man," Zalika says.

Afterword

Two years ago this book began with a complicated question: Why do teenagers do drugs, and what should we do about it? Behind that question were a couple of bigger, deeper, equally complicated ones. Why are Americans in so much trouble with our teenagers? And why was I in so much trouble with mine?

Following Mike, Tristan, and Zalika through the last days of their childhoods kindled memories, many of them excruciating, of chasing Jesse through his. Set against the backdrop of Jesse's "happy ending," there was healing as well as hurt for me in that. Admiring Mike's mom's good intentions, appreciating Tristan's mom's persistence, empathizing with Zalika's parents' desperation opened me to long overdue compassion for our family, my son, myself.

It's been several months, now, since I stopped "following" Mike, Tristan, and Zalika and started pondering the bigger tale their stories tell. I don't take notes anymore when I see or talk to them, but all three are still very much in my thoughts, my heart, my life. Our continuing relationships are as much their doing as mine. They all stay in touch with me, sporadically yet steadily. They've each become important to me, and I—an adult who's free to love and support them without the parental prerogatives of panic or punishment—have become important to them.

"You didn't bring your computer!" Tristan exclaimed happily when we met for our first post-research lunch. "You're not typing!" Zalika says sometimes, with obvious disappointment. "I want my story to have a happy ending,"

Mike told me, just before he took off on a crank-fueled road trip to the meth labs of Montana.

I want their stories to have happy endings too. But we're not there yet. I went into this project hoping that during the course of it, Mike, Tristan, and/or Zalika would deliver what every terrified parent, every weary treatment professional, every stymied researcher longs for: a tidy, replicable success story. We're not there yet. As I heard many drug counselors say during the years I worked on this book, it wouldn't be recovery if it were easy. "I learned a long time ago that most kids aren't gonna turn around in front of me," Choices Director Leo Kidd told me the day Zalika ran from the program and the law. "But that doesn't mean they won't turn around someday."

Leo's right, of course. Jesse and the legions of once-hell-bent-on-self-destruction kids who have grown into stable, healthy adults prove that's so. Still, it's hard—there is no word for how hard it is—to watch, and worry, and wait.

I believe in Mike, Tristan, and Zalika, even though just about every bad thing that every counselor predicted would happen to them, has. I wanted Mike to be the one kid who could kick crank for good without finishing a drug program. I wanted Tristan to be the one kid who could use drugs for positive, personal growth purposes only. I wanted Zalika to be the one teenage prostitute who could walk away from that life, never to return. We're not there yet.

Since Mike left Center Point and Juvenile Hall, he's gone through a few "I'm turning my life around" phases: working at the detail shop, living briefly with his mom, his dad, his grandma, abstaining from what he calls "the devil's drug." But apart from those dry spells, his life has been all about buying, selling, snorting, and smoking crank.

Throughout it all, our connection has stayed strong. When a drug deal in Sonoma went bad, Mike took the Greyhound to Oakland to chill out with me. He got off the bus grinning proudly. "I knew you'd want me to be hungry for dinner, so I didn't do any crank on the bus," he said, adding in the spirit of full disclosure, "I smoked hella weed, but that was just to help my appetite." We celebrated his eighteenth birthday with a shopping spree at the Santa Rosa mall, from which he emerged with a few items neither of us had paid for, although I'd been at his side the whole time. Two weeks later, Mike called to say that even though his mom was "hella pissed" about his DUI arrest, she'd come through for him "like she always does." She'd convinced the judge to reduce the charges to reckless driving, punishable by community service he has yet to serve. Sometimes Mike is too embarrassed, too preoccupied, or too high to call, but a holiday hasn't passed without a "Merry Christmas" or "Happy Easter" voice mail from him, no matter what state (literal or figurative) he's in.

Tristan's path, as always, resists easy analysis. His transition from Phoenix to his new alternative school, TEAM, was smooth; his year at TEAM—filled with camping trips and internships, free of drug tests and therapy groups—was idyllic. Tristan still does drugs. He still fights with his parents about drugs. And he still vacillates between believing that he can use a variety of drugs for his own betterment and believing that he's an addict who'd better not do any drugs at all. He was grounded for a month, recently, when his parents found out he'd been doing cocaine. "I can't believe how fast it took over my life," he told me. "And I didn't even *like* it!"

At Tristan's seventeenth birthday party a houseful of his siblings, cousins, aunts, and uncles munched on Rob's barbecued sausages and Marian's vegetarian salads, toasted Tristan with local microbrewery beer, and presented him with a video camera, which he's been using nonstop ever since. Next year, Tristan tells me, he plans to skip his last year of high school, take filmmaking classes at a junior college instead. As we brainstormed topics for his next video, Tristan radiating excitement, I wondered if addiction would haunt him always or if he'd be one of the lucky teenagers who simply grow out of drug abuse. Given everything Tristan has going for him—a supportive if eccentric family, a past and a future cushioned by middle-class comforts, and, now, his first vision of a career path—it wasn't hard to imagine that he might.

The same day that Tristan told me, "I feel like I finally found the thing I love to do," Zalika got arrested doing something she hates to do—but still does nonetheless. "They were gonna let me go for the prostitution," she told me, "but they found a stolen check in my purse." Since Zalika still has an outstanding warrant in the juvenile system—the warrant Judge Easton issued when she ran from the Richmond Drug Court a year ago—she gave the arresting officers a false name, told them she was nineteen, and held her breath while they ran her fingerprints. So much for the Information Age. Her prints came back clean, as they have each of the many times she's been stopped by the police since she joined the underworld of teenage fugitives.

When she got out of jail, Zalika went back to the motel room that's been "home" since her last attempt to live with her parents failed the same way all of her past attempts have: in a screaming fight with her father. For a few months before that, she'd given us reason to hope, honoring her parents' curfew, working at a pet store by day, going to junior college classes by night, dating boys her own age. Then she got bored, met an older man, and went back to the stroll. "Put my real name in the book, so I can go on TV and say how messed up those drug programs are," she instructs me when she's doing well. "Show me what you're writing about me," she says nervously when she isn't.

Mike, Tristan, and Zalika are unique, of course, but their experiences in drug rehab aren't. Every day kids like them are placed in, kicked out of, and graduated from residential, day treatment, and after-school drug treatment programs in cities, suburbs, ghettos, and small towns across the country. What can we learn from these teenagers' lives, from their experiences in rehab and out of it? Which part of "Why?" can Mike, Tristan, and Zalika help us to understand? More important, what do Mike, Tristan, and Zalika tell us that we should *do*?

Looking for answers is like pulling on a sweater's loose thread. The obvious solutions unravel in my hand. Fixing the profoundly flawed system of adolescent drug treatment—much as it needs to happen, complicated as doing it will be—will not solve the problem of teenage drug abuse. To do that we must untangle the mess of issues that draw our kids to drugs in the first place: the warp and weave of our materialistic culture, which at once extols the virtues of and assaults what Zalika so poignantly says she needs, a family.

And so I offer proposals that address the underlying causes of America's teenage drug epidemic, not just the malady itself. This critique may be difficult to accept; these proposals will certainly be difficult—some will say impossible—to achieve. But everything I've learned as a teenager, a mother, and a journalist, everything Mike, Tristan, and Zalika have taught me, has brought me to this analysis, these conclusions. This is the truth as I know it. I urge you to find and advocate for your own.

WHY DO TEENAGERS ABUSE DRUGS?

Because it's fun. Every teenager I asked gave me this answer. And no wonder. Teenagers are letting go of childhood, when fun is encouraged and abundant, and facing adulthood, which seems to prohibit it. Teenagers' natural appetites for laughter, adventure, and excitement are immutable (even admirable); the only variable is how they will be satisfied. Until we offer adolescents healthy ways to have fun—as they, not we, define it—they'll go on getting it where they can.

Because they have no hope. When kids have a history of failure—in school, in rehab, in their parents' eyes, in their peers', in their own—they see only failure in their futures, if indeed they see futures for themselves at all. When kids feel hopeless, the prospect of staying sober can't compete with the instant gratification of getting high. If we want our kids to make choices that will benefit them (and all of us), we need to ensure that they experience and anticipate success in their lives early and often.

Because they don't believe us. Every teenager knows what ample research has proved: exaggerating the risks of drug use doesn't keep kids sober; it just keeps them cynical. Still, our tax dollars fund prevention programs that equate the dangers of marijuana and heroin, and media campaigns that link recreational drug use to terrorism. Lying to kids is never a good idea. Lying to kids about drugs can be lethal.

WHAT SHOULD WE DO TO KEEP TEENAGERS FROM ABUSING DRUGS?

1. Support good parenting. The moral and economic realities of American life have made children the last item on many parents' to-do lists, with predictable and disastrous results. We can't legislate the unconditional lifetime guarantee of love and care that every child deserves, but we can make laws that increase the odds they'll get it. If families are to have dinner together (and you don't have to be a Republican or a researcher to know that they should), we need family-friendly government and workplace policies—a living wage, a forty-hour workweek, and paid maternity/paternity leave, for starters—that give parents access to the time and money it takes to raise children right.

Our nation's budget priorities have turned parenting necessities—quality child care, medical care, schools, enrichment programs, and safe, nurturing neighborhoods—into privileges available only to the affluent. George W. Bush's promise to "Leave No Child Behind" will remain the cynical campaign slogan it is until we make the resources required for good parenting available to all.

2. Support healthy communities. Kids who grow up living with and surrounded by homeless, unemployed, chronically criminal, mentally ill, and/or drug-addicted adults are being primed daily to repeat the cycle. To keep kids from getting into trouble, we need to take care of adults in trouble by providing employment, housing, medical care, and mental-health services to everyone who needs them, not just those who can afford them.

To keep our neighborhoods and families safe from the ravages of addiction, every community must offer drug treatment on demand—free, effective programs like Drug Courts, which offer holistic "wraparound" services, including vocational and therapeutic support, while closely monitoring their clients' progress toward recovery.

3. Revamp the school system. When kids are failed by their schools, irreparable harm is done to their self-esteem, their hopes, their intellect, their options—damage that even the most "hands-on" parenting can't overcome.

Our first priority should be to make every school a small school, no bigger than five hundred students, and every class a small class, with no more than twenty students. From the first day of kindergarten through high-school graduation, every child needs well-trained teachers and on-site school counselors who know and care about their students. Family involvement and collaboration among all the adults in each student's life must be integral to every school's agenda.

To help kids imagine, look forward to, and prepare to take their places in the world, middle and high schools should offer career guidance and vocational training, making use of community as well as campus resources.

The DARE program and its ilk have failed because kids rightly distrust the message and the messengers. School-based drug-education programs should model themselves instead on the many successful high-school sex education programs: those staffed by experienced professional and peer counselors, teaching emotional and social awareness, offering credible information and referrals in safe, confidential, on-campus settings.

4. Revamp the juvenile justice system. About half of American teenagers in drug treatment are referred by the juvenile justice system, so reforming one system requires reforming the other.

The realities of today's juvenile justice system—prosecuting younger and younger children as adults, warehousing kids in overcrowded, decaying detention centers, providing inadequate academic, vocational, and life-skills training—fly in the face of its mission of rehabilitation. Incarceration should be the recourse of last resort for any child, drug-involved or not. We need to spend more money on prevention, diversion, and treatment programs that keep kids in their families and communities, and far less on building new children's jails.

From arresting officer to sentencing judge, the juvenile justice system must be purged of the class and race discrimination that sends disproportionate numbers of poor kids and kids of color to Juvenile Hall—and eventually prison—to serve disproportionately long sentences. Perpetuating racism in the juvenile justice system perpetuates the rage, despair, and intolerance that lead, in turn, to drug abuse and other manifestations of human suffering.

5. Revamp the adolescent drug-treatment system. The biggest problem with the adolescent drug-treatment system is that far too many adolescents are in it. According to a January 2003 Slate.com story by Maia Szalavitz, "Trick or Treatment," 75 percent of American teens in drug treatment are sent there by courts or schools, not professionals; most don't fit the criteria for substance dependence. "Teen treatment programs remove teens from a healthy peer group and surround them with other problem kids,"

Szalavitz warns, adding, "Studies show that family therapy and individual counseling work better for teens than programs modeled on adult addicts."

We must immediately resolve to *send no more teenagers who don't need drug treatment into drug-treatment programs.* Keeping this promise means creating support systems for nondrug-abusing teenagers who are already in trouble—for example, the "Life Court" proposed by Tom Fleming of the Richmond Drug Court—and strengthening the support systems of home, school, and community for teenagers who aren't.

To make programs more effective, fundamental changes are necessary:

- **Tailor adolescent drug treatment programs to fit adolescents.** The starting point of any drug program should not be adult treatment protocols, but teenagers' unique needs. There is no one-size-fits-all treatment plan for adolescents, whose situations vary greatly depending on their age, gender, sexual orientation, family situation, academic progress, physical- and/or mental-health issues, and drug(s) of choice.

- **Tailor the twelve-step treatment model to fit adolescents.** "What teenager would admit to being 'powerless' over anything?" the Slate.com story asks. Since most adolescent treatment programs promote the AA philosophy and require attendance at AA meetings, the twelve-step tenets must be examined and amended to support the particular needs of teens in recovery.

- **Don't label teenagers as addicts.** Telling a fifteen-year-old that he's got an incurable disease and can never drink another beer does more harm than good—whether it's true or not. "Since teenage identities are fluid anyway," Szalavitz says, "encouraging them to view themselves as powerless addicts may cement an antisocial identity that a teen was just trying on for size."

- **Don't let kids run from treatment.** We can't afford *not* to monitor teenagers in treatment twenty-four seven, including after-hours and weekend spot checks. We can't afford *not* to allocate the labor power needed to find them when they run. Once kids know they'll be caught, running away will quickly become less popular.

- **Make family involvement mandatory.** "If we don't have the parents," Leo Kidd says, "we don't have a prayer with the kid." Conducting multifamily groups and family-therapy sessions at convenient times, in as many languages as necessary, with paid time off from work and child care provided, will encourage parents to support their kids' recovery. When all efforts to involve them fail, parents should face legal consequences.

- **Treat the whole person.** As Tristan says, he's recovering from more than drugs—and kids need more than sobriety to build happy, productive lives. Treatment programs should help kids discover what they can do and want to do, not just what they can't, offering career guidance, community service experience, mentor-matching, and fun.

- **Build continued care into every treatment program.** Given the prevalence of relapse and adolescents' need for guidance from and connection with adults outside their families, follow-up contact is crucial after teens are released from residential or day-treatment programs.

- **Give adolescent drug-treatment programs the funding they need.** Many kids really do need drug treatment. We're not, for the most part, giving it to them. Treatment programs have more applicants than openings; there are more needs to meet than resources with which to meet them. Adolescent drug programs must have the facilities, enforcement capabilities, and—most important—the well-trained, dedicated counselors it takes to engage and invest teenagers in their own recovery.

Today Mike called me from his mom's house, where he's been sleeping off his latest crank run. As he does often, he asked me, "How much longer till the book comes out?"

I never like to answer that question because I know why he's asking it. Mike's been looking forward to the book tour for two years. He wants to know how long he's got to come up with the "happy ending" he's planning to trot out on talk shows.

"Six months," I answer, gritting my teeth, imagining all the damage Mike can do to himself in that length of time. I've tried every other argument before; I try this one now. "Maybe you should check yourself into a program, Mike. You don't want to be tweaking on *Oprah*, do you?"

"*H-e-ell*, no," Mike answers heartily. "But I don't need no *program*. I'll get clean on my own, like I always do. That way I can talk about getting sober while it's still hella fresh in my mind."

Mike's logic leaves me shaking my head, muttering, "Unclear on the concept." And then I think, maybe it's not Mike who's unclear about what "drug recovery" is all about. Maybe it's the rest of us.

I believe that Mike *will* get clean for the book tour. I believe he *will* speak intelligently and even honestly about the sucking seduction of crank and the action-packed life that goes with it. Maybe he'll talk about how good he is at blowing crank pipes, about how popular that made him in high school, even when he was flunking out and feeling like the world's biggest loser.

But if an interviewer asks Mike about the bone-crunching effort it takes to kick crank, I'm afraid he'll play "recovery poster child," tell the adults what he believes they want to hear, spout the recovery rhetoric he learned at Center Point. He won't tell the truth: that he got clean without a drug program because he had reason to. Not anyone else's reason; his own.

When all is said and done, it could be that simple—and that complex. All Mike needs to stay off drugs is a reason to. Not anyone else's. His own.

If the world had been a better one when Mike was a baby with a stressed-out, single mother, when he was a student in an overcrowded classroom, an adolescent with alcoholics and crank addicts for role models, a "resident" of Juvenile Hall, a client in the treatment programs that gave him plenty of essays to write and rules to follow but scant hope of a meaningful future—maybe Mike would have his own reasons, now, to get off crank and stay off it. Maybe he wouldn't have gotten into drugs in the first place.

Maybe if our family-support systems, our schools, our national priorities were different—*better*—we wouldn't have an epidemic of teenage drug abuse in this country today. But they aren't, and we do. So (as if we don't have enough on our plates), it's our job as parents—as Americans who care about kids' futures, and our nation's—to work toward changing that: to fight for the policies that will help make parenting the joy that it should be, instead of the terrifying, overwhelming trial by fire that it too often is.

In the meantime, what's a parent to do? The personal solutions are every bit as complex—and as simple—as the political. Raising two very different sons with two very different outcomes, I learned the hard way that it's not enough to give what's easiest to give. The parenting style that came naturally to me worked well for one son, but not so well for the other. Schools, teachers, teams, and rules that worked for one son utterly failed the other. It takes time, attention, and money to treat each child as a unique individual, to meet each child's unique needs. We've got to find the time, the attention, and the money it takes. And we've got to insist that every person and institution in our kids' lives do the same.

Parents can't do it alone. It took "a whole village" to save my son and me. We couldn't have done it without the teachers and coaches who gave him second chances—and didn't, the church members who gave Jesse a home, the friends and relatives who drove around looking for Jesse at midnight, who drove me to hospitals, police stations, jails, the people who reassured both of us that there was a way out of this and that we would find it. We parents need to surround ourselves and our children with the "villagers" who support and don't undermine us and our families, who recognize and nurture our best intentions and our kids', who come to us offering the open hand of love, not the clenched fist of blame.

Raising my own teenagers, spending a couple of years with teenagers in rehab, I learned that teenagers excel at inducing panic in adults. It's a gift that accomplishes its purpose—it shows them how much we care; it shows us how autonomous they actually are—but it serves none of us well. Thrashing around blindly in fear's dark dungeons, I lost track of what I knew to be true about myself and my child. The truth is, raising teenagers is neither as simple nor as complex as the threat-mongers make it seem. You can do everything "right" with your child and have him grow up terribly wrong. You can make terrible mistakes with your child and have her grow up just right. Not every kid who smokes pot will suffer lifelong addiction. Not every kid who seems to be able to drink "responsibly" can. It's up to parents to know the difference, to know when there's a problem—even when everyone else says there isn't, even when everyone else says there is. It's up to us to find solutions when solutions are what's needed.

We live in a time and a culture that make it exceedingly difficult to raise a teenager, and exceedingly difficult to be one. It's our job to make sure that we and our children have what we need to do the best we can. Most challenging of all, it's our job to recognize when we, and our children, are doing exactly that.

Resources for Parents

When you're the parent of a teenager in trouble, your best resources are other parents who have been where you are: people who share your values, who have felt what you're feeling and faced what you're facing. These are the "experts" most qualified to recommend the treatment programs, professionals, and resources that match your needs and your child's. To find such people:

- Talk to your kids' friends' parents.

- Join a parenting class or support group.

- Attend twelve-step meetings and share your situation; invite people to talk to you afterward.

- Post messages and read other parents' messages on local electronic bulletin boards.

- Ask trusted teachers, school counselors, coaches, and clergy to connect you with parents in similar situations.

To supplement what you'll get from friends and neighbors, here's a list of resources I've used myself and resources that have been recommended to me by professionals I trust. I encourage you to visit Web sites, bookstores, and agencies within your own community to find what's helpful to you. And I advise you to check references before committing yourself or your child to any professional or program.

ORGANIZATIONS

Treatment Programs

- On the Internet, use any search engine (such as www.google.com or www.yahoo.com) and enter "adolescent drug abuse" or "adolescent drug treatment programs in [your city]."

- Look in your local phone book under "Alcoholism" or "Drug Abuse & Addiction."

- Contact:

  National 24-Hour Alcohol/Drug Treatment and Support Group Referrals
  800–234–0420

  National Alcohol/Drug Treatment Referrals for Adults and Adolescents
  800–454–8966, 4:00 AM to 10:00 PM PT

  Hazelden Foundation
  "A nonprofit organization providing high-quality, affordable addiction treatment, education, publishing and research for more than 50 years," Hazelden offers referrals to its own twelve step–based programs and others.

  www.hazelden.org
  e-mail: info@hazelden.org

  800–257–7810 or 651–213–4000, 6:00 AM to 10:30 PM CT, weekdays; 7:00 AM to 10:30 PM, weekends

Parents Universal Resource Experts (P.U.R.E.)

"We offer first-hand experience and recommend programs/schools that we would send our own children to. P.U.R.E. will assist you in evaluating what your specific needs are, and recommend placement (if needed) into the most appropriate program and/or school."

www.helpyourteens.com

954–349–7260

Twelve-Step Programs

- Look in your local phone book under "Alcoholism" or "Drug Abuse & Addiction."

- Contact:

Alcoholics Anonymous

"A fellowship of men and women who share their experience, strength and hope with each other that they may solve their common problem and help others to recover from alcoholism."

Check the phone book or call 411 for the AA office in your area.

www.alcoholics-anonymous.org

Al-Anon, Alateen

"To help families and friends of alcoholics recover from the effects of living with the problem drinking of a relative or friend. Alateen is our recovery program for young people."

www.al-anon.alateen.org

888–4AL–ANON, 8:00 AM to 6:00 PM ET, Monday to Friday

Parenting Support

Toughlove

"A nonprofit, self-help organization that provides ongoing education and active support to families, empowering parents and young people to accept responsibility for their actions."

P.O. Box 1069, Doylestown, PA 18901

www.toughlove.org

215–348–7090; fax: 215–348–9874

Families Anonymous

"A Twelve-Step, self-help, recovery and nonprofit fellowship of support groups for relatives and friends of those who have alcohol, drug, or behavioral problems."

www.familiesanonymous.org
e-mail: famanon@familiesanonymous.org

800–736–9805, 10:00 AM to 4:00 PM PT, Monday to Thursday; 10:00 AM to 2:00 PM, Friday

The Children's Defense Fund

"CDF's Parent Resource Network (PRN) can help you find the necessary resources to become a more effective parent. We have selected a variety of national Web sites that offer parents information about caring for their own children as well as getting involved in group efforts to help children in their own communities or states."

25 E Street NW, Washington, DC 20001

www.childrensdefense.org/parentresnet.php
e-mail: cdfinfo@childrensdefense.org

202–628–8787

Recovery High Schools

Association of Recovery Schools

"Brings together students, secondary and post-secondary schools, and helping professionals to support students in recovery from alcohol or other drug dependence."

117 Lyle Lane, Nashville, Tennessee 37210

Andy Finch, Director

www.recoveryschools.org
e-mail: a.finch@creativerecovery.org

615–248–8206; fax: 615–248–8762

Adolescent Drug Court Programs

- If your child is arrested, ask if an adolescent drug court program is available. (Even in counties that have adolescent drug courts, their existence may not be made known to teenagers or their parents.)

- Contact:

Justice Programs Office, American University

Offers publications on juvenile drug courts and referrals to local drug courts.

www.american.edu/justice
e-mail: justice@american.edu

202–885–2875, 8:00 AM to 6:00 PM ET, Monday to Friday

National Association of Drug Court Professionals

Offers publications on juvenile drug courts and referrals to local drug courts.

www.nadcp.org
e-mail: nadcp1@aol.com

703–575–9400

Therapists and Consultants Specializing in Adolescents and/or Drug Abuse

- Look in your local phone book under "Psychologists" or "Educational Consulting & Services."

- Contact:

American Psychology Association

"A scientific and professional organization that represents psychology in the United States. With more than 155,000 members, APA is the largest association of psychologists worldwide."

www.apa.org, click on "Consumer Help Center"

202–336–5500

National Association of Social Workers

"The largest membership organization of professional social workers in the world . . . NASW works to enhance the professional growth and development of its members, to create and maintain professional standards, and to advance sound social policies."

www.socialworkers.org

800–227–3590

National Board for Certified Counselors

"An independent not-for-profit credentialing body for counselors, incorporated in 1982 to establish and monitor a national certification system, to identify those counselors who have voluntarily sought and obtained certification, and to maintain a register of those counselors."

www.nbcc.org

336–547–0607

American Association of Marriage and Family Therapists

"The professional association for the field of marriage and family therapy, representing the professional interests of more than 23,000 marriage and family therapists throughout the United States, Canada and abroad."

www.aamft.org

Independent Educational Consultants Association

"A nonprofit, international professional association representing full-time experienced independent educational advisors [who] counsel students and their families in the selection of educational programs, based on the student's individual needs and talents."

www.iecaonline.org

800–808–4322

Federal Government Agencies Offering Free Informational Materials About Teens and Drugs

National Youth Anti-Drug Media Campaign

"The Office of National Drug Control Policy's National Youth Anti-Drug Media Campaign is a historic initiative created to educate and enable America's youth to reject illicit drugs." Publishes lists of Web sites related to "raising drug-free kids."

800–788–2800

Web sites include:

www.mediacampaign.org: Fact sheets, press releases, links related to the National Youth Anti-Drug Media Campaign.

www.whitehousedrugpolicy.gov: Current data on drug use, policies, programs.

www.theantidrug.com: "Drug-free children" parental strategies in Spanish, Korean, Vietnamese, Chinese, and Cambodian.

www.freevibe.com: "Helps kids 10–15 understand the dangers of substance abuse"; features moderated bulletin boards, media tools, drug facts.

Substance Abuse and Mental Health Services Administration's National Clearinghouse for Alcohol and Drug Information

"The nation's one-stop resource for the most current and comprehensive information about substance abuse prevention." Offers publications searches and referrals twenty-four seven in English and Spanish.

www.health.org
e-mail: info@health.org

800–729–6686

National Criminal Justice Reference Service

"NCJRS offers extensive reference and referral services to answer your questions about crime and justice-related research, policy, and practice. Staff can offer statistics and referrals, discuss publications, compile information packages, search for additional resources, and provide other technical assistance—all tailored to your particular information needs."

www.ncjrs.org
e-mail related to juvenile justice issues: askjj@ncjrs.org

BOOKS

Addiction and Recovery

Diller, Lawrence. *Running on Ritalin*. Bantam Books, 1998.

Dodes, Lance. *The Heart of Addiction*. HarperCollins, 2002.

Frey, James. *A Million Little Pieces*. Doubleday, 2003.

Hazelden Foundation. Various titles. P.O. Box 176 Center City, MN 55012. 800–328–9000. www.hazeldenbookplace.organization; e-mail: bookstore@hazelden.org.

Shavelson, Lonny. *Hooked*. New Press, 2001.

Teenagers in Trouble—Parents' Stories

Digges, Deborah. *The Stardust Lounge: Stories from a Boy's Adolescence*. Doubleday, 2001.

Dudman, Martha Tod. *Augusta, Gone*. Simon & Schuster, 2001.

Lara, Adair. *Hold Me Close, Let Me Go: A Mother, a Daughter, and an Adolescence Survived*. Broadway Books, 2001.

Teenagers in Trouble—Help for Parents

Drug Strategies. *Treating Teens: A Guide to Adolescent Drug Programs*. 1150 Connecticut Ave., NW, Suite 800, Washington DC, 20036. 202–289–9070. www.drugstrategies.org; e-mail: dspolicy@aol.com.

Goleman, Daniel. *Emotional Intelligence*. Bantam, 1995. (Especially sections on children and teenagers.)

Wolf, Anthony. *Get Out of My Life, but First Could You Drive Me and Cheryl to the Mall?* Farrar Straus & Giroux, 2002.

Notes

INTRODUCTION

Number of American teenagers using drugs

Center for Substance Abuse Treatment, *The Need for Developing and Evaluating Adolescent Treatment Models*, August 31, 2001.

Center on Addiction and Substance Abuse, *National Survey of Teens, Teachers and Principals*, September 1998.

Columbia University College of P & S Complete Home Medical Guide.

Robert Wood Johnson Foundation, *Reclaiming Futures*, 2002.

National Institutes of Health, *Monitoring the Future: National Survey Results on Drug Use, Overview of Key Findings*, 2001.

Partnership for Drug-Free America, "National Survey: Ecstasy Use Continues Rising Among Teens," press release, February 11, 2002.

Number of American teens arrested for drug violations

Robert Wood Johnson Foundation, *Reclaiming Futures*, 2002.

Office of Juvenile Justice and Delinquency Prevention, *Crime in the United States*, 2001.

Number of teens who need treatment but aren't getting it

Robert Wood Johnson Foundation, *Reclaiming Futures*, 2002.

National Institute on Drug Abuse (NIDA), *Preventing Drug Use Among Children and Adolescents*, 1997.

Number of Americans in treatment for drug abuse

Office of National Drug Control Policy, *Pulse Check: Trends in Drug Abuse, July–December 2001*, April 2002.

Schneider Institute for Health Policy, *Substance Abuse: The Nation's Number One Health Problem*, Brandeis University, February 2001.

Substance Abuse and Mental Health Services Administration (SAMHSA), report, August 2002.

Cost of drug abuse and the War on Drugs

Federal Bureau of Investigation, *Crime in the United States*, Uniform Crime Reports, 2000.

"Fighting Addiction," *Newsweek*, February 12, 2001.

William Finnegan, *Cold New World*, Random House, 1998.

Office of National Drug Control Policy, *Annual Report*, 2001.

Peggy Orenstein, "Staying Clean," *New York Times Magazine*, February 10, 2002.

Jonathan D. Salant, "Record-Setting 6.6 Million Americans Behind Bars or on Parole," *San Francisco Chronicle*, August 26, 2002.

Schneider Institute for Health Policy, *Substance Abuse: The Nation's Number One Health Problem*, Brandeis University, February 2001.

Substance Abuse and Mental Health Services Administration (SAMHSA), *Summary of Findings from the 2000 National Household Survey on Drug Abuse*, 2000.

"Your Body, Their Profits," *San Francisco Chronicle*, editorial, February 6, 2002.

The Middle Eastern heroin trade and the CIA

Reese Erlich, "From Berkeley to Kabul," *The Monthly*, April 2002.

RUNNING ON EMPTY

Number of American children regularly sharing meals with their families

Robin Toner, "Kids in the Balance," review of Al and Tipper Gore's *Joined at the Heart*, *New York Times*, November 17, 2002.

Alice Waters, "Happy Meals," *Utne Reader*, May/June 2002.

Children living in poverty, funding cut for children's health, education, and welfare

Alexander Cockburn, "Concerning Pee-Wee, Townshend and Ritter," *The Nation*, February 17, 2003.

William Finnegan, *Cold New World*, Random House, 1998.

WHY ARE WE HERE?

The history of drugs in the United States

The Consumers Union Report on Licit and Illicit Drugs, 1972.

"Drug Wars," *Frontline*, 2000.

"History of Heroin," HeroinAddiction.com by NarcAnon Arrowhead.

Los Angeles Times, August 23, 1996.

John P. Morgan, M.D., and Lynn Zimmer, Ph.D., "Marijuana Myths, Marijuana Facts: A Review of the Scientific Evidence," The Lindesmith Center, mjgate.htm, 1997.

National Institutes of Health, *Monitoring the Future: National Survey Results on Drug Use, Overview of Key Findings*, 2001.

Office of National Drug Control Policy, *Juveniles and Drugs*, Office of National Drug Control Policy Web site.

Richard Rudgley, *The Encyclopedia of Psychoactive Substances*, St. Martin's Press, 1999.

SAMHSA's Drug and Alcohol Services Information System (DASIS), *Coerced Treatment Among Youths 1993–1998*, August 10, 2001.

San Jose Mercury-News, August 18–20, 1996.

Substance Abuse and Mental Health Services Administration (SAMHSA), *Summary of Findings from the 2000 National Household Survey on Drug Abuse*, 2000.

U.S. Food and Drug Administration, *Milestones in U.S. Food and Drug Law History*, August 2002.

GOOD MORNING, FAMILY

Adolescents in drug treatment nationwide

Bob Curley, "Lack of Research, Capacity Plague Adolescent Treatment System," JoinTogether.org, May 15, 2001.

Michael L. Dennis, Ph.D., Senior Research Psychologist, Chestnut Health Systems, Bloomington, IL, personal correspondence, August 15, 2002.

Robert Wood Johnson Foundation, *Reclaiming Futures*, 2002.

SAMHSA's Drug and Alcohol Services Information System (DASIS), *Coerced Treatment Among Youths 1993–1998*, August 10, 2001.

SAMHSA's Drug and Alcohol Services Information System (DASIS), *Treatment Episode Data Set (TEDS)*, 1999.

"Reality Check," *People*, August 20, 2001. North Bay Regional Information Center, Sonoma State University.

Ritalin and ADD/ADHD

Lawrence Diller, *Running on Ritalin*, Bantam Books, 1998.

Lawrence Diller, interview, May 29, 2002.

"A Prescription for Disaster," Salon.com, April 27, 2000.

United States General Accounting Office, *Attention Disorder Drugs*, September 2001.

Funding for prisons nationwide growing, funding for education shrinking

Justice Policy Institute, *Cellblocks or Classrooms? National Summary Fact Sheet*, 2000.

History of Synanon

Rod Janzen, *The Rise and Fall of Synanon*, The Johns Hopkins University Press, 2001.

Lonny Shavelson, *Hooked*, The New Press, 2001.

SOBRIETY HIGH

Recovery high schools

Jim Cazarniecki, CEO of Sobriety High, personal correspondence.

Andrew Finch, President of the Association of Recovery Schools, personal correspondence.

Randolph Muck, Public Health Advisor, Center for Substance Abuse Treatment, SAMHSA, personal correspondence.

Meg Sherry, Director of Alcohol/Drug Services, Bay Area Community Resources, personal correspondence.

"Sobriety High," American News Service, May 1, 2000, reprinted on Wiretap.com.

Ecstasy, inhalants, and methamphetamines

"DEA Calls for Crackdown on Methamphetamine," JoinTogether.org, March 26, 2002.

William Finnegan, *Cold New World*, Random House, 1998.

Good Morning America, February 26, 2001.

"History of Ecstasy," Australian Broadcasting Corporation Online, June 4, 2001.

Office of National Drug Control Policy, *Annual Report*, 2001.

Substance Abuse and Mental Health Services Administration (SAMHSA), *Summary of Findings from the 2000 National Household Survey on Drug Abuse*, 2000.

"Survey Shows Increase in Marijuana, Cocaine Emergency Room Visits," JoinTogether.org, August 22, 2002.

JUVENILE DRUG COURT

Drug Courts

Melissa Hostetler, "Rethinking Drug Courts," *Friction Magazine*, March 12, 2002, reprinted on AlterNet.org.

Office of Juvenile Justice and Delinquency Prevention, *The Juvenile Drug Court Movement*, March 1997.

Office of National Drug Control Policy, *Annual Report*, 2001.

Lonny Shavelson, *Hooked*, The New Press, 2001.

Lonny Shavelson, interviews, January 2002–March 2003.

GOOD-BYE, FAMILY

Therapeutic communities

Center Point staff, personal correspondence.

Peggy Orenstein, "Staying Clean," *New York Times Magazine*, February 10, 2002.

Peggy Orenstein, interview, February 25, 2002.

Lonny Shavelson, *Hooked*, The New Press, 2001.

Lonny Shavelson, interviews, January 2002–March 2003.

Profitability of the rehab industry

"Boot-Camp Director Arrested on Murder, Other Charges," JoinTogether.org, February 20, 2002.

Bob Curley, "Lack of Research, Capacity Plague Adolescent Treatment System," JoinTogether.org, May 15, 2001.

Michael L. Dennis, Ph.D., "Advances in Adolescent Substance Abuse Treatment," abstract for presentation, Chestnut Health Systems, August 21, 2002; also personal correspondence.

"More U.S. Teens in Substance Abuse Treatment," *Reuters*, December 27, 2001.

"Parents of Troubled Youths Are Seeking Help at Any Cost," *New York Times*, September 10, 2001.

SAMHSA's Drug and Alcohol Services Information System (DASIS), *Coerced Treatment Among Youths 1993–1998*, August 10, 2001.

"Study Finds Long-Term Treatment Best for Teens," *Archives of General Psychiatry*, JoinTogether.org, July 12, 2001.

Maia Szalavitz, "Bush + Jesus = Unprotected Kids," *American Prospect*, July 17, 2001; "Drug Abuse Treatment or Drug Treatment Abuse," AlterNet.org, July 25, 2001.

Number of teens arrested, sentenced for drug abuse

Office of Juvenile Justice and Delinquency Prevention, *Drug Offense Cases in Juvenile Courts, 1989–1998*.

Office of Juvenile Justice and Delinquency Prevention, *Crime in the United States, 2001*.

Office of National Drug Control Policy, *Annual Report*, 2001.

MOVING VIOLATIONS

Punishment for juvenile drug offenders fits the criminal, not the crime

"Drugs Still Driving Growth in U.S. Prison Population," JoinTogether.org, August 5, 2002.

"Incarceration Rates Increasing," NPR station KQED–FM, August 29, 2002.

James A. Morone, "The Corrosive Politics of Virtue," *American Prospect*, May/June 1996.

Office of National Drug Control Policy, *Annual Report*, 2001.

"The State of Juvenile Crime, 2002," NPR station KQED–FM, April 8, 2002.

Substance Abuse and Mental Health Services Administration (SAMHSA), *Summary of Findings from the 2000 National Household Survey on Drug Abuse*, 2000.

Tim Wise, "School Shootings and White Denial," AlterNet.org, March 7, 2001.

Acknowledgments

Beginning this project, I faced a formidable challenge: to gain entry to several confidentiality-clad adolescent drug programs and their privacy-protected clients. Many treatment professionals, teachers, and parents paved the way, among them Dr. Susan Landes, Dr. Virginia Wolf, Gael Thompson, Dr. John Nickens (to whom I owe much more than thanks), and Coach David Manson—*compadre* in basketball, parenting, and life.

At each of the programs profiled in this book and others not named here, counselors, teachers, and line staff allowed me to observe their most intimate professional moments and made themselves available for endless after-hours questioning. Their openness is further evidence of their dedication to the work they do, and to the teenagers with whom they do it. Those teenagers, in turn, patiently ignored me as I sat in on their therapy groups, classes, and conversations, then answered my nosy questions with enthusiasm, thoughtfulness, and candor. If I've done my part as well as they did, those were their voices you heard ringing in your ears as you turned the pages of this book.

At Center Point I was invited in by Associate Director Marc Hering, then welcomed by Danny Ramirez, Tess Carpenter, and the entire staff—particularly the exemplary teacher and human being Stevo Lamott.

At Phoenix Academy I learned much about the power of love from Dr. Clara MacNamee, Mike Herrera, Bill Ashworth, Dr. Meg Sherry, Lisa Ahrens, Dana Leigh, and Susan Pease. I was honored to witness up close and personal the therapeutic alchemy of Floyd Jackson and Eric Olson, whose devotion to Tristan and to each of their clients simply took my breath away.

From the first time I sat in on the Richmond Juvenile Drug Court I was struck by the magnitude of the task undertaken by the Choices/Drug Court Team, and by the heart, soul, and tenacity with which they accomplish it. For this and for their active support, I thank Jim Bouquin, Cally Martin, Leo Kidd, Stacy Harris, Ursula Sanders, Colleen Wimmer, Mike Caldwell, Pam Collinshill, Commissioner Stephen Easton, and especially Tom Fleming and Kevin Charles, who gave unstintingly to Zalika and to this project.

When I was swimming in data, fellow journalist Peggy Orenstein threw me a lifeline, sharing her own meticulous research. Three student interns, Jessi Hempel, Ana Campoy, and Simon Leaver-Appelman, provided statistical research and analysis. Andrew Finch, of the Association of Recovery Schools, and Randolph Muck, of SAMHSA's Center for Substance Abuse Treatment, invited me to sit in on the first Recovery Schools Conference. Randy also accomplished the unthinkable: he put a (kind, caring) human face on the federal drug treatment bureaucracy.

I owe much to America's independent booksellers, those stalwart keepers of the free-speech flame. In particular I want to thank Andy Ross and Melissa Mytinger of Cody's Books in Berkeley, California, for their fierce support of writers like me, and communities like ours.

Journalist, photographer, doctor, and mensch Lonny Shavelson opened his files, his sources, and his considerable brainpower to me, becoming mentor, friend, and writing buddy in the process. Along with "Don't Ask Unless You Want Me to Tell" memoirist Susan Parker, our Small Writing Group provided me with invaluable criticism and encouragement, not to mention wine with a cork. Julie Whitten once again read and critiqued every word. Phenomenal photographer. Joe Pugliese contributed generously to the cause.

At two key moments during the writing of this book, I was offered the writer's ultimate luxury item: uninterrupted time and a beautiful place in which to work. The Mesa Refuge in Pt. Reyes, California, has been a sanctuary and a (solar) battery charger for me and hundreds of other activist writers since its inception in 1998. I thank founder Peter Barnes for this gift, and for the gift of his loyal, provocative friendship. At the Virginia Center for the Creative Arts, I was housed, fed, and sheltered within a vibrant community of artists: dark chocolate for the soul.

I'm sure I have the world's best agent, Amy Rennert. She proves this often, but she outdid herself the day she introduced me to the world's best editor, Gideon Weil. Gideon signed this book up on the promise that a writer he'd never met would somehow accomplish a lot of seemingly undoable things. Then he provided the shrewd strategizing, daily encouragement, brilliant editorial critiques, and human kindness it took to make my job not only possible but exhilarating.

Collaborating with the rest of the HarperSanFrancisco team—Jeff Hobbs, Margery Buchanan, Jim Warner, Calla Devlin, and Anne Connolly—has also been an unexpected delight.

My profoundly lovely wife, Katrine Andrée Simone Thomas, gives me everything and she is everything to me, *aujourd'hui et toujours*.

Since their births, my sons, Jesse Graham and Peter Graham, have been my two best reasons to be in the world, and my two best reasons to change it. Now they're both busy doing that themselves with great spirit, grace, and integrity. What more could a mother want? Only that they would willingly donate their privacy and their talents to help this book achieve our shared goals. The greatest gift I've been given is being Jesse and Peter's mom, and I am deeply grateful for the privilege.

I met the families of Mike, Tristan, and Zalika at desperate moments in their lives. Half past believing that they could save their own kids, Barbara, Michael, Marian, Rob, Asani, and June agreed to participate in a personally risky project in hopes of saving others. I admire and appreciate their generosity and courage; I thank them for their friendship and their trust.

Mike, Tristan, and Zalika gave me much more than a book. I count among the blessings of knowing them laughter, hugs, heartbreak, insights, adventures—and inspiration to tell the truth of children's lives until we get it right, in this country, and give our kids something to live for. Mike, Tristan, and Zalika knew what they were getting into, hooking up with me. They did it anyway, and they've honored their commitment. My greatest hope is that their faith in me, and in the world we've made for them, will prove well founded.

About the Author

Meredith Maran is the author of many magazine and newspaper articles and several books, including the *San Francisco Chronicle* best-sellers *Class Dismissed: A Year in the Life of an American High School* and *What It's Like to Live Now*. Expelled from the Bronx High School of Science in 1968, Meredith speaks frequently to organizations that serve and advocate for children and teenagers. She lives in Oakland, California, where she's always working on her next book.

TO CONTACT THE AUTHOR

You can reach Meredith Maran at www.meredithmaran.com, or by mail:

    c/o HarperSanFrancisco
       353 Sacramento Street, Suite 500
       San Francisco, CA 94111